KEY CONCEPTS IN MODERN

Palgrave Key Concepts

Palgrave Key Concepts provide an accessible and comprehensive range of subject glossaries at undergraduate level. They are the ideal companion to a standard textbook making them invaluable reading to students throughout their course of study and especially useful as a revision aid.

Key Concepts in Accounting and Finance
Key Concepts in Business Practice
Key Concepts in Cultural Studies
Key Concepts in Drama and Performance
Key Concepts in e-Commerce
Key Concepts in Human Resource Management
Key Concepts in Information and Communication Technology
Key Concepts in International Business
Key Concepts in Language and Linguistics (second edition)
Key Concepts in Law
Key Concepts in Management
Key Concepts in Marketing
Key Concepts in Operations Management
Key Concepts in Politics
Key Concepts in Psychology
Key Concepts in Sociology
Key Concepts in Strategic Management
Key Concepts in Tourism

Palgrave Key Concepts: Literature
General Editors: John Peck and Martin Coyle

Key Concepts in Contemporary Literature
Key Concepts in Medieval Literature
Key Concepts in Modernist Literature
Key Concepts in Postcolonial Literature
Key Concepts in Renaissance Literature
Key Concepts in Victorian Literature
Literary Terms and Criticism (third edition)

Further titles are in preparation

www.palgravekeyconcepts.com

Palgrave Key Concepts
Series Standing Order ISBN 1–4039–3210–7
(outside North America only)

You can receive future titles in this series as they are published by placing a standing order. Please contact your bookseller or, in the case of difficulty, write to us at the address below with your name and address, the title of the series and the ISBN quoted above.

Customer Services Department, Macmillan Distribution Ltd
Houndmills, Basingstoke, Hampshire RG21 6XS, England

Key Concepts in Modernist Literature

Julian Hanna

First published 2009 by
PALGRAVE MACMILLAN

Palgrave Macmillan in the UK is an imprint of Macmillan Publishers Limited, registered in England, company number 785998, of Houndmills, Basingstoke, Hampshire RG21 6XS.

Palgrave Macmillan in the US is a division of St Martin's Press LLC, 175 Fifth Avenue, New York, NY 10010.

Palgrave Macmillan is the global academic imprint of the above companies and has companies and representatives throughout the world.

Palgrave® and Macmillan® are registered trademarks in the United States, the United Kingdom, Europe and other countries.

ISBN-13: 978–0–230–55119–0
ISBN-10: 0–230–55119–X

This book is printed on paper suitable for recycling and made from fully managed and sustained forest sources. Logging, pulping and manufacturing processes are expected to conform to the environmental regulations of the country of origin.

A catalogue record for this book is available from the British Library.

A catalog record for this book is available from the Library of Congress.

10   9   8   7   6   5   4   3   2   1
18   17   16   15   14   13   12   11   10   09

Printed and bound in China

For Simone, Clyde, and Nico, with love

Contents

General Editor's Preface

The purpose of **Palgrave Key Concepts in Literature** is to provide students with key critical and historical ideas about the texts they are studying as part of their literature courses. These ideas include information about the historical and cultural contexts of literature, as well as the theoretical approaches current in the subject today. Behind the series lies a recognition of the need nowadays for students to be familiar with a range of concepts and contextual material to inform their reading and writing about literature.

But behind the series there also lies a recognition of the changes that have transformed degree courses in Literature in recent years. Central to these changes has been the impact of critical theory together with a renewed interest in the way in which texts intersect with their immediate context and historical circumstances. The result has been an opening up of new ways of reading texts and a new understanding of what the study of literature involves together with the introduction of a wide set of new critical issues that demand our attention. An important aim of **Palgrave Key Concepts in Literature** is to provide brief, accessible introductions to these new ways of reading and new issues.

Each volume in **Palgrave Key Concepts in Literature** follows the same structure. An initial overview essay is followed by three sections – **Contexts**, **Texts**, and **Criticism** – each containing a sequence of brief alphabetically arranged entries on a sequence of topics. **Contexts essays** provide an impression of the historical, social, and cultural environment in which literary texts were produced. **Texts essays**, as might be expected, focus more directly on the works themselves. **Criticism essays** then outline the manner in which changes and developments in criticism have affected the ways in which we discuss the texts featured in the volume. The informing intention throughout is to help the reader create something new in the process of combining context, text, and criticism.

Martin Coyle

General Introduction

The term 'modernism' has many varied and contradictory associations. For some it has an aura of difficulty and formal experimentation, while for others it connotes an exuberant celebration of the machine age; still others might imagine the kind of romantic disenchantment and alienation summed up in the title of British modernism's most famous poem, *The Waste Land*. But what the term primarily suggests is a sense of crisis and a will to innovation. In most cases this involves a break with traditional modes and subject matter. The desire to change and to reflect change, to 'make it new' in Pound's famous phrase, is modernism's defining characteristic. Paradoxically, the study of modernism generally involves treating the modernist spirit as something confined to history. In Harold Rosenburg's phrase, modernism is 'the tradition of the new'. This seems counterintuitive: how can 'modernism' end? Are we not modern? But fixing the boundaries, even in a seemingly arbitrary way – Virginia Woolf's famous suggestion, for example, that 'on or about December 1910 human character changed' – is usually considered to be a practical necessity. Modernism, like all terms, is defined by difference: 'modernist' literature is not Victorian or Edwardian, for example. Literature after the Second World War, meanwhile, is labelled 'postmodern' or 'contemporary' and given its own set of attributes.

Modernism may be defined, in one major view, as the reaction of artists and writers to the drastic changes that accompanied the onset of modernity. (Here a further distinction becomes necessary – between 'modernism', the cluster of artistic and literary tendencies; 'modernity', the period concerned and the conditions associated with it; and 'modern', the broadest of the three terms, which simply means 'current' and is not easily fixed to an historical period.) Far from being a self-contained aesthetic experiment, in this view, modernism describes a range of responses to the technological advances and rapid urbanization experienced across Europe and elsewhere at the turn of the twentieth century. Reactions expressed through art to the sweeping effects of modernization varied considerably: some, like the Italian futurists, were unabashed in their enthusiasm; others, including many of the British modernists, drew back in horror, especially after the First World War. But without exception they were fascinated by the changes brought to everyday life, especially in cities like London, Paris and Milan. Even in the Dublin of 1904 depicted in James Joyce's *Ulysses* (1922), the reader is assaulted by the noise of trams – an innovation reintroduced to the city exactly a century later, in 2004 – carrying commuters to and from the suburbs:

> Before Nelson's pillar trams slowed, shunted, changed trolley, started for Blackrock, Kingstown and Dalkey, Clonskea, Rathgar and Terenure, Palmerston park and upper Rathmines, Sandymount Green, Rathmines, Ringsend and Sandymount Tower, Harold's Cross. The hoarse Dublin United Tramway Company's timekeeper bawled them off:
>
> – Rathgar and Terenure!
> – Come on, Sandymount Green!
>
> Right and left parallel clanging ringing a doubledecker and a sin- gledeck moved from their railheads, swerved to the down line, glided parallel.
>
> – Start, Palmerston park!

Similar scenes take place in many other novels of the period. In the opening pages of Woolf's *Mrs. Dalloway* (1925), Clarissa Dalloway takes in the excitement of a June morning in central London, 'the bellow and the uproar; the carriages, motor cars, omnibuses, vans, sandwich men shuffling and swinging; brass bands; barrel organs…and the strange high singing of some aeroplane overhead'. The first futurist manifesto of 1909 celebrates 'the beauty of speed' and champions war, factories, crowds, shipyards, railway stations, locomotives, steamships, bridges, and other features of modernity. The pre-war manifestos of vorti- cism give their blessings to 'the great ports' of Britain, that 'industrial island machine'. These reactions echo the description in *The Communist Manifesto* of the revolutionary nature of bourgeois capitalism, the foun- dation of modernity. The capitalist era, in the words of Marx and Engels, 'accomplished wonders far surpassing Egyptian pyramids, Roman aque- ducts, and Gothic cathedrals'. This period of upheaval saw venerable institutions crumble and firmly held convictions disintegrate. With the old order 'stripped of its halo', a new world of uncertainties and possibilities was revealed. 'The lies of centuries have got to be discarded', Mina Loy declared in her 'Feminist Manifesto' of 1914. She asks: 'Are you prepared for the wrench?'

Modernism is best described as a set of tendencies, rather than one particular style. Some of its traits include formal experimentation and complexity; a sense of crisis or apocalypse; the evocation of dynamism and speed; sexual openness; scepticism about traditional social, moral, and religious values and systems; an interest in alternative cultures, distanced by geography or history; confidence in aesthetic doctrines; and suspicion of progress, rationalism, and notions of fixed identity. Descriptions of modernism often reveal striking contradictions. In one view, for example, modernism is radically subversive, earning the label 'degenerate art' from Adolf Hitler in 1937, a label many modernists would have worn with pride. In his essay 'The Ideology of Modernism' (1955), the Hungarian Marxist critic Georg Lukács attacked precisely this 'asocial' quality of modernism, albeit from the opposite end of the political spectrum. Modernist literature's 'surrender to subjectivity', Lukács complained, came at the cost of historical context and depicted a 'nightmare world' of alienation and impotence that did little to encourage social change. In contrast to its image of degeneracy, modernism can also be seen as coldly formal, difficult, elitist, produced and understood by the few, and concerned only with its own perfection, a survival of nineteenth-century aestheticism. T. S. Eliot, for example, when surveyed by the *Left Review* in 1937 for his opinion concerning the Spanish Civil War, put himself firmly in the 'neutral' category with the statement that 'at least a few men of letters should remain isolated, and take no part in these collective activities'.

It is important to keep in mind that modernist literature was only a small fraction of the literature produced in Britain during the first half of the twentieth century. It was the voice of a small band of revolutionaries – Joyce, Eliot, Pound, Woolf – whose work represented an alternative to the mainstream novels of H. G. Wells, Arnold Bennett, and John Galsworthy, the three writers Woolf chose to illustrate the stodgy realism she objected to in her essay 'Modern Fiction' (1919). Successful self-promotion by modernist writers, especially Eliot and Pound, and the critics who took up their cause, from Edmund Wilson and F. R. Leavis to Hugh Kenner, resulted in a distorted picture of the literature of the period that still persists to this day. Other forms, including social chronicles, humour, romance, and detective fiction, travelogues, and historical novels, have only recently been brought back into the picture by new surveys, and they account for the vast majority of literature in this period. At the same time, the lines of modernism have been redrawn in recent decades to include a much broader and more diverse group of writers: no longer the preserve of the 'Men of 1914', modernism now includes, in Bonnie Kime Scott's phrase, the 'Women of 1928', as well as other groups like the Harlem Renaissance writers that were either considered distinct from the modernism of Pound and Eliot (as in a sense they surely are) or were neglected by literary scholars entirely.

Setting the boundaries for this book, as the preceding points should suggest, has not been an easy task. As the field of modernist literature grows in many productive directions, its characteristics become harder to define in any clear and meaningful way. Modernism has in fact become 'modernisms', a set of often contradictory and even irreconcilable movements. The dates chosen for other books on modernism give some sense of the flexibility of the field: Malcolm Bradbury and James McFarlane's classic study covers the years 1890–1930; Michael Levenson's *A Genealogy of Modernism* covers the crucial years of development 1908–1922, from Ford Madox Hueffer's *English Review* (1908–1909) to the launch of T. S. Eliot's *Criterion* and the publication of *The Waste Land* and *Ulysses* in 1922; Marjorie Perloff understands the period as 'roughly 1900–1930' but also considers it in some ways 'not yet finished'. Jane Goldman's recent study extends the end date to 1945 but also concurs with Woolf that the year 1910 signalled an important point of origin for modernism. The Second World War is accepted as the (latest) end date by the majority of modernist scholars for obvious historical reasons: the years 1939–1945 saw the deaths of numerous key figures of modernism, including Yeats, Woolf, Joyce, Ford (Hueffer), Marinetti, Freud, and Bergson, along with the incarceration for treason of Ezra Pound in 1945. What Perloff means when she says it is 'not yet finished' is that the modernist project and its innovations were 'deferred by two world wars and then the Cold War so that many of its principles are only now being brought to fruition' (Perloff, 2006, p. 571). Thankfully, the format of this book allows for a flexible timeframe. While some discussions of context will go as far back as the mid-nineteenth century, most works under discussion will have been published between 1909 and 1939. The primary focus will be on the key works and 'key concepts' of Anglo-American modernism, with important digressions on European movements whose importance was felt in Britain and America.

Further Reading

Baldick, Chris, *The Oxford English Literary History: Vol. 10. 1910–1940* (Oxford and New York: Oxford University Press, 2004).

Berman, Marshall, *All That is Solid Melts Into Air: The Experience of Modernity* (London: Verso, 1983).

Bradbury, Malcolm and James McFarlane, eds, *Modernism: 1890–1930* (Harmondsworth: Penguin, 1976).

Goldman, Jane, *Modernism, 1910–1945: Image to Apocalypse* (Basingstoke and New York: Palgrave Macmillan, 2003).

Levenson, Michael, *A Genealogy of Modernism: A Study of English Literary Doctrine 1908–1922* (Cambridge and New York: Cambridge University Press, 1984).

Nicholls, Peter, *Modernisms: A Literary Guide* (Berkeley: University of California Press, 1995).

1 Contexts: History, Politics, Culture

Introduction

The term 'crisis' is often used to describe aspects of modernism: literature of crisis, crisis of value, crisis of language, crisis of knowledge, crisis of belief. The sense of being at a critical turning point is also a defining characteristic of the broader context of modernity. For the historian Eric Hobsbawm, modernity was the product of a 'dual revolution': the French and the Industrial. This, however, was only the start. The first half of the twentieth century in Europe saw a string of interrelated crises. In Russia, Vladimir Ilyich Lenin called for the formation of a revolutionary party in his pamphlet, *What Is to Be Done?* (1902). There followed the failed bourgeois-democratic revolution of 1905, and later the successful Bolshevik revolution of 1917. In Ireland, the 1916 Easter Rising and its brutal suppression culminated in the Anglo-Irish Treaty of 1921, resulting in the partition of Ireland, and the Civil War of 1922–1923. The German revolution of 1918–1919 saw the abdication of Kaiser Wilhelm II and the inauguration of the Weimar Republic (1918–1933). There were also revolutions or rebellions in Romania (1907), Turkey (1908), Portugal (1910), Mexico (1910), China (1911), Hungary (1919), Brazil (1930), and Spain (1936). Anarchist violence at the turn of the century took the form of frequent bombings and resulted in numerous assassinations, including the heads of state of France, Spain, Italy, and the United States.

In his classic study of English politics before the war, *The Strange Death of Liberal England* (1935), George Dangerfield argued that Britain was also on the verge of revolution from 1910 to 1914. Events reached a climax in the spring and summer of 1914, which saw the threat of mass strikes by miners, transport, and railway workers; violent demonstrations by suffragettes; and near civil war in Ireland. The first seven months of 1914, not coincidentally perhaps, also saw the most concentrated activity of the English avant-garde, culminating at the end of June in the eye-catching debut of the vorticist magazine *Blast*. Certainly the modernist period as a whole can be seen as a revolutionary phase in the arts, parallel in some ways to the political and social upheaval of the time. In purely formal terms, modernism broke with all of the major conventions of the Victorian era, exchanging intimacy for sweeping narratives and fragmentation for artificial cohesion. Yet in Britain, being a revolutionary in the arts did not necessarily mean being a revolutionary in politics, at least not in the usual sense. In fact, many giants of modernism, including T. S. Eliot, Ezra Pound, and Wyndham Lewis, are better described as politically conservative or, to use T. E. Hulme's preferred term, reactionary. They called into question the basic tenets of humanism and liberal democracy, which they saw as decaying and outmoded vestiges of an earlier Romanticism. For many, the horrors of the First World War only served to confirm this perception: Pound's *Hugh Selwyn Mauberley* (1920) describes how the war brought 'disillusions as never told in the old days', and how 'a myriad' were killed 'For an old bitch gone in the teeth, For a botched civilization' – or returned 'home to old lies and new infamy'. During the 1920s and 1930s, artists and writers increasingly abandoned liberal democracy for extremes at either end of the political spectrum.

The term revolution, in fact, implies a circular motion rather than continuous forward progress. Hulme, for example, described the pre-war rise of abstraction not in terms of artistic progress but as a return to the abstract art of so-called primitive societies, and associated it with a desire for permanence rather than change. In sharp contrast to European movements like futurism, which called for liberation through the destruction of cultural heritage, Pound and Eliot tried to reconnect with distant traditions and to repair lost links with the past in the hope, especially after the First World War, of finding a way to rebuild the degraded, ruined present. The ideas of the Italian philosopher Giambattista Vico (1688–1744) were influential for James Joyce, William Butler Yeats, and other modernists who believed in a cyclical model of history. Vico wrote of a history that proceeds by stages, through *corsi* and *recorsi*, beginning with a poetic, mythologizing phase and moving through a rational, humanistic phase before declining into decadence and returning to a primitive state. (Most modernists, whether they were familiar with Vico or not, felt that they were living in a phase of decline.) Other thinkers who exerted a strong influence on modernism, such as Friedrich Nietzsche and Georges Sorel, were similarly pessimistic about romantic ideas of progress. Whether rebelling or reacting, few put faith in gradual transitions or democratic reforms. The prevalence of manifestos, with their urgent appeals to dramatic change, is indicative of the widespread impulse to reform, rethink, and renew, even without the comfort of faith in progress.

The early twentieth century saw the rapid development of consumer culture, and modernist literature responded to this and other signs of massification with a mixture of fascination and ambivalence. Thorstein Veblen, author of the groundbreaking sociological study *The Theory of the Leisure Class* (1899), invented the phrase 'conspicuous consumption', and evidence of the phenomenon was everywhere to be seen. The 'high' period of modernism coincided with the decadence of the 'roaring twenties', fueled by a booming American stock market; F. Scott Fitzgerald chronicled the excesses of the 'jazz age' in stories like 'A Diamond as Big as the Ritz' (1922). In his 1931 recording of 'Minnie the Moocher', Cab Calloway, the 24-year-old sensation of the Cotton Club in New York, sang of opium dreams of unimaginable wealth: 'He gave her a home of gold and steel / A diamond car with a platinum wheel.' In Ernest Hemingway's short story 'Hills Like White Elephants' (1927), meanwhile, the female protagonist ('Jig') complains: ' "That's all we do, isn't it – look at things and try new drinks?" '

In Eliot's *The Waste Land* (1922), the new consumer culture is equated with emptiness and amorality. As the 'typist' recovers from her meaningless sexual encounter with 'the young man carbuncular', a clerk, 'She smoothes her hair with automatic hand, And puts a record on the gramophone.' In *Ulysses* (1922), Leopold Bloom sells advertising for a living, and sees Dublin through an adman's eyes. He is also a consumer of advertising, getting the newspaper ad for Plumtree's Potted Meat stuck in his head: 'What is home without Plumtree's Potted Meat? Incomplete.' (With its euphemistic reference to sex, the ad is a poignant reminder of Bloom's marital problems.) In Virginia Woolf's 'Mrs. Dalloway in Bond Street' (1923), the short story that formed the nucleus of *Mrs. Dalloway* (1925), a shopping trip becomes a meditation on changes brought by the war: to class and gender relations, religious faith, fashion trends and consumer products, and general confidence. 'Thousands of young men had died that things might go on', Clarissa Dalloway muses, then shifts abruptly back to the present and her dealings with the shop assistant: 'My dear slow coach...do you think I can sit here the whole morning?'

The entries in this section provide significant background information on a variety of cultural contexts relating to modernism. Each entry begins with essential facts: 'Science and Technology', for example, features a list of some of the many discoveries and inventions beginning at the turn of the century. Then we get into deeper questions of the impact such inventions had on people's psyches at the time, and how these effects, the 'shocks' of modernity, filtered into literature. Finally, specific examples are provided from modernist texts to illustrate the relationship between text and context in understandable terms. Several of the entries in this section describe disciplines – anthropology, psychology, and linguistics, for example – that had evolved relatively recently, over the previous few decades, and whose rapid growth continued in the modernist period. The professionalization of literature and the rise of literary criticism were also part of this wider phenomenon. Questions of value raised by George Gissing in *New Grub Street* (1891), about art and commerce, the role of the critic, and the author as producer, would become central to modernist literature's crisis of identity in the early twentieth century.

Further Reading

Armstrong, Tim, *Modernism: A Cultural History* (Cambridge: Polity, 2005).
Bell, Michael, ed., *The Context of English Literature 1900–1930* (London: Methuen, 1980).
Bradbury, Malcolm, *The Social Context of Modern English Literature* (New York: Schocken, 1971).
Dangerfield, George, *The Strange Death of Liberal England 1910–1914* (New York: H. Smith and R. Haas, 1935).
Hobsbawm, Eric, *The Age of Extremes 1914–1991* (London: Michael Joseph, 1994).
Hynes, Samuel, *The Auden Generation: Literature and Politics in England in the 1930s* (London: Bodley Head, 1976).
Kolocotroni, Vassiliki, Jane Goldman, and Olga Taxidou, eds, *Modernism: An Anthology of Sources and Documents* (Edinburgh: Edinburgh University Press, 1998).
Rabaté, Jean-Michael, *1913: The Cradle of Modernism* (Oxford and Malden, MA: Blackwell, 2007).

Anthropology

In Britain, the field of anthropology, most broadly defined as the study of humankind, dates back to the mid-nineteenth century. The Ethnological Society of London, founded in 1843, was a splinter group of the Aborigines' Protection Agency, a Quaker-based anti-slavery organization founded in 1837. In 1871 it merged with the rival Anthropological Society to become the Anthropological Institute, which in turn became the Royal Anthropological Institute (1907) that still exists today. What began as an amateur pursuit in the Victorian era rapidly transformed into a professional activity in the first decades of the twentieth century. Anthropology in Victorian and Edwardian Britain was broadly comparative in nature. From its inception, it was closely tied to a pair of hotly debated issues: colonialism and evolutionary theory. Encounters with the 'other' brought about by colonial expansion produced a growing curiosity among Europeans about non-European cultures. Early anthropological narratives often attempted to legitimize colonial rule on the basis of two broadly evolutionary models (both of which placed Europe at the pinnacle): racial, according to which other peoples were viewed as biologically inferior; and cultural, which argued that different societies, though biologically equal, were at different stages of development along one continuous axis of progress. The British Quaker anthropologist E. B. Tylor's influential book, *Primitive Culture* (1871), exemplifies the latter position. In Joseph Conrad's *Heart of Darkness* (1902), the Tylorian narrator describes the African workers on his boat in just these terms: ' "I don't think a single one of them had any clear idea of time, as we at the end of countless ages have. They still belonged to the beginnings of time – had no inherited experience to teach them".' Another Tylorian, the anthropologist Sir James Frazer (1854–1941), is the figure with the closest ties to modernism. *The Golden Bough* (1890–1915) was a bestseller even in its full 12-volume format, and T. S. Eliot famously acknowledged its impact on his generation of writers in the 'Notes' section of *The Waste Land* (1922).

The year 1922 was the *annus mirabilis* of modern anthropology as much as it was the apex of literary modernism. In modernism, it was the year that saw the publication of *Ulysses* and *The Waste Land*, the debut of Eliot's *Criterion* magazine, and Woolf's first major excursion into modernist experimentation with *Jacob's Room*. In anthropology, the year was marked by the publication of Bronislaw Malinowski's *Argonauts of the Western Pacific*, an ethnographic study of the Trobriand Islanders (in particular the *kula* system of exchange with neighbouring groups), and A. R. Radcliffe-Brown's *The Andaman Islanders*. Together these groundbreaking studies signalled a new direction for the discipline, towards the use of fieldwork over library (or 'armchair') research, and away from the biological determinism and crude evolutionary models that marked earlier studies. In the same year, a single-volume edition of *The Golden Bough* was published. Frazer's epic work had already sold 36,000 copies of the full edition between 1915 and 1922, and the newly abridged edition promised even greater success. Originally subtitled *A Study in Comparative Religion*, *The Golden Bough* represented the older comparative (as opposed to analytical) approach. Nevertheless, it remains one of the most famous and influential works of anthropology ever published, and is the closest link between anthropology and literary modernism. Perhaps because it was published over such a long period, and because it is so vast, the book has meant different things to different readers. The earlier editions, for example, might have reassured readers that the forces of progress and rational science would always prevail over superstition and magic. One of Frazer's most controversial ideas (introduced in the second edition) was that of 'mental evolution' – the journey of all human societies from magic, through religion, to science. This in itself might be unsettling for its implication that religion was merely a stage of development linked to more 'primitive' forms of ritual and superstition. But *The Golden Bough* could also be read, following on the discoveries of Freudian psychoanalysis and in the aftermath of the First World War, as unsettling proof of the irrationality that lurks beneath the thin veneer of civilization.

The impact of *The Golden Bough* on modernism has long been recognized. 'Perhaps no book has had so decisive an effect upon modern literature as Frazer's', Lionel Trilling once wrote (Trilling, 1965, p. 14). *The Waste Land* is the most obvious representation of the modernist interest in myth and ritual fed by anthropology, in this case by Frazer and his disciple, Jessie Weston. Her book, *From Ritual to Romance* (1920), traced the medieval Grail legend back to its roots in ancient fertility rituals of the kind documented by Frazer. Briefly stated, the Fisher King of the Grail myth and the barren lands he oversees parallel the figure of the poet in his modern 'waste land'; the poet, like the injured King, must attend to his wounds. Though it is open to dispute, religious faith seems to offer hope at the end of the poem for the restoration of health to both the individual and society. The poem also uses various figures and symbols from Frazer, including those of the Hanged Man and the corpse planted in the garden, and draws parallels to other myths of death and resurrection, including the resurrection of Christ. Using a comparative approach not unlike Frazer's, Eliot connects individual stories of faith, suffering, and desire to other instances across literature and history. The following year, Eliot expanded on the association between anthropology and modernism in an essay for the *Dial*, 'Ulysses, Order, and Myth' (1923), where he applauded Joyce for his revolutionary use of the mythical framework. (Episodes of Joyce's novel had appeared in serialized form between 1918 and 1920, and Eliot himself had borrowed from its innovations while composing *The Waste Land*.)

In his notes to *The Waste Land*, Eliot called *The Golden Bough* a 'work of anthropology . . . which has influenced our generation profoundly', and indeed the interest in Frazer and anthropology was widespread among modernists. A key point for Eliot and Ezra Pound, who famously edited *The Waste Land*, was the idea of tradition and continuity; that Christianity, for example, is simply the latest incarnation of much more ancient rituals and beliefs. (Borrowing from Frazer, Pound sometimes overlaid or used interchangeably the names of Christ and the Sumerian vegetation god, Tammuz.) Language and literature also retained the wealth of the past, something emphasized by Pound, Eliot, and others. Ideas of a Golden

Age, fleshed out by anthropology, were also popular at the time, as in Yeats's poem 'Sailing to Byzantium' (1927). In this view, the modern West was not the pinnacle of development as it was in Victorian narratives of progress, but a time of barbarism and decadence that awaited a rebirth. T. E. Hulme was also interested in Byzantium, specifically for its geometrical mosaics, in which he saw a precursor to the new abstraction of artists like Wyndham Lewis and the sculptor Jacob Epstein.

At the other end of the modernist period, in the 1930s, a very different kind of impact was seen in the Mass Observation experiment in Britain. This movement, headed by an anthropologist, Tom Harrisson, and two surrealist poets, Charles Madge and Humphrey Jennings, enlisted hundreds of observers to collect ethnological data on their fellow citizens, with the aim of producing a kind of self-portrait of British society and its unconscious. The movement's first report was published in 1937, and afterwards it moved increasingly away from ethnological surrealism and towards popular anthropology, until in 1949 it became a standard market-research company. French surrealism also had close ties with anthropology. The work of Georges Bataille, for example, a student of the great anthropologist Marcel Mauss, borrowed from ethnographic studies in its radically primitivist celebration of 'baseness' and physicality, and its rejection of 'civilized' bourgeois values. In the United States, Zora Neale Hurston (*Their Eyes Were Watching God*, 1937) studied under the founding figure of modern American anthropology, Franz Boas, and was an accomplished folklorist as well as a leading figure of the Harlem Renaissance. Modernism's interest in anthropology speaks to the broader theme of looking elsewhere to revitalize Western society and culture, and in this respect it has been implicated in the colonizing tendencies and logocentric position of early anthropology (and of the West generally). More positively, perhaps, anthropology and modernism shared a healthy scepticism of the notion of civilization, and it was this, more than the impulse towards mastery, that drove their common search for alternative belief systems and other ways of life.

See also: *Contexts*: Culture, Empire, Race; *Texts*: Allusion, Dada and surrealism, Harlem Renaissance, Primitivism.

Further Reading

Fraser, Robert, ed., *Sir James Frazer and the Literary Imagination: Essays in Affinity and Influence* (New York: St. Martin's Press, 1990).
Manganaro, Marc, ed., *Modernist Anthropology* (Princeton, NJ: Princeton University Press, 1990).

Censorship

In the modernist period, the issue of censorship was linked to an important debate about modern art. Some felt that modernism was an accurate and important reflection of the changing society. Others, however, viewed modern art and literature as symptomatic of a broader social decline, or even as a source of the problem. The Marxist critic Georg Lukács argued that modernism provided at best a negative, distorted picture of the world; that it represented, in his words, 'a glorification of the abnormal and...an undisguised anti-humanism' (Lukács, 1964, p. 32). Other critics attacked what they saw as 'deviant' behaviour. Max Nordau, in his best-selling book *Degeneration* (1892), singled out Oscar Wilde as the leading figure in England of a pan-European trend towards decadence. The book was translated into English in 1895, coinciding with Wilde's trials and his eventual conviction for gross indecency. Nordau asked this question:

> It is easily conceivable that the emotion expressed by the artist in his work may proceed from a morbid aberration, may be directed, in an unnatural, sensual, cruel manner, to what is ugly or loathsome. Ought we not in this case to condemn the work and, if possible, to suppress it?

His answer was clear: 'beauty without morality is impossible' (Nordau, 1985, p. 326). Wilde himself admitted, in the prison letter known as *De Profundis*, that his subversive aesthetics mirrored his transgressions of social and sexual norms. 'What the paradox was to me in the sphere of thought,' he wrote, 'perversity became to me in the sphere of passion.' In the courtroom, however, Wilde argued that art should be judged solely on aesthetic and not moral grounds, just as a few years earlier, in the 'Preface' to *The Picture of Dorian Gray* (1891), he had declared: 'There is no such thing as a moral or an immoral book. Books are well written, or badly written. That is all.' Wilde's contemporaries, the 'New Woman' authors George Egerton and Sarah Grand, provoked controversy for their frank treatment of sexuality, which involved depictions of female desire (in Egerton's short stories) and the risk of venereal disease for women (in Grand's novel *The Heavenly Twins* [1893]).

It was common in the late nineteenth century for serialized fiction to be sanitized for publication in book form: examples include *The Picture of Dorian Gray* and Hardy's *Jude the Obscure* (1895). In the first decades of the twentieth century the situation shifted as modernist periodicals like the *Little Review* were seized, or their publishers were threatened with fines for trafficking in obscene material. Obscenity, a highly controversial term in its own right, can be viewed as a way of instigating cultural change. To effect a forceful break with the timid past and generate publicity using taboo language and subject matter is a method that is still widely used today, and still with surprising success. In the early twentieth century, however, many authors had difficulty getting even moderately *risqué* subject matter past increasingly nervous publishers. As George Orwell wrote in 'The Freedom of the Press', originally intended as a preface to *Animal Farm* (1945): 'The sinister fact about literary censorship in England is that it is largely voluntary.' Joyce fought word by word for the unaltered publication of *Dubliners* (1914) and *A Portrait of the Artist as a Young Man* (1916), but it was *Ulysses* (1922) that brought the real storm of controversy. The first battle with the censors erupted when *Ulysses* was serialized in the American *Little Review* between 1918 and 1920. During the first year, copies were seized and burnt by the US Post Office. Two years – and 23 installments – later, serialization was halted by a court order resulting from a complaint lodged by the New York Society for the Suppression of Vice. In 1921 the editors of the *Little Review*, Margaret Anderson and Jane Heap, were arrested and convicted over the 'Nausicaa' episode. When the intrepid Sylvia Beach published the book in 1922 through her Paris bookshop, Shakespeare and Company, it was immediately banned in Britain and America, and imported copies were frequently confiscated. *Ulysses* was finally released in America in 1934, after Joyce's publisher Random House successfully challenged the importation ban. Two years later Britain followed suit, largely on account of the American ruling. In his summing up of the case, Judge John M. Woolsey famously remarked: 'my considered opinion, after long reflection, is that whilst in many places the effect of *Ulysses* on the reader undoubtedly is somewhat emetic, nowhere does it tend to be an aphrodisiac.' One of the more notorious passages in *Ulysses*, in which Bloom 'wipe[s] himself' with a copy of *Tit-Bits*, the penny weekly founded by George Newnes in 1881, during his morning ritual, has been read as a reflection of Joyce's view of popular fiction. What might seem today like a relatively innocent, if too scatological, piece of cultural commentary, was then considered almost unspeakably coarse. Even a fellow writer like Virginia Woolf, who read *Ulysses* in manuscript form for the Hogarth Press, privately deplored the 'underbred' book.

  D. H. Lawrence had a similarly strong reaction to *Ulysses*. He judged Molly Bloom's closing soliloquy to be 'the dirtiest, most indecent, obscene thing ever written'. (The judgement was no doubt influenced by his personal animus against Joyce.) But Lawrence shared with Joyce a notable distinction: the trials of *Ulysses* and *Lady Chatterley's Lover* were two of the most important and talked about literary events of the last century. Lawrence's first foray into modernism, *The Rainbow* (1915), was also initially banned under the notorious Obscene Publications Act of 1857. Like many other works of the period, it was only published with substantial, unauthorized cuts. The alternative, which Lawrence also succumbed to on occasion, was self-censorship. The Act was finally modified in 1959, to allow a defence on the basis of literary or artistic merit. *Lady Chatterley's Lover* became the first test case in 1960, and was cleared for publication. When in the last year of his life an exhibition of his paintings was raided by police, Lawrence responded fiercely and eloquently in a long essay entitled 'Pornography and Obscenity' (1929). Here he reiterated a theme previously expressed in 'Art and Morality' (1925), that the unreflective, hypocritical morality of the 'mob', and the mass culture that it consumed, was to him far more 'obscene' than the work of any 'serious' artist. In 1928, the same year that saw the publication, in Florence, of *Lady Chatterley's Lover*, lesbian author Radclyffe Hall's *The Well of Loneliness* became the subject of another high profile obscenity trial. Unlike the works of Joyce and Lawrence, Hall's novel featured neither the detailed depiction of private bodily functions nor any trace of explicit sexual content. The ban and subsequent destruction of printed copies resulted from a warning by the medical establishment that it would encourage female homosexuality and thus erode the moral bedrock of Britain. *The Well of Loneliness* was only published in Britain in 1949, after the author's death.

See also: *Contexts*: Culture, Sex and sexuality, Women and gender; *Texts*: Aestheticism and decadence, Irish literature, Realism and naturalism; *Criticism*: Cultural materialism/New Historicism, Feminist and gender criticism, Psychoanalytic criticism.

Further Reading

Dollimore, Jonathan, *Sexual Dissidence: Augustine to Wilde, Freud to Foucault* (Oxford: Clarendon Press, 1991).

Parkes, Adam, *Modernism and the Theatre of Censorship* (Oxford and New York: Oxford University Press, 1996).

Showalter, Elaine, *Sexual Anarchy: Gender and Culture at the Fin de Siècle* (New York: Viking, 1990).

Cities and Urbanization

In 1915, the Scottish city planner and social evolutionist Sir Patrick Geddes coined the term 'conurbation' to describe Greater London and other areas of urban aggregation. Rapid expansion and merging together of urban areas was one indication that the age of the city had truly arrived. London's population nearly doubled between 1851 and 1901, and reached its highest point just before the Second World War. The increasing complexity of urban space is memorably conveyed in the labyrinthine central episode of Joyce's *Ulysses* (1922), 'The Wandering Rocks'. According to Frank Budgen, Joyce composed the episode with a map of Dublin in front of him, tracing the paths of his characters in red ink and timing their journeys down to the minute. (The young Stephen Dedalus, too, creates 'a skeleton map of the city in his mind' in *A Portrait of the Artist as a Young Man* [1916].) The 19 sections of 'Wandering Rocks', intercut with glimpses of other sections, each follow a different character or group of characters as they make their way through the city. Woolf used a similar technique in *Mrs. Dalloway* (1925), with the narrative view shifting constantly from one character to the next as they move through London or stop to witness one of the spectacles of modernity, like the airplane that appears overhead in the opening scene: 'actually writing something! making letters in the sky!'. Midway through the novel, the young Elizabeth Dalloway breaks away from her tutor Miss Kilman to explore the city by omnibus. On her journey, she contemplates the many career options now open to a woman of her generation and class: 'She would become a doctor, a farmer, possibly go into Parliament, if she found it necessary.' She ventures up the Strand, 'a pioneer', anonymous, conscious of herself in the gaze of others, exploring the main thoroughfares but stopping short of entering the 'queer alleys' and 'tempting bye-streets' of London.

Alongside efforts by writers like Joyce and Woolf to portray the subjective experience of urban life, the relatively new fields of sociology and psychology produced numerous studies of the effects of mass living on the average city dweller. Gustave Le Bon's *The Crowd: A Study of the Popular Mind* (1895) traced the rise of the modern masses, while Georg Simmel's 'The Metropolis and Mental Life' (1903) posited a protective intellectualism that sought to preserve the fragile psychology of the individual from 'the intensification of emotional life' one encounters with urban living. How to 'preserve the autonomy and individuality of his existence', in other words, was Simmel's primary concern. In his investigation of the effects of the mass economy on the individual, Simmel draws upon Marx, who declared with Engels in *The Communist Manifesto* (1848) that bourgeois capitalism 'left remaining no other nexus between man and man than naked self-interest, than callous "cash payment"'. Meanwhile, Emile Durkheim, a pioneering figure of both sociology and anthropology, wrote (especially in *Suicide*, 1897) of the personal sense of *anomie* many city dwellers experienced – the lack of a sense of purpose or belief, and feelings of loneliness, isolation, and despair.

Earlier in the nineteenth century, Edgar Allen Poe had written a short story entitled 'The Man of the Crowd' (1840). Poe's unnamed narrator, seated in a coffee house in London (at that time the most populous city in the world), observes in great detail the appearance and behaviour of individuals caught in the 'press' outside. Some passersby seem to be alone in the crowd; they 'talked and gesticulated to themselves, as if feeling in solitude on account of the very denseness of the company'. Various urban types are registered, including businessmen, clerks, pick-pockets, gamblers, beggars, and prostitutes, along with the change in the crowd from afternoon to evening. One particularly striking face suddenly captures his attention: he pursues an old man unobserved through the gas-lit streets until dawn, but learns nothing about the restless figure except that he appears to be guilty of a nameless crime. In his book on Charles Baudelaire, Walter Benjamin, another theorist of urban life, wrote of the 'shock experience' – the sensory experience of being jostled by a crowd of innumerable strangers – that had become the norm by the nineteenth century. Benjamin expanded this idea of 'shocks' into a theory of modernity itself, including the art it produces: the shock experience of the cinema, for example, or of a surrealist painting.

Modernist literature was almost entirely an urban phenomenon. Yet as Malcolm Bradbury has argued, London was not a particularly vibrant metropolis, nor was it hospitable to the arts. Bradbury claims that while London

> is the obvious centre of English-language Modernist activity...it is also in the record as one of the dullest and most deadening of capital cities, one with no real artistic community, no true centres, no coteries, no cafés, a metropolis given to commerce and an insular middle-class life-style either indifferent or implacably hostile to the new arts. (Bradbury and McFarlane, 1976, p. 172)

In 1914, confronted with the challenge of Italian futurism, whose leader Marinetti made several appearances in London during the pre-war years, the vorticist magazine *Blast* reacted with jealous anger, declaring that England was the rightful home of 'the modern movement'. 'Machinery, trains, steam-ships, all that distinguishes eternally our time, came far more from here than anywhere else', *Blast* declared. The city was conceived as an environment, a replacement for nature, the air which the new art would breathe. In its desire to distinguish itself from futurism's worship of technology, however, vorticism set itself a difficult task – to appear unmistakably modern, but to convey this with a studied nonchalance, to resist succumbing to the illusory notion of progress. Vorticism 'blessed' Britain's major ports – Hull, Liverpool, London, Newcastle, Bristol, Glasgow – while it 'blasted' the Victorian optimism that created them. This ambivalent view of modernity is at the heart of modernism. To be 'modern' meant embracing and in some way reflecting the stimulating urban environment without bowing to ideas of progress. The novels of D. H. Lawrence, for example, faithfully render the earth-shattering psychological experience of modernity ('all that is solid melts into air', in the words of *The Communist Manifesto*), while remaining scathingly critical on the subject of industrialization. The *energy* of modernity is a cause for celebration, if not its achievements. This sentiment may be traced back to nineteenth-century France and Baudelaire's famous essay, 'The Painter of Modern Life' (1863). In England, since Oscar Wilde, whom *Blast* recognized for praising the beauty of the automobile long before futurism did, artists and writers no longer fled to the pastoral: instead, they plunged headlong into the urban chaos.

See also: *Contexts*: Psychology, Science and technology; *Texts*: Aestheticism and decadence, Consciousness, Stream of, Imagism and vorticism; *Criticism*: Cultural materialism/New Historicism, Marxist criticism, Postmodernism.

Further Reading

Benjamin, Walter, *Reflections: Essays, Aphorisms, Autobiographical Writings,* ed. Peter Demetz (New York: Schocken, 1986).

Class

The modern three-tier class system, a product of the Industrial Revolution, underwent significant changes in the early twentieth century. There was progress, for example, in the areas of workers' rights, public education, and extension of the vote. Trade union membership doubled between 1913 and 1920, and the first Labour government was formed in 1924. In 1918, women won the right to vote, and by 1928 suffrage had been extended to everyone over 21. At the same time, the General Strike of 1926 revealed that inequality and class tensions still ran deep. All this, however, had less impact on literary modernism than might have been expected. One reason was the fact that so few modernists were British. American expatriates, from James McNeill Whistler and Henry James to Ezra Pound and T. S. Eliot, enjoyed freedom from the dictates of social norms that was denied to the native-born. This freedom was further emphasized by the outbreak of war in 1914. Americans like Pound escaped conscription and, along with women, who were also judged unfit to serve, quickly took over the London literary scene. Another important reason was the emphasis the modernists themselves placed on a different kind of social hierarchy: the division between artists and non-artists, elites and Philistines. This idea can be traced back to the Romantic idea of genius, and indeed a belief in the privileged role of the artist survived as a feature of modernism. Charles Baudelaire, in 'The Painter of Modern Life' (1863), proposed an aristocracy of the intellectual elite, based on 'the divine gifts that neither work nor money can give'.

In one view, of course, this separation of elites and masses was simply class prejudice by another name. Nevertheless, the fact remains that modernism paid little heed to traditional class lines, preferring to draw its own. For example, Wyndham Lewis's iconoclastic pre-war magazine, *Blast*, attacked all classes, suggesting that the artist lived apart from these mass social groupings. It declared: 'Curse abysmal inexcusable middle-class.' But it added – 'also Aristocracy and Proletariat'. Similarly, D. H. Lawrence, a collier's son from Nottinghamshire, was caustic in his criticism of what he called the 'mob', but this group was defined by its narrow-mindedness and intellectual poverty, not by its economic poverty. When the American artist Whistler, who influenced Pound in particular, lamented in his 'Ten O'Clock' lecture (1885) that ' "the many" have elbowed "the few", and the gentle circle of Art swarms with the intoxicated mob of mediocrity', his disdain was directed as much at the well-heeled crowd of non-artists who paid to hear his sold-out lecture as it was at the democratization of culture in general. (Wilde, who was in attendance, called him 'a miniature Mephistopheles mocking the majority'.)

The arrival of mass democracy, strongly felt on both sides of the Atlantic, was responsible for some anxiety on the part of writers and artists, but mainly from a market perspective. For example, writers in Britain had to consider, if not necessarily cater to, the much larger reading public that grew up in the wake of the 1870 Education Act, with its seemingly insatiable demand for popular fiction and journalism. While many writers celebrated the arrival of mass democracy and adapted to the new demands, others, especially among the modernists, reacted against the perceived threat to culture. They lamented the passing of the old order, particularly the patronage system and an audience with a shared frame of reference. The declining aristocracy could no longer provide large-scale support of the arts, though a lucky few writers, including James Joyce, did benefit from patronage on a smaller scale. Modernism is very nearly defined by its hatred for the 'mob', and its corresponding interest in models of society that featured a powerful ruling elite. Yeats had a romantic longing for pre-industrial Ireland, with its uneducated peasant class. Wyndham Lewis's vision for the post-war future, outlined in *The Caliph's Design: Architects! Where is Your Vortex?* (1921), was a ruling Caliphate. On the other hand, the reactionary philosopher T. E. Hulme gained a new interest in democracy during the war. Hulme fought in the trenches as an enlisted man before seeking and gaining a commission in the Royal Marines, and the experience softened his outlook on the 'masses'. Shortly before he was killed in battle in 1916, he wrote in his diary: 'this war has greatly, to their own surprise, converted many men to democracy'.

Where class-consciousness in modernism did exist, its clearest manifestation was in the novel, which continued to function as the primary site for the exploration of social dynamics. The novels of Virginia Woolf provide many examples. In her essay 'Mr. Bennett and Mrs. Brown', she elaborated her famous remark that 'on or about December 1910 human character changed' by stating: 'All human relations have shifted – those between masters and servants, husbands and wives, parents and children.' ('Mrs. Brown' is herself a working-class woman, like Mrs. McNab in the central 'Time Passes' section of *To the Lighthouse*, and Woolf equates the new style of representation with her emancipation.) That the style of the novel must reflect changes in society is borne out by the representation of diverse characters and their views in *Mrs. Dalloway* (1925). The 'shift', however, is by no means complete, and characters are still judged and pigeonholed according to their appearance. Septimus Smith is, in class terms, 'a border case, neither one thing nor the other', according to the narrator; 'he might have been a clerk, but of the better sort; for he wore brown boots'. His future might hold a suburban existence, 'a house at Purley and a motor car', or he might 'continue renting apartments in back streets...one of those half-educated, self-educated men'. In her diary of 1922, Woolf famously (and mistakenly of course) wrote that *Ulysses* was 'the book of a self-taught working man, & we all know how distressing they are, how egotistic, insistent, raw, striking, and ultimately nauseating'. In Woolf's last novel, *Between the Acts* (1941), her narrator takes an almost anthropological view and sets such judgements in their place. Following the description of a couple exchanging knowing glances at the appearance of the eccentric Mrs. Swithin, the narrator declares: 'Snobs they were; long enough stationed that is in that one corner of the world to have taken indelibly the print of some three hundred years of customary behaviour.'

See also: *Contexts*: Culture, Race, Women and gender; *Texts*: Bloomsbury, Realism and naturalism; *Criticism*: Cultural materialism/New Historicism, Marxist criticism.

Further Reading

Carey, John, *The Intellectuals and the Masses* (London: Faber, 1992).
Tratner, Michael, *Modernism and Mass Politics: Joyce, Woolf, Eliot, Yeats* (Stanford, CA: Stanford University Press, 1995).

Culture

For the modernists, as for the Victorians, the term 'culture' usually meant 'high culture'. Famously defended against its enemies by Matthew Arnold in *Culture and Anarchy* (1869), culture was associated with the idea of perfectibility, and its products were the highest achievements of civilization. At the same time, however, another sense was developing: what the pioneering British anthropologist Edward Tylor, in *Primitive Culture* (1871), called culture in the 'ethnographic sense', in other words: 'that complex whole which includes knowledge, belief, art, morals, law, custom and any other capabilities and habits acquired by man as a member of society'. The idea of 'popular', 'mass', or 'low' culture draws on both these descriptions, the hierarchic and the anthropologic, in that it posits levels of culture, but also broadens the idea of culture and reintegrates it with everyday life. The era of modernism, a movement often represented by its writers as being of and for the few, was not coincidentally also the era of mass culture: the popular press, advertising, cinema, radio, and popular fiction.

Beginning with the Education Act of 1870, it was also the era of mass literacy. As Tim Armstrong has argued, 'Modernity is constituted by mass activity, cutting across work, leisure, politics and intellectual life', from 'typists' pools' and 'Ford factories' to mass political rallies and the Mass Observation project (Armstrong, 2005, p. 47). The line drawn by modernist writers between elite and mass culture was in many ways a line of defence against this new reality, just as Arnold in the previous century wrote in response to the changes brought by an earlier phase of industrialization. Literary critics of the time, F. R. Leavis in particular, reinforced this distinction between the many and the few. Leavis wrote in *Mass Civilization and Minority Culture* (1930): 'In any period it is upon a very small minority that the discerning appreciation of art and literature depends.' The phrase 'discerning appreciation' signals the crisis of value that was a focal point for much of the anxiety among writers and critics at the time. How to protect 'true' art, and by extension the civilization it stands for, from a wave of inferior culture apparently flooding the marketplace – that was the question.

The nature of the split between high and mass culture has been theorized in different ways in the past century. In 1944, Frankfurt School critics Theodor Adorno and Max Horkheimer introduced the term 'culture industry' in their *Dialectic of Enlightenment* to refer to commercial entertainment such as Hollywood movies and popular songs. Their arguments about the culture industry developed from Marx's theory of commodity fetishism, where exchange-value rather than use-value is the motivating concern. Although they approached culture from a Marxist perspective, Adorno in particular has been criticized (by John Carey and others) for upholding modernism's view of mass culture as worthless and corrupt. More recently, in *After the Great Divide* (1986), Andreas Huyssen sought to provide an updated account of modernism's difficult relationship with mass culture, especially as compared with attempts by the avant-garde and postmodernism to reopen the dialogue with pop cultural forms. 'Modernism', Huyssen argues, 'constituted itself through a conscious strategy of exclusion, an anxiety of contamination by its other: an increasingly consuming and engulfing mass culture.' Huyssen focused attention on two theorists of the 'great divide', Adorno and the art historian Clement Greenberg, whom he described as 'uncompromising enemies of modern mass culture'. (Although he is a self-described postmodernist, Huyssen is sympathetic to the historical reasons for Adorno's hostility to mass culture, which include its appropriation by Hitler and Stalin, and its perceived degradation by American commercialism.) In Huyssen's view, postmodernism was an extension of the historical avant-garde as described in Peter Bürger's *Theory of the Avant-Garde* (1974). Bürger argued that in contrast to modernism, avant-garde movements like futurism and dada tried to mend the 'divide' that was first created by aestheticism in the nineteenth century. The work of another important theorist of postmodernism, Fredric Jameson, has also described in Marxist terms the blurring of the lines and reintegration of high and mass culture after modernism.

'THE PLAIN READER BE DAMNED', declared the Paris expatriate magazine *transition* in its manifesto, 'The Revolution of the Word' (1928). It is in many ways a summary statement of modernism's regard for public taste. The response by modernist writers to the rise of mass culture was not simply anxiety, but aggressive attack. 'The Day of the Rabblement' (1901), written and published in pamphlet form while James Joyce was still a university student, declared: 'No man…can be a lover of the true or the good unless he abhors the multitude; and the artist, though he may employ the crowd, is very careful to isolate himself.' The specific example Joyce had in mind was Yeats's nascent Irish Literary Theatre. Starting out, it had 'proclaimed war against commercialism and vulgarity', but 'after the first encounter it surrendered to the popular will'. The Theatre's capitulation was only temporary. In 1925, standing before an angry crowd at the production of J. M. Synge's *The Playboy of the Western World*, Yeats delivered a famous speech, which began: 'You have disgraced yourselves again. Is this to be an ever-recurring celebration of the arrival of Irish genius?'

In *The Birth of Modernism* (1993), Leon Surette perceived that modernist elitism had important roots in the occult and the idea of esoteric doctrine, secret knowledge accessible only by initiates. (Yeats and Pound are the key figures of the study.) In the occult view, Surette argues: 'history is seen as a story of conflict between superior individuals of small number ("the few", whether defined genetically or by enlightenment) and an oppressive inferior mass (whether defined genetically or by ignorance). The few are identifiable by their cultural attributes' (Surette, 1993, p. 38). It is not, then, so much a matter of class as of cultural difference: hence the invocation of the Philistine, and the targeting of the bourgeoisie, the Academy, and 'middlebrow' taste. The idea of the enlightened and the ignorant was found by some modernists to be as useful as it was malleable. Ursula Brangwen in D. H. Lawrence's *The Rainbow* (1915), for example, felt 'the grudging power of the mob lying in wait for her, who was the exception'. The Brangwens in general are shown to be targets of resentment for their natural superiority, victims of 'brutish resentment'. During the First World War, the idea of the privileged artist was manifested in petitions for combat exemption, as T. E. Hulme campaigned on behalf of the sculptor Jacob Epstein. (In the end it was Hulme who was killed.) As Stephen Dedalus tells his friend and fellow aesthete Lynch in Joyce's *A Portrait of the Artist as a Young Man* (1916): 'We are right...the others are wrong.'

See also: *Contexts*: Class, Fascism; *Texts*: Aestheticism and decadence, Irish literature.

Further Reading

Chinitz, David E., *T. S. Eliot and the Cultural Divide* (London and Chicago: University of Chicago Press, 2003).

Huyssen, Andreas, *After the Great Divide: Modernism, Mass Culture, Postmodernism* (Bloomington and Indianapolis: Indiana University Press, 1986).

Leavis, F. R., *The Great Tradition: George Eliot, Henry James, Joseph Conrad* (London: Chatto and Windus, 1948).

Williams, Raymond, *Culture and Society* (London: Chatto and Windus, 1958).

Empire

The British Empire, the largest empire in history, reached its greatest size in terms of land mass (roughly a quarter of the earth) and governed population (about a fifth) around 1920, also the peak of the modernist period. Indeed, it could be said that modernity itself is a product of colonialism: not only in material terms, for the wealth, goods, and knowledge gained through global trade and exploitation, but in metaphysical terms, for the self-image that developed of the West as rational and enlightened, an emissary of progress. The greatest phase of colonial expansion took place in the last decades of the nineteenth century, and was marked by the so-called Scramble for Africa and the Berlin Conference of 1884–1885, where the African continent was largely divided among the major European powers. This was also the period in which Britons took the most pride in British imperialism, sometimes leading to jingoistic extremes – indeed, the phrase 'by jingo' first appeared in a music hall song of the 1870s. Perhaps the most familiar literary expressions of this sentiment are Rudyard Kipling's popular poems, including the two series of *Barrack-Room Ballads* (1892, 1896), 'Recessional' (1897), and 'The White Man's Burden' (1899). The colonizers portrayed by Joseph Conrad in *Lord Jim* (1900) and *Heart of Darkness* (1902), by contrast, revealed the ugly effects of imperialism on both the colonizers and the colonized. The early twentieth century saw expansion give way to consolidation, and public enthusiasm for the Empire began to wane along with other aspects of the Victorian legacy. This was particularly true after the First World War; even before the War, however, the tide of public opinion was turned by revelations of systematic abuse and genocide contained in the Casement Report on the Belgian Congo (1904) and other documents.

Strong ambivalence, if not outright condemnation, is the most common reaction towards British imperialism in modernist literature. In *Heart of Darkness*, for example, the 'darkness' and Kurtz's famous last words ('The horror! The horror!'), suggest the terrible reality of colonization in Africa. Marlow decides at the end of the story not to reveal Kurtz's final utterance to his Intended because ' "It would have been too dark – too dark altogether" '. Kurtz was an expert ivory hunter, but he also represented a new type of high-minded colonialism that emphasized the 'morality' of its civilizing mission rather than pursuing simple exploitation. At one point a character in the book quotes Kurtz as saying: ' "Each station should be like a beacon on the road towards better things, a centre for trade of course, but also for humanizing, improving, instructing." ' Whether this was a cynical cover (as it was for

King Leopold II of Belgium) or misguided idealism, the intellectual pretense dissolves when faced with the situation on the ground. In Virginia Woolf's novel *Mrs. Dalloway* (1925), meanwhile, Peter Walsh, Clarissa's former suitor who ran away to India to become a colonial official, notes on his return to London the 'triumphs of civilization' he sees everywhere: an efficient health care system, for example. This simple binary of civilized Europe and its implied opposite (India), however, breaks down as the reader realizes that Peter's vision is false: the ambulance he sees has been called to take away the body of Septimus Warren Smith, the war veteran turned shell-shock victim and suicide. The idea of civilization suffered greatly after the atrocities of the war, and with it went any belief in the civilizing power of Europe with regard to its colonies.

Ireland represents a special case in terms of modernism and empire. On one hand, it may be seen as a 'settler colony' like Canada or Australia, whose writers were British subjects (whether or not they considered themselves as such) until Partition in 1922. In another view, the idea of linguistic, cultural, and racial difference – of Irishness and Englishness – was often exploited in a way that emphasized the relationship of colonizer and colonized. Joyce in particular has proved fertile ground for postcolonial readings. A cosmopolitan writer above all else, meditations on issues of nation and empire appear in all of Joyce's major works. In *A Portrait of the Artist as a Young Man* (1916), the built environment of Dublin reveals its colonial history. Stephen's father 'lingers' in the Bank of Ireland when Stephen claims his cash reimbursement for a school prize, and tells Stephen 'that they were standing in the house of commons of the old Irish parliament'. Later Stephen recalls a phrase he learned in Latin class: *India mittit ebur*, or 'India sends ivory' (as if willingly). In conversation with the Dean of Studies, who is also an Englishman and a Jesuit priest, Stephen thinks:

> The language in which we are speaking is his before it is mine.... His language, so familiar and so foreign, will always be for me an acquired speech. I have not made or accepted its words. My voice holds them at bay. My soul frets in the shadow of his language.

In *Finnegans Wake* (1939), Joyce's subversion of the language of the colonist reaches its highest point: it is not the English language we are reading but the language of Joyce, a slippery, punning, polyglot language.

See also: *Contexts*: Nationalism, Race; *Texts*: Irish literature, Primitivism; *Criticism*: Postcolonialism.

Further Reading

Cheng, Vincent J., *Joyce, Race, and Empire* (Cambridge and New York: Cambridge University Press, 1995).
Hobsbawm, Eric, *The Age of Empire 1875–1914* (New York: Random House, 1987).
Said, Edward, *Culture and Imperialism* (New York: Vintage, 1994).

Fascism

Modernism has long held an unfortunate, but not unfounded, association with fascism. Most obviously, there are the coinciding timeframes. On the fascist side, Mussolini formed his party in Milan in 1919, the same year Hitler joined the nascent Nazi party. Hitler became leader of the Nazi party in 1921, and was appointed Chancellor of Germany in 1933. Oswald Mosley formed the National Union of Fascists in Britain in 1932. In 1936, General Franco led his military coup, setting off the Spanish Civil War. The two movements, modernism and fascism, share a simultaneous progression from radical roots in the pre-war period to a 'high' or institutionalized period in the 1920s and 1930s. Shared philosophical influences are also cited as evidence of their affinity: from Nietzsche, whose influence was pervasive in Europe during the early twentieth century, to the French syndicalist Georges Sorel, author of *Reflections on Violence* (1908), which was published in an English translation by T. E. Hulme in 1914. More striking are the explicit links: perhaps most notoriously Ezra Pound's broadcasts in support of Mussolini on Rome radio between January 1941 and July 1943. Pound's wartime activities resulted in his detention at Pisa, during which time he wrote the *Pisan Cantos*. There followed charges of treason, deportation to America, and 12 years at St. Elizabeth's Hospital for the Criminally Insane in Washington, D. C.

Marinetti's futurists, who had their own revolutionary political party, were among the earliest and most boisterous supporters of fascism in Italy. They joined forces with Mussolini in 1918 and helped to establish the *Fasci di Combattimento* in Milan the following year. In England, Wyndham Lewis's misguided praise in *Hitler* (1931) dealt a lasting blow to his reputation; he later reversed his judgement in *The Hitler Cult* (1939), but to little effect. In the case of D. H. Lawrence, some have found his frequent talk of 'blood consciousness' too close to the blood metaphors of fascism, and his 'leadership' novels of the 1920s, notably *Kangaroo* (1923), too enthusiastic in their depiction of extreme-right politics. Yeats's support for the Irish Blueshirts, an openly xenophobic and anti-Semitic fascist organization, extended to writing marching songs for the movement, which were reportedly sung by Blueshirts fighting for Franco alongside a Nazi tank regiment in Spain. One of the most open supporters of Spanish fascism was the South African poet Roy Campbell, a friend of Lewis's and author of the pro-Franco epic *Flowering Rifle: A Poem from the Battlefield of Spain* (1939). It is perhaps a reminder of the complexity of some of these cases that Campbell was also a translator of the poet Federico García Lorca, a leftist homosexual who was executed by Franco's Falangists in 1936.

The turn to fascism must be seen in the context of the turn against liberal democracy, especially after the failures of the First World War. A sense of crisis and the legitimate fear of collapse into anarchy motivated the movement towards political extremes in the interwar period. Yeats wrote in 1933: 'I find myself constantly urging the despotic rule of the educated classes as the only end to our troubles' (Yeats, 1954, pp. 811–12). It should be remembered that a large number of Left-leaning writers and artists flew to communism for similar reasons, and many remained faithful to the Party long after Stalin took control in the late 1920s. There was a sense that democracy and the Enlightenment belief in progress and rationality had been invalidated by the mass carnage of the First World War and state of chaos into which Europe had fallen. There needed to be, in Nietzsche's words, a 'revaluation of values'. Because fascism is fundamentally opposed to the bourgeois ideals of liberalism and democracy, any reaction against these values, especially in the 1920s and 1930s, would naturally have made one appear to share common cause with fascist ideology, even if there were disagreement in the details. Other interests common to modernism and fascism include order, social hierarchy, myth, regeneration, and the occult. (Leon Surette usefully explores the links between modernism, fascism, and the occult in *The Birth of Modernism*.)

Less common was the treatment of fascism as a theme. One exception is Lawrence, who had witnessed violent clashes between fascists and communists in Italy after the war, and transposed the rise of extreme politics to Australia in his novel *Kangaroo*. More common were ideological debates conducted in newspapers and magazines in the 1930s, when the binary opposition of fascism versus communism reached its height. In 1937, for example, the *Left Review* published its landmark pamphlet *Authors Take Sides on the Spanish War*, which boasted 148 contributions including many first-rank writers. The anti-fascist statements made up the overwhelming majority, and ranged from Samuel Beckett's '¡UPTHEREPUBLIC!' to the West Indian writer C. L. R. James's reply: 'Against Fascism, against Franco, but against Bourgeois democracy too.' Only five supported Franco, one of whom was Evelyn Waugh. The 'Neutral' category, meanwhile, featured T. S. Eliot, Ezra Pound (who dismissed the whole exercise as 'an escape mechanism for young fools who are too cowardly to think'), and others including Sean O'Faolain, Robert Byron, H. G. Wells, Vita Sackville West, and Oscar Wilde's son Vyvyan Holland. Writers who fought against Franco in the International Brigades included George Orwell, Ernest Hemingway, the poet John Cornford, the Marxist critic Christopher Caudwell, and Julian Bell, who was Virginia Woolf's nephew and the son of Clive and Vanessa Bell.

The many links between modernism and fascism have been examined in books with titles like *Fables of Aggression: Wyndham Lewis, the Modernist as Fascist* (1979), *Fascist Modernism: Aesthetics, Politics, and the Avant-Garde* (1993), *The Poetics of Fascism: Ezra Pound, T. S. Eliot, Paul de Man* (1996), *Thinking Fascism: Sapphic Modernism and Fascist Modernity* (1998), and, more broadly, *Bad Modernisms* (2006). Some scholars defend their authors' fascist tendencies as a product of the time, while others argue that claims are exaggerated or judgements have made unfair use of hindsight following the Second World War. Defenders of poets like Pound, Eliot, and Yeats have sometimes insisted that political affiliations are irrelevant, especially when considering the work of a movement that often emphasized formal innovation and autonomy over political engagement or issues of morality. But it is clear that there existed a modernist flirtation with fascist ideas, and that this flirtation developed into a more serious relationship for Pound in particular. With the exception of Pound, however, most of these figures could more accurately be referred to simply as conservatives or reactionaries, or 'proto-fascists', as Fredric Jameson has called Wyndham Lewis. In 1943, George Orwell, who fought in the International Brigades against Franco, wrote of Yeats that 'long before Fascism was ever heard of, he had had the outlook of those who reach Fascism by the aristocratic route. He is a great hater of democracy, of the modern world, science, machinery, the concept of progress – above all, of the idea of human equality' (Orwell, 1946, p. 116). In this sense, 'fascism' is too historically limited a term, and it seems more accurate to say that the views held by Yeats and other modernists with anti-democratic, anti-humanist tendencies had similar origins and followed a similar path of development to those of the European fascist movements.

See also: *Contexts*: Class, Culture, Nationalism, Philosophy, Race, War; *Texts*: Anti-Semitism, Apocalypse, Futurism, Imagism and vorticism, Violence; *Criticism*: Cultural materialism/New Historicism, Marxist criticism.

Further Reading

Hewitt, Andrew, *Fascist Modernism: Aesthetics, Politics, and the Avant-Garde* (Stanford, CA: Stanford University Press, 1993).

Jameson, Fredric, *Fables of Aggression: Wyndham Lewis, the Modernist as Fascist* (Berkeley: University of California Press, 1979).

Payne, Stanley G., *A History of Fascism 1914–1945* (Madison: University of Wisconsin Press, 1996).

Redman, Tim, *Ezra Pound and Italian Fascism* (Cambridge and New York: Cambridge University Press, 1991).

Language

Ferdinand de Saussure (1857–1913), a pioneering Swiss linguist whose work led to the development of structuralism, is a name that is often mentioned in relation to modernism and language. The main source of his ideas is the *Course in General Linguistics* (1916), which was assembled from his papers and from the notes and recollections of students who had been present at his lectures in Geneva between 1907 and 1911. (Saussure died in 1913.) According to Saussure, language is a system of signs. These signs can be broken down into two components: the 'signifier' (the written or spoken part), and the 'signified' (the idea in the mind of the speaker). The connection between signifier and signified is arbitrary, which allows shifts in meaning to occur over time. Most relevant to modernist art and literature, aside from the linguistic self-consciousness that Saussure's ideas represent, was his idea of linguistic autonomy: that the meaning of words derived from their context, the language system, and not from the thing to which they referred. Language, much like abstract art, is a closed system, where meaning is relative and does not necessarily relate to or derive from the outside world. Our language shapes and bounds our world. This theory was akin to James McNeill Whistler's declaration, in his famous court case with the critic John Ruskin in 1878, that rather than producing a faithful rendering of a particular scene from nature, his only goal was to create a perfectly coherent world within the painting, 'to bring about a certain harmony of colour'. It also resonates with Gustave Flaubert's expressed desire to write 'a book about nothing, a book without external attachments which would hold together by itself through the internal force of its style'. Virginia Woolf also attempted to achieve such formal balance in her novels. In *To the Lighthouse* (1928), for example, the first and third parts are almost literally balanced by a thin passage down the middle, 'Time Passes'. The artist character Lily Briscoe mirrors this balance in the novel's famous closing passage: 'With a sudden intensity, as if she saw it clear for a second, she drew a line there, in the centre.'

In the pre-war period, avant-garde literary manifestos called for radical changes, especially to poetic language. Some of the more influential manifestos included Marinetti's 'Technical Manifesto of Futurist Literature' (1912), Mayakovsky's 'Slap in the Face of Public Taste' (1912), and Pound's 'A Few Don'ts by an Imagiste' (1913). Mayakovsky and the Russian futurists called on poets to enlarge the language with neologisms, and 'To feel an insurmountable hatred for the language existing before their time.' Marinetti presented a highly detailed programme for renewal, which advocated 'words in freedom', the destruction of syntax, and dispensing entirely with adverbs and adjectives, punctuation, and the pronoun 'I'. Analogy, the essence of poetry, would be elevated to fill the place of all this grammatical scaffolding. More conservatively, and indeed partly in reaction to Marinetti, Pound instructed the poet simply to 'Use no superfluous word' and to 'Go in fear of abstractions'. All of these poetic commandments, with their calls to strip language down to its elements and build it up afresh, can be seen as a reaction against the excesses of the previous generation. Pound and other Anglo-American modernists differed from their Russian and European counterparts not in concept but only in degree, and in their continued reverence for past masters like Shakespeare and Dante. In another articulation of Pound's slogan, the Russian critic Viktor Shklovsky observed in avant-garde literature the attempt to 'estrange' language (his concept, *ostrenenie*, translates as 'estrangement' or 'defamiliarization'). He contrasted everyday language with literary language, where the goal, at least if it was done right, was to make strange and thereby revitalize the language.

The modernist project of renovation encapsulated in Ezra Pound's exhortation to 'make it new' applies, above all, to language itself. Language, as opposed to what it represents, became the central focus of much modernist writing; language itself became the subject. This will be evident to anyone who has reached the second half of Joyce's *Ulysses* (1922), where the mode of telling increasingly threatens to eclipse the tale itself. Each chapter is written as a pastiche or burlesque of one or more styles: the musical, 'fugue' style in 'Sirens'; the succession of generic styles in 'Cyclops' (journalistic, epic, legal, scientific, all filtered through the nameless narrator's Dublin street slang); or the sentimental style of a popular women's magazine in 'Nausicaa' ('mayhap he would embrace her gently, like a real man, crushing her soft body to him, and love her, his ownest girlie, for herself alone').

Other modernists were less confident than Joyce was about the power of language. They felt that even if language could still represent the 'real' world, the picture of this world was no longer shared. In the opening scene of Woolf's *Mrs. Dalloway*, for example, onlookers vary widely in their interpretations of two spectacles: an impressive automobile taking someone, possibly the Queen or the Prime Minister, to Buckingham Palace; and an airplane writing something in the sky overhead. How to describe the world accurately when everyone sees it differently? For other modernists, the relationship between words and their referents, signifier and signified, had broken down. Narrators lost their reliability, or they lost the ability to describe anything with confidence. In Samuel Beckett's early novel *Murphy* (1938), Celia, talking to Murphy, feels 'spattered with words that went dead as soon as they sounded; each word obliterated, before it had time to make sense'. The experimental novelist B. S. Johnson, an heir to Joyce and Beckett, grew so disillusioned with the task of communicating with his readers that when it came time to describe the protagonist of his final novel, *Christie Malry's Own Double-Entry* (1973), he threw up his hands and declared: 'Make him what you will: probably in the image of yourself.' The struggle with language, whether or not it is seen as hopeless, goes back to Flaubert's famous struggle, in the writing of his foundational modernist text, *Madame Bovary* (1856), to find just the right word. As Prufrock exclaims in Eliot's 'The Love Song of J. Alfred Prufrock' (1915): 'It is impossible to say just what I mean!'

See also: *Contexts*: Censorship; *Texts*: Allusion, Fragmentation, Futurism, Imagism and vorticism; *Criticism*: Deconstruction, New Criticism, Structuralism, Poststructuralism.

Further Reading

Saussure, Ferdinand de, *Course in General Linguistics*, trans. Wade Baskin (New York and London: McGraw-Hill, 1966).

Market

Drastic changes to the publishing industry that began in the Victorian era continued to have their effect in the modernist period. Literacy rates had climbed steadily since the Education Act of 1870, and by the early twentieth century literacy in Britain stood at about 80 percent. Newspapers and magazines accounted for much of the growth in reading material: at the turn of the century, the *Daily Mail* famously achieved circulation of a million copies a day. 'For her generation', the narrator of Virginia Woolf's last novel, *Between the Acts* (1941), relates about a character born in 1900, 'the newspaper was a book'. For those who still read books, as of course many did, private lending libraries offered the most affordable way for people to consume fiction. Boots' Book-Lovers Library, for example, was founded in 1900. This was as it had been in the previous century; however, public libraries were gradually extending their branches from large cities to smaller towns, particularly after the Public Libraries Act of 1919. The three-decker novel had suffered a sudden collapse in the 1890s, when circulating libraries withdrew their support of the format, but the single-volume novel that replaced it continued to thrive and diversify into different genres.

In the first decades of the twentieth century, cheap editions (sixpenny or even lower) were printed in the tens of thousands. Popular authors could expect to sell their books at various prices – half a crown, one shilling, sixpenny – simultaneously to capture different readerships. The advent of compact, affordable reprint editions, including the World's Classics (1901, bought by Oxford University Press in 1905) and Everyman's Library (1906), was another significant change to publishing. The World's Classics were priced as low as one shilling in 1905, when the pocket edition was also introduced. The average literary novel, however, might sell only 1000 copies, and the hardbound edition was usually priced at a fairly expensive six shillings. During the inter-war years, the price of these novels rose to seven shillings and sixpence, further widening the gap between middle-class fiction and mass-market cheap editions. Penguin Books, which arrived on the scene in 1935, revolutionized the industry by offering 'high-culture' titles in a paperback edition that cost only sixpence.

Throughout this period, modernism's relationship with the market was complex and often marked by outright hostility. Of course, what was then called 'modern' literature amounted to only a small fraction of the publishing industry. By 1914, more than 1000 novels were published in Britain each year, but very few of them offered the challenge of Wyndham Lewis's *Tarr* or Joyce's *A Portrait of the Artist as a Young Man*, both of which were serialized in Harriet Shaw Weaver's *Egoist* magazine and then published by the Egoist Press during the war. These writers rejected the novelistic conventions of best-selling authors like H. G. Wells and Arnold Bennett, who appealed to middle-class readers, while also shunning the 'mass' culture represented by everything from popular romance novels to the newer media of cinema and radio. To hear the writers tell it, modernism made few if any concessions to either audience expectations or commercial concerns. The familiar modernist pose was to defy reader expectations and the demand for a familiar plot, characters, and style.

Writers actively taunted readers by breaking taboos and placing rigorous demands on the reader's knowledge and patience. In the *Manifesto of Futurist Theatre* (1910), subtitled *The Pleasures of Being Booed*, the Italian futurist leader F. T. Marinetti, who was a regular visitor to England during the pre-war years, called on authors to 'despise the public' as fickle and mediocre. 'Playwrights should have no other concern than that of an absolute, innovative originality.' This dictum summarized the view of most modernists. It can also be seen in earlier works like George Gissing's bleakly pessimistic *New Grub Street* (1891), with its somewhat simplistic binary of money versus art in the London literary world.

Recent studies in publishing history, most notably Lawrence Rainey's *Institutions of Modernism* (1998), have uncovered in careful detail the truth behind claims that modernism existed outside of market pressures. According to Rainey, the show of contempt for mass culture was simply part of modernism's broader cultural economy, in which value and demand tied in with collectability, new forms of patronage, coterie audiences, and a general aura of exclusivity. Far from resisting commodification, in other words, these texts invited it, albeit on their own terms. Modernism, as conceived by Ezra Pound and others, was like a fashionable nightclub: the stricter the door policy, the longer the queue, the higher the entrance fee, the greater the interest was generated. Of course, modernism made all sorts of demands: a higher price and hard-to-find copies were only the first difficulties the contemporary reader-consumer would have encountered. Quality, small-scale publishing did not originate in the twentieth century. In the 1890s, for example, William Morris's Kelmscott Press had produced its finely crafted editions partly in reaction to the mass market.

The publishing history of T. S. Eliot's *The Waste Land* (1922) serves as Rainey's chief example of modernist exclusivity as a marketing technique. A combination of money and reputation led Eliot to place his poem in the *Dial* for its initial US publication rather than the *Little Review*, where payment was nil and circulation was too limited, or *Vanity Fair*, which had ten times the *Dial*'s circulation but lacked its exclusivity and seriousness. Pound acted not only as editor of *The Waste Land* but also as its agent, negotiating between various offers. (The professionalization of literature in Britain had begun in the previous century with the founding of the Society of Authors by Walter Besant in 1884.) Following the careful re-examination of print culture in the early twentieth century by Rainey and others, it is now generally accepted that modernism was more deeply entangled in commercial concerns than was previously thought. Even before he sold *The Waste Land*, Eliot perceived with clarity the relationship between supply and demand: in a letter from 1919 he remarked:

I write very little, and I should not become more powerful by increasing my output...each [poem] should be an event. (Eliot, 1988, p. 285)

See also: *Contexts*: Censorship, Class, Culture; *Texts*: Aestheticism and decadence, Futurism, Imagism and vorticism; *Criticism*: Cultural materialism/New Historicism, Leavisite criticism, Marxist criticism.

Further Reading

Dettmar, Kevin J. H., and Stephen Watt, eds, *Marketing Modernisms: Self-Promotion, Canonization, and Rereading* (Ann Arbor: University of Michigan Press, 1996).
Rainey, Lawrence, *Institutions of Modernism: Literary Elites and Public Culture* (New Haven and London: Yale University Press, 1998).
Willison, Ian, Warwick Gould, and Warren Cherniak, eds, *Modernist Writers and the Marketplace* (Basingstoke and New York: Palgrave Macmillan, 1996).

Nationalism

The issue of nationalism in this period is complicated by the rise of two new tendencies, both of which are strongly present in modernist literature: transnationalism and cosmopolitanism. Transnationalism may be defined as extending beyond national boundaries, or cutting across boundary lines, as modernism certainly did. Cosmopolitanism, often linked with decadence and used as a term of derision by conservatives in the period (much as 'liberalism' is used in America today), similarly denotes a lack of regard for international boundaries. It can also describe a city with a highly diverse ethnic makeup or cosmopolitan outlook: a 'cosmopolis' or world city. It has often been noted that none of the so-called 'Men of 1914' – Joyce, Pound, Eliot, and Lewis – were born in England. Joyce in particular was defiantly cosmopolitan, an outlook that is reflected in many of his characters. The idea expressed by Hugh Kenner that 'English' modernism was a movement of Irish exiles and American expatriates is of course only partly true: Lawrence, Woolf, Hulme, and Ford were born in England, as were Dorothy Richardson, May Sinclair, and Rebecca West. British-born modernists were also prone to periods of self-imposed exile: Lawrence lived in Sicily and New Mexico, for example, while Mina Loy moved between Florence and New York. It is perhaps more accurate to say that Anglo-American modernism was primarily a literature of exiles and outsiders: if not exiles of another nation, then outsiders in terms of class, sex, or gender.

Modernism elsewhere in Europe is in some ways a different story. Italian futurism was extremely nationalistic and supported Italy's colonial interests in Libya and Ethiopia, for example. Futurism was vehemently opposed to the family; instead, it considered the nation to be the ideal grouping. Marinetti wrote of the nation in 1919: 'It is generous, heroic, dynamic, and Futurist, while...the family is small-minded, fearful, static, conservative, and...bound by tradition' (Marinetti, 2006, p. 322). Italy and Germany were both newly formed nation states, having come into existence roughly at the end of the Franco-Prussian War in 1871, and it was not by accident that these nations also saw the strongest support for fascism, with its dependence on national and racial mythologies. In Scotland, meanwhile, the leading figure of the Scottish renaissance, Hugh MacDiarmid, wrote approvingly of Italian fascism in 1923, calling for Scotland to welcome a similar marriage, as he saw it, of socialism and nationalism. The Irish literary revival also flirted with fascism, seen in Yeats's support for the Blueshirts in the 1930s. However, the revival was by no means uncritical in its nationalism, and protests over plays deemed insulting to Ireland were a common occurrence at the Abbey Theatre.

Modernist literature is generally marked by its reaction against nationalism and its advocacy of the writer's and the individual's freedom from institutional restraints. This is perhaps best seen in Joyce's *A Portrait of the Artist as a Young Man* (1916). Stephen Dedalus undertakes to free himself from a series of 'nets' that would hamper his development as an artist, namely: 'nationality, language, religion'. When Davin, a member of the Gaelic League, challenges Stephen's Irishness he replies: 'This race and this country and this life produced me.... I shall express myself as I am.' Stephen, like Joyce, is mindful of the fate of nationalist heroes like Wolfe Tone and Charles Stewart Parnell, whose death occurs at the beginning of the book. In Joyce's view, these men tried to save Ireland from itself, and were betrayed and martyred at the hands of their own people. As Stephen tells Davin with bitterness: 'Ireland is the old sow that eats her farrow.' Despite his obvious reservations, Stephen is in some ways modeled on past nationalist heroes, and the novel's famous penultimate line, 'to forge in the smithy of my soul the uncreated conscience of my race', makes one form of allegiance clear. A similar concern for the artist's autonomy was expressed in England at this time in Wyndham Lewis's *Blast* (1914–1915). On the eve of the First World War, the vorticist magazine made the audacious declaration: 'We fight first on one side, then on the other, but always for the SAME cause, which is neither side or both sides and ours.' (The 'War Issue' that followed in 1915, however, made some concessions to patriotic duty.)

The impact of the First World War was a major factor in the erosion of nationalist sentiment among writers and public alike. Bloomsbury writer and conscientious objector Lytton Strachey published his ironic biography *Eminent Victorians* shortly before the Armistice in 1918, and with it laid to rest four pillars of Victorian England – Cardinal Manning, Thomas Arnold, Florence Nightingale, and General Gordon – and set the tone for the post-war period. In Woolf's *Mrs. Dalloway* (1925), the new post-war attitude is signalled by a description of the brief swell of patriotic interest created as a luxurious motorcar carrying 'Queen, Prince, or Prime Minister' passes through the crowd on its way to Buckingham Palace. The narrative tone is anything but reverential, noting the gossip-mindedness of the onlookers, and if some still doff their caps and stand to attention, they just as quickly lose interest when a skywriting airplane advertising toffee flies overhead, at which point 'the car went in at the gates and nobody looked at it'. The old symbols of Queen and country still survive, but they are largely nostalgic. Meanwhile, for another of Woolf's characters, the shell-shocked Septimus Smith, the war has killed off his romantic patriotism. Septimus went to war for the England of Shakespeare, but came back to find in the same plays only 'loathing, hatred, despair'. D. H. Lawrence's wartime short story 'England, My England' (1922) takes its title from W. E. Henley's patriotic poem 'England' (1900), and indeed starts out in the idyllic and timeless setting of Crockham Cottage in Hampshire. This place is described as being 'savage as when the Saxons first came', and life there is 'like a chapter of living romance'. When the modern world interrupts this idyll, in the form of trench warfare, Egbert, the lazy, idealistic Englishman, 'born and bred free', goes to war as if in a daze and is soon killed by a German shell. Lawrence later wrote, in *Kangaroo* (1923): 'It was in 1915 the world ended.'

See also: *Contexts*: Empire, Fascism, Race; *Texts*: Anti-Semitism, Futurism, Irish literature; *Criticism*: Cultural materialism/New Historicism, Leavisite criticism, Marxist criticism, Postcolonialism.

Further Reading

Esty, Jed, *A Shrinking Island: Modernism and National Culture in England* (Princeton and Oxford: Princeton University Press, 2004).

Gervais, David, *Literary Englands: Versions of 'Englishness' in Modern Writing* (Cambridge: Cambridge University Press, 1993).

Lewis, Pericles, *Modernism, Nationalism and the Novel* (Cambridge: Cambridge University Press, 2000).

Nolan, Emer, *James Joyce and Nationalism* (London and New York: Routledge, 1995).

Psychology

Like the fields of anthropology and sociology, psychology was an emerging profession in the modernist period and was very much tied up with modernist concerns. Sigmund Freud (1856–1939) was a contemporary of the modernists and published his most influential writings, including *Three Essays on the Theory of Sexuality* (1905), *Totem and Taboo* (1912), *Beyond the Pleasure Principle* (1919–1920), and *The Ego and the Id* (1923), in the first decades of the twentieth century. Freud's groundbreaking study, *The Interpretation of Dreams* (1900), introduced the idea that our dream life is intimately connected with, and revelatory of, our waking life – that, for example, dreams may represent repressed sexual desires and the wish fulfillment of desires. Far from being trivial and nonsensical, dreams were revealed as dense texts that could be 'translated' from their symbolic or 'picture-puzzle' state into the accessible language of our conscious wishes or 'dream-thoughts'.

One of Freud's earliest successes was the technique of 'free association', later to become the psychoanalytical method. It was developed as an alternative to hypnosis used in the recovery of repressed memories. In 1910 Freud established the International Psychoanalytical Association, with the Swiss psychologist and psychiatrist Carl Jung as its first president. Jung's *Psychology of the Unconscious* (1912), which marked the beginning of his break with Freudian psychoanalysis, was another influential work of psychology for modernism. Jung's ideas of the 'collective unconscious' as a source of dreams, and the recurring images or symbols ('archetypes') manifested in dreams and myths, led among other things to the practice of archetypal or myth criticism. Like Freud, Jung was influenced by the anthropology of E. B. Tylor and James Frazer, particularly on the subject of myth, and for both of them myth was seen as a key to the universal unconscious. This is the side of Freud (and of Frazer) that influenced T. S. Eliot, seen in *The Waste Land* (1922) and his influential review of *Ulysses*, '*Ulysses*, Order, and Myth' (1923). Jung also wrote a review of *Ulysses*, in 1932, and in 1934 he became the twentieth doctor to be consulted by James Joyce about his daughter Lucia's mental illness. Joyce's *Finnegans Wake* (1939) contains several references to Jung, as well as to Freud.

The dissemination of Freud's theories sparked widespread interest in the unconscious, and this extended to modernism. The 'inward turn' or exploration of the psyche often said to characterize modernist literature is difficult to imagine without Freud. That is not to say that Freudian influence was necessarily direct or explicit; such an assertion would be not only difficult to prove, it would be anachronistic. Like Einstein or Darwin,

Freud's ideas of the unconscious, the libido, and repression were partly a product of their time. Once published, they quickly became so popular that they were in some form or other simply 'in the air'. Translations of Freud into English became available shortly before the War, and by the 1920s most writers would have been familiar with the central tenets of his work. The London Psychoanalytic Society was founded in 1913, followed by the British Institute of Psychoanalysis in 1924, which published the International Psychoanalytic Library Series in partnership with the Woolfs' Hogarth Press.

In 1909, Freud made a celebrated trip to the United States, his first and only visit. The trip came at the invitation of G. Stanley Hall, a fellow psychologist and President of Clark University in Massachusetts, where a major conference was taking place. Jung accompanied Freud, and at the conference they met the psychologist William James, who coined the term 'stream of consciousness', and the anthropologist Franz Boas, among other pioneering figures of the social sciences. Freud's visit began a longstanding relationship with America, where interest in psychoanalysis was always greater than on the other side of the Atlantic. The First World War, with its many psychological as well as physical casualties, did contribute to Freud's notoriety in Britain. The shell-shocked character Septimus Smith in Woolf's *Mrs. Dalloway* (1925), for example, is symptomatic of a wider fascination in the post-war period with the causes of psychological trauma. Septimus's doctors, Holmes and Bradshaw, struggle and ultimately fail to treat their suicidal patient, and Woolf's portrayal of the medical establishment is highly critical. It was C. S. Myers, an experimental psychologist and a consultant to the British Army during the war, who first used the term 'shell shock' in 1915. Myers considered the condition treatable, but was frustrated by strong opposition to this view. Since shell shock was not widely recognized or understood, it was often equated with cowardice, and in some cases soldiers exhibiting signs of mental distress on the battlefield were simply shot. Nervousness as a symptom of modern life can be traced back at least as far as Baudelaire's conception of the modern subject as 'nerve-ridden', and Max Nordau's infamous study *Degeneration* (1892) associated nervousness and hysteria – signs of an 'artistic temperament' – with moral and spiritual decay. This view only increased after the war, and persisted well into the 1930s: in 1936, for example, the American reporter Michel Mok called F. Scott Fitzgerald 'The poet-prophet of the post-war neurotics'.

Importantly for modernist writers, Freud's theories suggested that our identity was fluid and changing rather than fixed and permanent. (The French philosopher Henri Bergson also articulated this view.) Neither was self-knowledge something to take for granted; it seemed suddenly that people were at the mercy of complex desires and hidden drives. This contradicted the Victorian idea of a stable and knowable identity, and in fact it was Oscar Wilde who presented an early challenge to this notion in *The Importance of Being Earnest* (1895), where Jack discovers at the end of the play that in fact he is not Jack, the person he thought he was, but Ernest, the person he pretended to be. Clarissa Dalloway, too, reveals her unified self to be merely a mask: she 'tried to be the same always, never showing a sign of all the other sides of her'. Moreover, Freud saw the formation of identity as something that occurred mostly in childhood. Woolf's 'tunneling' method of characterization, flashing back to her characters' formative experiences, suggests that she shared this view. Other remarkable episodes depicting the unconscious at work in modernist literature include: the dream sequence in Thomas Mann's *Death in Venice* (1912), with its obvious symbolism and themes of homosexual desire and repression; the 'Time Passes' section of Woolf's *To the Lighthouse* (1927), with its astonishing invention of the dream life of an empty house; the 'Circe' episode of *Ulysses* (1922), in which Bloom and Stephen lose themselves in 'Nighttown', Dublin's carnivalesque brothel quarter; and indeed virtually all of what John Bishop has called Joyce's 'book of the dark', *Finnegans Wake* (1939). D. H. Lawrence wrote two Freud-inspired books, *Psychoanalysis and the Unconscious* (1921) and *Fantasia of the Unconscious* (1922), and the basic theme of freedom versus repression, of the quest for the instinctual self, is central to many of his works. The modernist novelists May Sinclair and Dorothy Richardson were two of the first writers in England to digest Freud's ideas. Of course, Freud did not win the admiration of all modernists. Some, like Pound and Lewis, reacted against what they saw as another excuse for romantic introversion, infantile regression, and a morbid overemphasis on sex.

See also: *Contexts:* Cities and urbanization, Sex and sexuality; *Texts:* Consciousness, Stream of, Fragmentation, Memory; *Criticism:* Feminist and gender criticism, Psychoanalytic criticism.

Further Reading

Valentine, Kylie, *Psychoanalysis, Psychiatry, and Modern Literature* (Basingstoke and New York: Palgrave Macmillan, 2003).

Race

Race was a subject of great interest in this period among scientists and scholars, artists, and the general public alike. It was part of a broad network of issues relating to nationalism, colonialism, war, population and migration, and new directions in science and the humanities that had emerged in the Victorian period – Darwin's theory of evolution, psychology, anthropology, and so on. Though racial prejudice even in its modern form developed much earlier, the term 'racist' only entered common usage in the 1930s. (Its predecessor, 'racialist', dates back to 1907.) The relationship between modernism and race has many different aspects. The 'primitivism' of white European and American modernists attempting to 'make it new', for example, has long been a subject of interest. What was often simply called Negro Art, and might have included anything from African masks to jazz or the poetry of the Harlem Renaissance, enjoyed immense popularity at the time. Many artists viewed it as the antidote to a dying European culture: it was seen as a source of vitality, or as a rich repository of abstract motifs ripe for plundering – even as the roots of abstraction.

A very different aspect of the relationship between race and modernism can be found in the Harlem Renaissance itself. This movement of the 1920s and 1930s married stylistic innovation to cultural nationalism and ideas of 'race consciousness', 'uplift', and W. E. B. DuBois's idea of an active and assertive black cultural elite, the so-called 'talented tenth'. The contribution of Harlem Renaissance writers was so great, in fact, that this body of writing is often seen as a distinct, in a sense parallel literary movement, not to be easily subsumed under the broader definition of a predominantly white Anglo-American modernism. The questions of race and empire contribute to the ongoing discussion of what constitutes modernism: where did it take place, who were the important figures, how was its early history written, and how should we redraw its boundaries to bring it into line with contemporary scholarship.

Another important and controversial aspect of this topic is modernism's engagement with eugenics, the study of racial engineering. As David Bradshaw makes clear, the eugenics movement that reached its height in Britain and America in the 1920s was anything but marginal. Eugenicist themes are present in the writing of Yeats, Eliot, Woolf, Stein, Lawrence, and other modernists, and in the more popular works of Wells and Shaw. High profile advocates of eugenics in the 1920s came from across the political spectrum, and included many 'progressive' thinkers such as the economist John Maynard Keynes, the philosopher Bertrand Russell, and the birth control advocate Marie Stopes. Compulsory sterilization for certain groups became law in countries like Denmark, Sweden, Norway, Finland, Canada, and Switzerland, as well as in many American states, though it never got that far in Britain. It was Darwin's cousin, Sir Francis Galton, who coined the term 'eugenics' in *Inquiries into Human Faculty* in 1883. The anxiety that drove this phenomenon was the perceived deterioration of the race, which some believed was reaching epidemic proportions. Evidence was found in the declining health of the working classes in industrial cities like Manchester and Birmingham. This fear was compounded by studies showing a decline in the birth rate for the upper and middle classes, while the birth rate among the poor and immigrant populations remained steady. 'Positive' and 'negative' eugenic strategies were proposed to combat this differential decline: the former included incentives to encourage breeding among the 'better' classes, while the latter sought to limit (or eliminate) breeding among 'less desirable' or 'unfit' groups. Much has been written about modernism's flirtation with fascism, and this theme is often tied – for obvious reasons – to eugenics. The interest in selective breeding ultimately led to, and also ended with, the eugenics-inspired ideology of the Nazis and the genocide of the Holocaust, an event many scholars (most recently Vicki Mahaffey in *Modernist Literature: Challenging Fictions*, 2007) have identified as marking the end of modernism.

The modernist period was one of enormous cultural hybridity, cosmopolitanism, and expatriation. There were Irish writers in London, American writers in Paris, and Caribbean writers in New York, and a constant flow of migration was stirred up by two world wars. Take, for example, the byline at the end of Joyce's *Ulysses* (1922): '*Trieste-Zurich-Paris*, 1914–1921'. Joyce had chosen exile from Ireland, and first settled his family in Trieste, which was then part of the Austro-Hungarian Empire. Forced to leave Trieste at the outbreak of the First World War because he was a citizen of the United Kingdom, and was therefore considered an enemy, he moved to neutral Zurich to sit out the war. He finally settled in Paris shortly after the Armistice. In 1940, when Joyce tried to move his family back to Switzerland from France, he was initially denied entry on the grounds that he was suspected of being Jewish. The cosmopolitanism of this period resulted in new breakthroughs, but also new anxieties about the policing of national and ethnic boundaries. Britain lagged behind the rest of Europe in the registration of resident aliens, which it instituted in 1914, and the country had long been considered a safe haven for anarchists and other radicals. The English poet and philosopher T. E. Hulme, who arrived in London in 1908, was keenly cosmopolitan despite his reactionary reputation. This cosmopolitanism was reflected in the guest lists at his weekly Frith Street salon, which included an array of continental European visitors and expatriates. Hulme was, according to his biographer Robert Ferguson, 'a leading importer into England of intellectual goods, in the form of French *vers libre*, Bergson's dignified and dignifying metaphysics, and the artistic theories of the German aestheticians'.

The concept of 'otherness' that is so central to an understanding of Victorian literature also lies at the heart of modernism. In Victorian literature, the English sense of self is often constructed in contrast to its foreign other – Indian or Irish, or for that matter female or working class. However, a major shift in the concept of race and otherness can be seen to occur in literature between the height of the colonial period at the end of the nineteenth century and the period of decolonization beginning with the Second World War. Increasingly, the other is not encountered outside of oneself, but rather it is found within: the self *as* other. New discoveries in science and psychology were one factor in this shifting sense of self, as uncertainty and inwardness replaced Victorian confidence to become distinguishing marks of modernist literature. Another factor was the increased movement of people between countries. As Marjorie Perloff has argued recently, 'the diaspora literature of our own time begins in the early twentieth century' (Perloff, 2006, p. 576). At the turn of the century, the sociologist and activist DuBois, who (like Gertrude Stein) studied under William James at Harvard University, pioneered the idea of 'double consciousness' – an idea which later gained a more general application – to describe the African-American experience of alienation from the self. 'An American, a Negro; two souls, two thoughts, two unreconciled strivings; two warring ideals in one dark body', DuBois intoned in *The Souls of Black Folk* (1903), the collection of essays in which he famously predicted that 'the problem of the Twentieth Century is the problem of the color-line'. This quintessentially modern form of alienation, 'double consciousness', DuBois argued, came from being raised in the mindset of the majority culture while at the same time being excluded from it. This split identity produced a sense of otherness towards oneself. Two meanings of otherness, both of which are central to modernism, are present in the concept of 'double consciousness': the view of the exotic 'other' that was a legacy of the nineteenth century and earlier, here internalized; and the feeling of alienation from the larger society, of being an outsider, that is already present in early modernists like Baudelaire and Dostoevsky. The interest in primitivism that was pervasive in the modernist period carried on the old ways of the colonial era, but it also suggested a new recognition of, and identification with, the authenticity of the other: the other was now seen as being one facet of ourselves.

See also: *Contexts*: Anthropology, Class, Empire, Fascism, Nationalism; *Texts*: Anti-Semitism, Harlem Renaissance, Primitivism; *Criticism*: Postcolonialism, Postmodernism, Poststructuralism, Psychoanalytic criticism.

Further Reading

Bradshaw, David, 'Eugenics: "They Should Certainly Be Killed" ', in Bradshaw, ed., *A Concise Companion to Modernism* (Oxford and Malden, MA: Blackwell, 2003).

Childs, Donald J., *Modernism and Eugenics: Woolf, Eliot, Yeats, and the Culture of Degeneration* (Cambridge: Cambridge University Press, 2001).

Gilroy, Paul, *The Black Atlantic: Modernity and Double Consciousness* (London: Verso, 1993).

Said, Edward, *Orientalism* (New York: Pantheon, 1978).

Religion

'It is a curious thing, do you know, Cranly said dispassionately, how your mind is supersaturated with the religion in which you say you disbelieve.' The line from James Joyce's *A Portrait of the Artist as a Young Man* (1916) speaks not only to Stephen Dedalus's situation, and to Joyce's own, but also to a generation born into religion and raised in an age of doubt. In the Victorian era, Christian belief was most famously shaken by Charles Darwin's theory of evolution through natural selection, detailed in *The Origin of the Species* (1859) and *The Descent of Man* (1871). The more literal, historical sort of Christianity was further undermined by textual scholarship on the Bible itself, which revealed its gradual production by numerous authors over an extended period of time. The new field of comparative religion was also widely perceived as a threat to Christianity. In 1889, the anthropologist James Frazer wrote to his publisher describing the first edition of *The Golden Bough* (1890–1915), a book that would have a profound effect on modernist literature, and acknowledging one of its possible side effects. He wrote: 'The resemblance of savage customs and ideas to the fundamental doctrines of Christianity is striking. But I make no reference to this parallelism, leaving my readers to draw their own conclusions, one way or the other.' Then, in addition, there was Nietzsche's sustained attack on Christianity in the last decades of the century. This was neatly summed up in the bold and quotable declaration 'God is dead', which first appears in *The Gay Science* (1882). The fact that the phrase was usually taken out of context is overshadowed by the substantial currency it gained with the general public.

Given the rise of secularism in Britain and the West during the late nineteenth and early twentieth century, the extent to which religious themes and imagery still appear in modernist literature and art may be surprising. However, if the language and iconography of religion were still used, the treatment and function of religion in modernism changed dramatically. Religious belief, like most other areas of thought at the time, was perceived to be in a state of crisis. The directions modernist writers took in responding to this crisis varied, but they generally fell into three categories: embracing secularism, usually in tandem with challenging or attacking religious institutions; exploring spiritual alternatives to Christianity, including pantheism, the occult, and Eastern religion; and calling for the return to some sort of Christian tradition. The secularists were led by James Joyce, whose wife Nora refused last rites on his behalf at his deathbed, and Virginia Woolf, along with most of Bloomsbury. The occultists included W. B. Yeats, Ezra Pound, and the influential *New Age* editor A. R. Orage, although Joyce and D. H. Lawrence also employed the occult tradition in different ways. Yeats was a member of the Hermetic Students of the Golden Dawn and the Theosophical Society, both led by Madame Blavatsky, the key figure of the occult fad of the 1890s. His dedication to the occult lasted throughout his life, and was reflected in the automatic writing experiments with his wife, Georgie Hyde Lees, and in the system outlined in *A Vision* (1925).

The traditionalists, meanwhile, included Eliot and the philosopher and critic T. E. Hulme. Hulme upheld the doctrine of Original Sin – though arguably more as a philosophical idea than a specifically religious one – against what he considered false optimism and the notion of progress. In the essay-lecture 'Romanticism and Classicism' (1912), he famously denounced Romanticism as 'spilt religion'. Eliot's decisive embrace of Christianity came in 1927, the year he gave up his American citizenship and became a British subject, when he was baptized into the Church of England. The following year, in the 'Preface' to *For Lancelot Andrewes: Essays on Style and Order* (1928), Eliot described his 'point of view' as 'classicist in literature, royalist in politics, and anglo-catholic in religion', an English gloss on a slogan that originated with the French reactionary thinker Charles Maurras (*classique, catholique, monarchique*). Eliot's conversion can been seen as part of a greater effort to escape what he called the 'futility and anarchy' of the present age, including the growing secularism and materialism of Western society. This deliberate move into orthodoxy seemed like an abrupt departure from his earlier bohemianism, but in fact it had deeper roots than many realized at the time. Eliot's embrace of Christianity and its institutions contrasted greatly with Lawrence's very personal, pantheistic view. Lawrence summed up this view in 1912: 'I worship Christ, I worship Jehovah, I worship Pan, I worship Aphrodite .... I want them all, all the gods.' He goes on: 'If I take my whole passionate, spiritual and physical love to the woman who in turn loves me, that is how I serve God.' Here the prophetic influence of William Blake is clearly evident, representing another very different strain of modernist belief. Both of these differ again from the view expressed by Stephen Dedalus (to the Englishman Haines) in Joyce's *Ulysses* (1922).

When Haines tells Stephen, 'You are your own master', Stephen replies: 'I am the servant of two masters...an English and an Italian.' Stephen equates the power of the Roman Catholic Church in Ireland with English colonial rule, and tries, as the younger Stephen did in *A Portrait*, to free himself from these 'nets'. In *A Portrait*, Stephen goes so far as to tell Cranly, 'I will not serve', echoing Satan's *non serviam*; as Cranly says: 'That remark was made before.'

Spiritual alternatives aside, the majority of modernists believed that art itself represented the last, best chance for Western civilization. Like many modernist beliefs, this can be traced back to Romanticism, and to the aestheticism of the late-Victorian period. Whistler, the American expatriate artist, cast his influential 'Ten O'Clock' lecture of 1885 in the style of Genesis, and himself in the role of the preacher declaiming the doctrine of art. He also spoke of 'false prophets' and the 'Gentle priest of the Philistine' (alluding to Wilde), who convinced the public that they should take an interest in art – an unhealthy interest, in Whistler's view. The artist was given the raw materials of nature by God, but surpassed God (or 'the Gods') in the masterpiece he created: 'and the Gods stand by and marvel, and perceive how far and away more beautiful is the Venus of Melos than was their own Eve.' Whistler's typically outrageous assertion, that the artist not only equalled but actually surpassed and improved upon God's work in the creation of beauty, is a testament to the strength of modernist confidence in the redemptive power of art.

See also: *Contexts*: Anthropology, Culture; *Texts*: Aestheticism and decadence, Apocalypse, Bloomsbury, Epiphany, Fragmentation, Primitivism; *Criticism*: Leavisite criticism, Marxist criticism.

Further Reading

Surette, Leon, *The Birth of Modernism: Ezra Pound, T. S. Eliot, W. B. Yeats, and the Occult* (Montreal and Kingston: McGill-Queen's University Press, 1993).
Wright, T. R., *D. H. Lawrence and the Bible* (Cambridge and New York: Cambridge University Press, 2000).

Science and Technology

It is common for modernist criticism to draw parallels between advances in science and literature: use of the word 'experiment' is one such gesture. However, tracing a line of influence can be difficult. What is clear is that innovations in the two fields, and the new ways of seeing they introduced, bear some striking resemblances. 'Relativity' and 'uncertainty', for example, evoke defining features and achievements of both. In science, as in the arts, 'reality' was dealt a heavy blow at the turn of the century by a rapid succession of new discoveries. Beginning in the 1890s, Wilhelm Roentgen discovered X rays (or Roentgen Rays) in 1895; Henri Becquerel, investigating Roentgen's work, discovered radioactivity in 1896; J. J. Thomson announced his discovery of the electron in 1897; Marie and Pierre Curie followed with radium in 1898; and in 1900 Max Planck first proposed the quantum theory, which reached maturity in the1920s. These discoveries among many others, including Earnest Rutherford's successful splitting of nitrogen atoms in 1910, had profound implications for empirical science. As in the work of Freud, these new lines of inquiry dealt, disconcertingly for some, more with the unseen than the seen. Abstract, speculative theory increasingly replaced old-fashioned observation. Moreover, with the advent of Einstein's special (1905) and general (1916) theories of relativity, high-level physics no longer appeared to obey reasonable laws. After Einstein, the physical (Newtonian) universe was never the same. Even if writers did not necessarily understand Einstein's theories, they understood that everything previously held to be true was now subject to revision and would remain ambiguous at best, just as Darwin's theories had turned natural science on its head in the previous century. Even more unsettling was the idea that, in fact, Newton's laws still held for everyday life; Einstein's theories applied to extreme situations, such as travel near the speed of light. Had everything changed, or not? The existence of two apparently contradictory theories in tandem furthered the impression that science (like religion at the time) could no longer be thought of as a single, conclusive explanation, but only a series of 'stories' made up to account for the workings of the universe.

If science had suddenly been rendered 'all too human', to borrow Nietzsche's phrase, the new doctrine of relativism was in many ways liberating. Einstein published a layman's version of his work, *Relativity, the Special and the General Theory*, in 1920. Several other popular introductions followed. Relativism is perhaps the key identifying factor of modernist literature: what 'happens' in a modernist novel or poem is highly speculative and subjective, owing to unreliable narrators, shifts in perspective, and other techniques suggesting epistemological uncertainty. Werner Heisenberg's 'uncertainty principle' of 1927, another step forward in quantum mechanics, only added to this general outlook. Rather than one reliable, omniscient perspective, readers were shown several limited ones, often with nothing more than the distant and ambiguous presence of an 'arranger' (as this figure has been called in studies of Joyce) to watch over things. Even taken together these multiple perspectives do not necessarily add up to an objective view of the world. Characters witness events from their particular position in the world, and this position influences their view, just as Einstein and Heisenberg's theories suggested that the observer's position would always render scientific laws relative and contingent. In the 'Lestrygonians' episode of *Ulysses* (1922), Bloom contemplates the word 'parallax', which in astronomical terms refers to a 'change in the apparent position or direction of an object [e.g. a star] as seen from two different points' (*Oxford English Dictionary*). In the novel, it signals an important element of relativism, that what you see depends on who you are and where you are standing, not unlike the multiple perspectives of a cubist painting. Bloom, however, professes his ignorance of the term ('I never exactly understood') and moves on. Another version of the new *Weltanschauung* can be seen in the philosopher T. E. Hulme's early work 'Cinders', a collection of notes begun in 1906 and unpublished in his lifetime, which described a new outlook of uncertainty, plurality, and only local comprehension. 'The *absolute*', Hulme states, 'is to be described not as perfect, but if existent as essentially imperfect, chaotic, and cinder-like'. Hulme adds to this the very modern sounding statement that 'all a writer's generalisations and truths can be traced to the personal circumstances and prejudices of his class, experience, capacity and body.' Our knowledge, in other words, is partial, contingent, and highly subjective. Attempts at outright explanation were now seen as hopelessly naïve.

The impact of technology on daily life in the first decades of the twentieth century can scarcely be overstated. Technological innovations brought profound changes to every aspect of human existence in Europe and North America. In a section of *The Education of Henry Adams* (1907) entitled 'The Dynamo and the Virgin', for example, the American Adams recorded the shock he felt at the Great Exposition of 1900 in Paris: 'he found himself lying in the Gallery of Machines... with his historical neck broken by the sudden irruption of forces totally new'. In manufacturing, Henry Ford pioneered the moving assembly line in 1913, which dramatically increased the production capacity and affordability of the Model T (first built in 1908). Mass production was advanced not only by 'Fordism' but also by 'Taylorism', the management theory developed by Frederick Winslow Taylor in the 1880s and 1890s to increase productivity through division of labour. It was the dehumanizing, repetitive work promoted by Taylorism that Charles Chaplin parodied in the film *Modern Times* (1936). Domestic life was altered, especially in the United States, by inventions like the lightweight electric iron (1903), the domestic vacuum cleaner (1907), the electric toaster (1909), and the electric dishwasher (1911). This was also the age of mass communication, which meant cheaper and more plentiful printed matter (books, magazines, newspapers, posters, pamphlets), telegraph, telephone, radio, film, phonograph, and television, as well as the increased communication that accompanied easier travel. When the *Titanic* sunk in the mid-Atlantic on the night of 14–15 April 1912, New Yorkers read about it in their morning papers. Some significant landmarks in communications in this period include Guglielmo Marconi's transmission of radio signals from Cornwall to Newfoundland in 1901, the first transcontinental telephone call from New York to San Francisco in 1915, and John Logie Baird's demonstration of televised images at Selfridges department store in London in 1925.

Travel was revolutionized by the internal-combustion engine (1876) and the diesel engine (1896), along with advances in steam power. These laid the groundwork for the appearance of motorcars and buses in Britain at the turn of the century. There were over 750,000 passenger journeys by bus in 1914, and roughly the same number by tram and trolleybus. The London Underground, one of the great achievements of the Victorian era, was gradually electrified starting with the District and Circle lines in 1905, and by 1914 most lines had come under common ownership, making connections easier. The first escalators were built in Earl's Court Station in 1911, followed by the appearance of the familiar Underground logo, the 'roundel', in 1913. Charles Rolls and Henry Royce launched the Silver Ghost in 1907, the year before Ford introduced the popular Model T. Twentieth-century aviation began with the first zeppelin flight in 1900, followed by the Wright brothers' first sustained flight in a controlled airplane at Kitty Hawk, North Carolina in 1903. The French aviator Louis Blériot, later to become a major designer and manufacturer of airplanes, was the first to fly across the English Channel in 1909. Aircraft technology made a great leap during the First World War, where it was used in reconnaissance, air to air combat, and bombing missions. Civil aviation increased steadily after the war, with daily flights between London and Paris established in 1919. Airplanes feature prominently in literature of the 1920s and 1930s, often as a symbol of modern technology. A skywriting plane is watched by a crowd in the opening scene of *Mrs. Dalloway* (1925), while in Woolf's last novel, *Between the Acts* (1941), the first page mentions the ancient 'scars' on the landscape, which are visible from the air. Stephen Spender's poem, 'The Landscape Near an Aerodrome' (1933), begins with an admiring description of a passenger airplane in descent, 'More beautiful and soft than any moth'. William Faulkner was a keen aviator, and airplanes appear in many of his stories. He joined the Royal Canadian Air Force in 1918, but the war ended before he saw action; he resumed flying in the 1930s. *Pylon* (1935) depicts the world of air shows and barnstorming stunt pilots that Faulkner knew from personal experience.

See also: *Contexts*: Cities and urbanization, Culture, Market; *Texts*: Cinema, Futurism, Music, Primitivism; *Criticism*: Cultural materialism/New Historicism, Marxist criticism, Postmodernism.

Further Reading

Armstrong, Tim, *Modernism, Technology, and the Body: A Cultural Study* (Cambridge and New York: Cambridge University Press, 1998).
Benjamin, Walter, *Illuminations: Essays and Reflections*, ed. Hannah Arendt, trans. Harry Zohn (New York: Schocken, 1987).
Whitworth, Michael, *Einstein's Wake: Relativity, Metaphor, and Modernist Literature* (Oxford and New York: Oxford University Press, 2001).

Sex and Sexuality

The language of sex as we know it originated to a large extent in the modernist period. Words like 'sexology' (1902), 'sex-obsessed' (1914), 'sex act' (1918), and 'sexy' (1925; first in French in *La Nouvelle Revue Francaise* referring to Joyce's *Ulysses*, and shortly thereafter in English), as well as 'sex-talk' and 'sexual orientation' (both 1931), entered regular usage at this time. Even 'sex' meaning 'sexual intercourse' ('to have sex') is first recorded in the D. H. Lawrence poem 'Sex and Trust' from *Pansies* (1929), which begins: 'If you want to have sex, you've got to trust / at the core of your heart, the other creature.' In his 'Introduction' to *Pansies*, Lawrence registered his surprise at the power some words still have to shock. 'The words themselves are clean, so are the things to which they apply', he wrote. 'But the mind drags in a filthy association, calls up some repulsive emotion. Well then, cleanse the mind, that is the real job.' The slogan of the *Egoist* (1914–1919), a London-based little magazine that published the work of Joyce, Eliot, and many other modernists, was 'Recognises no taboos'. This new sexual frankness marked yet another departure from the Victorian era, where euphemism held sway until the end of the century despite inroads made by writers like Havelock Ellis, whose seven-volume series *Studies in the Psychology of Sex* (1897–1928) began with *Sexual Inversion* (co-authored with John Addington Symonds), the first major study of homosexuality to be published in Britain.

The open discussion of sexual matters was encouraged in Britain by the growing awareness of Freud and psychoanalysis. In the 1915 edition of his book *Three Essays on the Theory of Sexuality* (1905), Freud introduced the concept of the sexual instinct or libido (Latin for 'desire' or 'lust'), which he argued was the motivating energy behind much of human behaviour. The first translations of Freud into English appeared before the War, and in the 1920s the Woolfs' Hogarth Press began publishing the International Psychoanalytic Library Series in partnership with the newly formed British Institute of Psychoanalysis. By this time authors had become bold enough with the censors that legal action was taken in high-profile cases involving Joyce's *Ulysses* (1922), Radclyffe Hall's *The Well of Loneliness* (1928), and D. H. Lawrence's *Lady Chatterley's Lover* (1928). Language, of course, was not the only issue. Risqué themes of the period included adultery, homosexuality, prostitution, illegitimacy, venereal disease, abortion, rape, and incest. Adultery figures in many key modernist novels, and is central to *Ulysses* and *Lady Chatterley's Lover*, as well as Ford's *The Good Soldier* (1915). Prostitution is a rite of passage in Joyce's *A Portrait of the Artist as a Young Man* (1916), while incestuous desire in the father–daughter relationship is a theme in *Ulysses* (1922) and *Finnegans Wake* (1939). Homosexuality is a significant theme in such works as *The Well of Loneliness*, Lawrence's *The Rainbow* (1915), Marcel Proust's *In Search of Lost Time* (1913–1927), Thomas Mann's *Death in Venice* (1912), Djuna Barnes's *Ladies Almanack* (1928), and E. M. Forster's *Maurice* (privately circulated from 1913, published posthumously in 1971). Shortly before the war the futurist leader Marinetti attacked English prudery and hypocrisy in his 'Lecture to the English on Futurism' (1911). After the war, however, changes to mainstream society became more and more apparent, as Peter Walsh notices on his way back to England in Woolf's *Mrs. Dalloway* (1925). He sees 'lots of young men and girls...carrying on quite openly; and the old mother sitting and watching them with her knitting, cool as a cucumber'. Nevertheless, Lawrence would continue to battle 'sexless' England through his writing and painting until his death in 1930.

The new atmosphere of sexual openness was not always seen as a cause for celebration. Rather, it was often used to symbolize decadence and decline, or the triumph of shallow materialism over a more meaningful existence. In the poetry of T. S. Eliot, for example, sex is a source of anxiety, abjection, and ennui. Masculinity in 'The Love Song of J. Alfred Prufrock' (1915), like everything else in the poem, is diminished and doubtful. 'I have heard the mermaids singing, each to each', Prufrock thinks, but then: 'I do not think that they will sing to me.' After the First World War, the sense of trauma and loss was frequently portrayed in sexual terms, particularly in the form of impotence or injury. Jake Barnes is left impotent by an unnamed war wound in

Ernest Hemingway's first novel, *The Sun Also Rises* (alternatively titled *Fiesta*, 1926). The war fills Septimus Smith with a feeling of revulsion in Woolf's *Mrs. Dalloway* (1925). He remains unable to consummate his marriage with Rezia after five years, party due to his reluctance to 'bring children into a world like this'. In the novel this parallels the Dalloways' sexless marriage, Clarissa's residence in the attic room, and her feeling of 'virginity preserved through childbirth'. In *The Waste Land* (1922), the theme of impotence is evoked by the myth of the Fisher King and the pagan fertility rituals from which it was believed to have derived: to revitalize his 'arid' lands, the king must first heal his own (sexual) wounds. Society in the poem is seen to be ill – exhausted, debased, fragmented – and it is the poet who might offer the chance of a cure, if there is to be one at all.

See also: *Contexts*: Censorship, Psychology, Women and gender; *Texts*: Aestheticism and decadence, Bloomsbury, Primitivism, Realism and naturalism; *Criticism*: Feminist and gender criticism, Poststructuralism, Psychoanalytic criticism.

Further Reading

Baldick, Chris, 'Sex and Sexualities', *The Oxford English Literary History: Vol. 10. 1910–1940* (Oxford and New York: Oxford University Press, 2004), pp. 364–90.

War

The modernist period is a period of wars, including their build up and aftershocks. Beginning in the wake of the Franco-Prussian War (1870–1871) and the Boer War (1899–1902), it was cut in half by the First World War (1914–1918), then progressed through the Anglo-Irish War (1919–1921), the Irish Civil War (1922–1923), and the Spanish Civil War (1936–1937). It was brought to a close, in most accounts, by the Second World War (1939–1945). Primarily, however, it was the First World War, which Britain entered on 4 August 1914, that left its mark on modernist literature. For many writers and artists, as for the wider public, the initial reaction in 1914 was stoic acceptance or even outright enthusiasm. Rudyard Kipling's 'For All We Have and Are' (1914), with the line 'The Hun is at the gate!', is an extreme example of the literary output in this phase. In addition, a long list of authors, including Kipling, G. K. Chesterton, and Arthur Conan Doyle, as well as Thomas Hardy, H. G. Wells, and May Sinclair, signed a petition in September 1914 supporting Britain's entry into the war.

By the mid-point of the war, however, when the endless slaughter in the trenches became an unavoidable reality, attitudes had changed considerably. This later view, captured in Wilfred Owen's 'Dulce et Decorum Est' and 'Anthem for Doomed Youth' (both written in 1917 and published posthumously), extended to the eruptions of nihilist outrage by members of the dada movement that began in neutral Zurich. Conscription was introduced in Britain in January 1916. Unmarried men of military age had the choice of either enlisting voluntarily, which sometimes carried the benefit of a preferred assignment, or being placed automatically in a reserve group to be called upon when needed. One of the greatest massacres of the Western Front, the battle of the Somme, with more than a million casualties, occurred in the summer and autumn of 1916. The following year, more than a quarter of a million Allied casualties were recorded at the disastrous battle for control of Passchendaele, a small and relatively insignificant Belgian village near the town of Ypres. These events marked a grim new phase of the war.

'Then down came the lid – the day was lost, for art, at Sarajevo.' Wyndham Lewis's bleak judgement of the effect the war had on art may be surprising given the achievements of modernist art and literature in the 1920s. The First World War is considered by many to be the defining historical event, even the primary source, of modernism. But the war had a catastrophic impact on the burgeoning avant-garde scene of the pre-war period, including Lewis's own vorticist movement. Looking back, Lewis described the pre-war avant-garde as a game played between artists, press, and public, where everyone 'felt as safe as houses'. Then the war entered, and swept away these antics. Modernism may have recovered, and even thrived, enjoying its 'high' period after the war, but it was a different kind of modernism – less exuberant, less open, and less optimistic. The post-war literature is characterized by a keen sense of lost innocence; a deep nostalgia for a world now vanished. D. H. Lawrence wrote in a letter to Mary Cannan in June 1918: 'Something inside one weeps and won't be comforted. But it's no good grieving.... there was *something* in those still days, before the war had gone into us...something very good, and poignant to remember, now the whole world of it is lost' (Lawrence, 1962, p. 558). Woolf's greatest novels, *Mrs. Dalloway* (1925) and *To the Lighthouse* (1927), are both divided – literally down the middle in the case of *To the Lighthouse* – between pre- and post-war settings. Woolf's writing entered a new phase immediately after the war, and *Jacob's Room* (1922), a fragmented portrait of a young man killed in battle (the aptly named Jacob Flanders), was her first truly experimental novel.

Relatively few major artists and writers actually died in the war. They included the poets Rupert Brooke (from an illness), Charles Hamilton Sorley, Isaac Rosenberg, and Wilfred Owen, the critic and philosopher T. E. Hulme, and the sculptor Henri Gaudier-Brzeska (remembered in the second issue of *Blast*). Wyndham Lewis served at the Front as an officer in the Royal Artillery and then as a war artist. Four of the central figures of modernism, two American and two Irish – Eliot, Pound, Joyce, and Yeats – had little involvement with the war. Voices opposed to the war included Bertrand Russell (who went to prison), D. H. Lawrence and Lytton Strachey (both judged unfit for service), Leonard and Virginia Woolf, Clive and Vanessa Bell, George Bernard Shaw, and Aldous Huxley. E. M. Forster, a pacifist, worked for the Red Cross, while Gertrude Stein and Alice B. Toklas transported medical supplies in their Ford automobile for the American Fund for the French Wounded (AFFW). Ernest Hemingway, John Dos Passos, May Sinclair, and E. E. Cummings served in the ambulance corps in Europe. A list of modernist fiction of the First World War might include, in addition to the novels by Woolf already mentioned: Hemingway's *In Our Time* (1925), with its vignettes of war scenes between the stories, and *A Farewell to Arms* (1929); Rose Macaulay's *Non-Combatants and Others* (1916); Rebecca West's *The Return of the Soldier* (1918); Mary Butts's story 'Speed the Plow' (1922); Lawrence's 'England, My England' (1922); Faulkner's *Soldier's Pay* (1926); Cummings's *The Enormous Room* (1922); Ford Madox Ford's tetralogy *Parade's End* (1924–1928); and Richard Aldington's *Death of a Hero* (1929). There were also many autobiographical accounts, including Robert Graves's *Good-bye to All That* (1929), Wyndham Lewis's *Blasting and Bombardiering* (1937), and Herbert Read's *In Retreat* (1925).

The endpoint of the modernist era is often given as 1939, the start of the Second World War. In her last novel, *Between the Acts* (1941), set in the summer of 1939, Virginia Woolf described one character's foreboding 'vision of Europe, bristling with guns'. If the Second World War was not necessarily the end of a modernist style, it was for all practical purposes the end of a generation. Yeats, Ford, and Freud died in 1939; Fitzgerald, Nathanael West, and the critic Walter Benjamin (fleeing the Nazis) in 1940; Joyce, Woolf, and Bergson in 1941; Kandinsky and Marinetti in 1944; and Stein in 1946. Pound was arrested in Italy on charges of treason in 1945.

See also: *Contexts*: Empire, Fascism, Nationalism, Psychology, Race, Science and technology, Women and gender; *Texts*: Apocalypse, Bloomsbury, Dada and surrealism, Fragmentation, Futurism, Imagism and vorticism, Violence; *Criticism*: Cultural materialism/New Historicism.

Further Reading

Fussell, Paul, *The Great War and Modern Memory* (Oxford and New York: Oxford University Press, 1975).

Hynes, Samuel, *A War Imagined: The First World War and English Culture* (London: Bodley Head, 1990).

Sherry, Vincent, ed., *The Cambridge Companion to the Literature of the First World War* (Cambridge and New York: Cambridge University Press, 2005).

Women and Gender

The modernist era saw momentous gains for women in society, but it was also a period of struggle and reaction. The movement for women's suffrage in Britain dates back to the formal exclusion of women from the 1832 Reform Act. It began to gather momentum after 1866, when a group of women petitioned the philosopher and Member of Parliament John Stuart Mill to introduce a bill for enfranchisement. (Mill put forward an amendment to the Second Reform Act of 1867, but it was defeated.) The campaign for suffrage gathered momentum in Britain towards the end of the nineteenth century, with the National Union of Women's Suffrage Societies (NUWSS) founded by Millicent Fawcett in 1897. Associated with this movement were the so-called 'New Woman' writers of the 1890s, including Sarah Grand (*The Heavenly Twins*, 1893) and George Egerton (*Keynotes*, 1893). The New Woman was also a subject of plays and novels by male writers, both sympathetic (Hardy, Gissing, Shaw, and Ibsen) and satirical (Sydney Grundy's play *The New Woman*, 1894).

In 1903 a militant offshoot of the NUWSS, the Women's Social and Political Union (WSPU), also known as the suffragette movement, was formed. The suffragettes were represented in literature and polemical pamphlets by a new generation of writers, notably Cicely Hamilton (*Diana of Dobson's*, a play, 1908), Elizabeth Robins (*Votes for Women*, a play, 1907), Evelyn Sharp (*Rebel Women*, 1910), Gertrude Colmore (*Suffragette Sally*, 1911), Constance Elizabeth Maud (*No Surrender*, 1912), and Margaret Wynne Nevinson (*In the Workhouse*, a play, 1911). As the dates of these works suggest, the suffragette movement was a phenomenon of the immediate pre-war years, reaching its peak intensity with the direct action campaigns of 1912–1914, which began with the smashing of shop and government office windows, and escalated to acts of arson and bombing. It not only coincided with the artistic and literary avant-garde, vorticism in particular, but also influenced their militant tactics. (Marinetti, the Italian futurist leader, marched with the suffragettes on a visit to London in 1912.) The right to vote was granted in the UK to women over 30 in 1918, and in the US in 1920. In 1928 the vote in Britain was extended to women over 21. The suffrage movement was supported by the majority of women modernists, including May Sinclair, Rebecca West, and Violet Hunt.

The modernist canon was, for much of the twentieth century, a masculine domain. Surprisingly, even Virginia Woolf's place in modernism was rejected by no less significant a scholar than Hugh Kenner, who mentioned her only three times in his magnificent but unapologetically partisan magnum opus, *The Pound Era* (1971). Kenner called her a 'shade' and a 'treacly mind' in two of these passages, and in the third offered a snide passing remark ('a cultivated person – the kind Virginia Woolf found fit to talk to') as he discussed Eliot's *The Waste Land*. For Kenner, she is merely a personality: none of her works are mentioned by name. Part of this antipathy has to do with Kenner's anti-Bloomsbury bias and his thesis that the 'real' British modernists were all foreigners. On the other hand, he was almost equally dismissive of the American Gertrude Stein. Similarly, essays by only two women authors, Woolf and George Eliot, were chosen for Richard Ellmann and Charles Feidelson's landmark anthology, *The Modern Tradition* (1965), totaling nine out of 948 pages. Bonnie Kime Scott made this observation in the Introduction to her equally significant revisionist anthology, *The Gender of Modernism* (1990). Scott's work, which was built on two decades of challenges to the canon, altered the course of modernist studies. The authors included Djuna Barnes, Nancy Cunard, Katherine Mansfield, Mina Loy, Nella Larsen, Charlotte Mew, H. D., Gertrude Stein, Marianne Moore, Jean Rhys, Dorothy Richardson, May Sinclair, Rebecca West, Zora Neale Hurston, Sylvia Townsend Warner, and others. A recent follow up anthology, *Gender in Modernism* (2007), also edited by Scott, offered further revisions to the field. These revisions acknowledged the flood of scholarship on gender and modernism since 1990, and offered a more thematic arrangement in keeping with current pedagogical trends.

The anxiety among male modernist writers caused by the campaign for women's rights is evident in the literature of the time. The first issue of the vorticist magazine *Blast* (1914), for example, included 'To Suffragettes', a notice advising women to 'stick to what you understand' and calling on them to 'Leave art alone'. The notice was prompted by Mary Richardson's high-profile attack on Velasquez's *Rokeby Venus* in the National Gallery, which she slashed seven times with a meat cleaver in March 1917. There were also attacks on pictures in the National Portrait Gallery, and in the Doré Gallery, where Wyndham Lewis and other vorticists had works on display. *Blast*, edited by Lewis, warned condescendingly: 'You might some day destroy a good picture by accident.' The use of heavily gendered language was another feature of the reaction by writers like Lewis,

Ezra Pound, T. E. Hulme, and D. H. Lawrence to changes in male–female relations. 'Masculine' language was used to describe the modern and stylistically innovative, while 'feminine' terms were used to describe either the products of mass culture or anything outdated or passé – in other words, whatever modernism opposed. Hulme's notorious opposition, delivered in a lecture in 1912, between the masculine, 'dry, hard, classical verse' of the new generation and the feminine, 'damp' Romanticism of the old, is one example. Despite Marinetti's participation in a suffragette march in 1912, the first futurist manifesto of 1909 had declared 'scorn for women' as one of its founding principles, and women were usually associated in futurist manifestos with timidity, sentimentality, and threats to masculinity. Marinetti later attempted to clarify what he actually opposed. He insisted that it was not women *per se* that he rejected, but the feminine ideal as conceived by society: woman as the object of sentimental love. (Being opposed to parliamentary democracy, Marinetti stated that he cared little whether women won 'the ridiculous, miserable little right to vote'.) Whatever the explanation, futurism and vorticism in particular established a vocabulary in which the modern was masculine and the past – Romanticism, aestheticism, or the entire Victorian era – was feminine. Femininity was earlier linked to decadence in the writings of Nietzsche and in Max Nordau's *Degeneration* (1892, trans. 1895). The anxiety surrounding Oscar Wilde and homosexuality, after his highly publicized conviction for gross indecency in 1895, almost certainly contributed to this discourse.

See also: *Contexts*: Class, Culture, Sex and sexuality; *Texts*: Aestheticism and decadence, Bloomsbury, Consciousness, Stream of, Futurism, Imagism and vorticism; *Criticism*: Deconstruction, Feminist and gender criticism, Marxist criticism, Poststructuralism.

Further Reading

Garrity, Jane, *Step-Daughters of England: British Women Novelists and the National Imaginary* (Manchester: Manchester University Press, 2003).

Nelson, Carolyn Christensen, ed., *Literature of the Women's Suffrage Campaign in England* (Peterborough, Ont.: Broadview, 2004).

Scott, Bonnie Kime, ed., *The Gender of Modernism: A Critical Anthology* (Bloomington and Indianapolis: Indiana University Press, 1990).

2 Texts: Themes, Issues, Concepts

Introduction

The pre-war social and political upheaval described in the 'Contexts' section was matched in the arts by an explosion of new forms and perspectives. One important catalyst of early modernism in Britain was Ford Madox Hueffer (later Ford), whose editorship of the *English Review* in 1908–1909 was marked by the 'discovery' of D. H. Lawrence, Wyndham Lewis, and Ezra Pound, who had recently arrived from America. The magazine also served as an important meeting place for the older and younger moderns: the poems and stories of Pound, Lewis, and Lawrence appeared alongside those of Henry James, Joseph Conrad, and Thomas Hardy. A number of the older writers, in fact, had contributed to the *Yellow Book*, that bible of 1890s aestheticism. Ford complained in a memoir, with only partial accuracy, of the way the younger modernists took over the magazine almost immediately: 'The control of the *English Review*, which I had started mainly with the idea of giving a shove to Impressionism and its literary form, was really snatched from my hands by Mr Pound and his explosive-mouthed gang of scarcely-breeched filibusters' (Ford, 1938, p. 281).

Meanwhile in Paris, 1909 saw the publication in *Le Figaro* of the first futurist manifesto, which set a new standard for avant-garde provocation. The futurists called not only for a poetics of 'audacity and revolt' but also for action beyond the realm of art, including the destruction of 'libraries and museums' and the call for war. Nevertheless, it is 1910 that is most often cited as the turning point in Anglo-American modernism: 'December 1910', after all, was the month that Virginia Woolf would pinpoint in 'Mr Bennett and Mrs Brown' (1924), half seriously, as the moment 'human character changed'. Two key events marking this change were the accession of a new king, George V, and an eye-opening exhibit of modern French art at the Grafton Galleries in London. *Manet and the Post-Impressionists*, curated by Woolf's friend Roger Fry, who coined the term 'post-impressionism', provided British audiences with their first chance to view paintings by Paul Cézanne, Paul Gauguin, and Vincent van Gogh. Fry was also curator of the *Second Post-Impressionist Exhibition* in 1912, which displayed the work of contemporary British, French, and Russian artists, including Duncan Grant, Vanessa Bell, Stanley Spencer, Wyndham Lewis, and a number of cubist works by Pablo Picasso and the Russian cubo-futurist Natalia Goncharova. A similarly influential exhibition, the Armory Show, took place the following year in New York. The years 1910–1914 were a time of promise and optimism in the arts, when it was felt that almost anything could be done. Imagism and vorticism, not to mention futurism, cubism, and other European movements, bloomed in this interval. The outbreak of war in August 1914 cut short many of the aspirations, and in some cases the lives, of the early modernists. The assassination on June 28 of Archduke Franz Ferdinand, heir to the Austro-Hungarian throne, happened within days of the publication of the first issue of the vorticist magazine *Blast*, the quintessential symbol of the pre-war avant-garde in Britain. With the onset of the war, 'blasting' in the arts quickly became obsolete.

Modernism entered its 'high' phase in the 1920s, attaining a level of prestige and maturity that it did not possess before the war. T. S. Eliot's *Criterion*, launched in 1922, exemplified the new respectability of modernism, which was quickly becoming an institution. *Ulysses* and *The Waste Land*, both published this same year, employed what Eliot called (in '*Ulysses*, Order, and Myth', 1923) the 'mythical method'. Rather than enacting a break with the past, as the pre-war avant-garde was fond of doing, Eliot argued for continuity between past traditions and the 'new', something F. R. Leavis would reinforce in his landmark study *The Great Tradition* (1948). As Michael Levenson explains, 'After its Impressionist, Imagist and Vorticist avatars, modernism returns to classicism . . . avoiding the technical stipulations of earlier programmes and avoiding polemical violence' (Levenson, 1984, p. 210). At the same time, Bloomsbury's upper-middle-class bohemia was in full swing: Woolf published her first truly experimental novel, *Jacob's Room*, in 1922, followed by her best known works, *Mrs. Dalloway* (1925), *To the Lighthouse* (1927), *Orlando* (1928), 'A Room of One's Own' (1929), and *The Waves* (1931), in quick succession. The Hogarth Press, run by the Woolfs in Tavistock Square from 1924, published an innovative list of authors through the 1920s and 1930s, including translations of the works of Sigmund Freud and Russian novelists like Dostoevsky and Tolstoy.

London, however, had to compete with Paris in the 1920s as a rival centre of Anglo-American modernism. Pound decided to move there in 1921, citing the presence of 'the intelligent nucleus for a movement . . . which there bloody well isn't in England' (qtd in Carpenter, 1988,

p. 402). The Paris expatriate scene thrived until the 1929 stock market crash, and counted among its writers Pound and Joyce, who moved there from Trieste in 1920 with Pound's encouragement and soon afterward published the first edition of *Ulysses* through Sylvia Beach's Left Bank bookshop, Shakespeare and Company. Mina Loy, Ford Madox Ford, Jean Rhys, and Nancy Cunard were among the British expatriates who lived in Paris after the war. Of the American modernists, Gertrude Stein was the central figure: she had lived in the city since 1903, knew all the most important artists and writers, and held a popular weekly salon in her apartment at 27 Rue de Fleurus. Stein would later declare that 'Paris was where the twentieth century was', and for many expatriates, Stein was where Paris was (Stein, 1940, p. 11). Other Americans included Natalie Clifford Barney, whose salon at 20 Rue Jacob ran until the 1960s, as well as Peggy Guggenheim, Djuna Barnes, and Ernest Hemingway. Ford Madox Ford's *Transatlantic Review* (1924–1925) and Eugene Jolas's *transition* (1927–1938) were both based in Paris, providing plenty of opportunity for the productive exchange of ideas between Anglo-American and European modernists.

If modernism became in some ways an acceptable institution in the 1920s, it was also being tested and 'refigured' by new groups of writers. These groups brought a new social urgency to what had been, under Eliot's guiding hand, an expressly apolitical movement. In New York, Harlem Renaissance writers such as Langston Hughes, Jean Toomer, and Zora Neale Hurston married formal experimentation, including the use of an African-American vernacular and the rhythms of jazz and blues, with ideas of radical social uplift. In contrast to Eliot's *Criterion*, the title of the Harlem Renaissance journal *Fire!!* (1926) alone suggests a return to the pre-war sense of militant urgency in the arts. Manifestos of the Harlem Renaissance, such as Langston Hughes's 'The Negro Artist and the Racial Mountain' (1926), in turn inspired the *négritude* movement of Aimé Césaire and Léopold Senghor in Paris during the 1930s. Modernism was also 'refigured' in the 1920s and 1930s by a number of modernist women, including Woolf, Djuna Barnes, Rebecca West, H. D., Katherine Mansfield, Dorothy Richardson, Mary Butts, and Jean Rhys. The 1930s brought other important changes to British literature, including the rise of the so-called Auden Generation and the dominance of leftist politics and a new spirit of engagement in the arts. Themes of this decade include a sense of generational transition, a growing sense of crisis and apocalypse with the long run-up to the Second World War, and an interest in mass movements and mass consciousness that was present only as an object of hatred among earlier modernists like Eliot and Pound. Far from displaying a sense of resignation in the face of growing turmoil, the younger generation of writers felt compelled to seize the opportunity to make a new, better world before the old world destroyed itself. The Spanish Civil War (1936–1937) served as the defining event for the younger generation, as the First World War had been for the previous one. George Orwell, John Cornford, Julian Bell, and others went off to fight, and in some cases to die, for the Spanish republic.

'Don't bother about the plot: the plot's nothing.' This typically Woolfian recommendation to the reader comes in the thoughts of Isa Oliver, who is watching the pageant-play in *Between the Acts* (1941). But Woolf was not the only writer giving out advice and diagnoses for what was perceived to be a serious crisis of the novel in the modernist period. In '*Ulysses*, Order, and Myth' (1923), Eliot makes the provocative declaration: 'The novel ended with Flaubert and with James.' He cites Joyce's *A Portrait of the Artist as a Young Man* (1916) and Wyndham Lewis's *Tarr* (1918) as indications, even before *Ulysses* (1922), that the conventional novel that came of age in the Victorian period was an outmoded form. Eliot's statements added to an important discussion on the 'state of the novel' in the 1920s, with H. G. Wells, E. M. Forster, Ford Madox Ford, and D. H. Lawrence among the other contributors. Lawrence outlined his views in several essays including 'Surgery for the Novel – Or a Bomb' (1923), in which he attacked the extreme self-consciousness of modernist contemporaries like Joyce, Marcel Proust, and Dorothy Richardson, arguing that the novel must 'present us with new, really new feelings, a whole line of new emotion, which will get us out of the emotional rut'. Despite their differences, what united most modernist novelists, starting perhaps with James (who in turn studied Flaubert), was their representation of consciousness. In her essay 'Modern Fiction' (1919), Woolf sums this up in the following sentence: 'Let us record the atoms as they fall upon the mind in the order in which they fall, let us trace the pattern, however disconnected and incoherent in appearance, which every sight or incident scores upon the consciousness.' One radical exception is the fiction of Wyndham Lewis: in *Tarr*, Lewis speaks through the title character at one point, summing up his theory of a coldly external art that is focused on anything but the depiction of interior states: '*Deadness* is the first condition of art', Tarr states. 'The second is absence of *soul*, in the sentimental human sense. The lines and masses of the statue are its soul. . . . It has no inside.'

The short story was still a very young form at the start of the twentieth century, less bound by tradition than poetry, drama, or the novel. It was, like modernity itself, dynamic and fleeting. Authors could sell their stories to magazines or newspapers for a quick profit: the form seemed tailored to meet increasing demands on time and could be easily digested on the morning commute. In this sense, the short story was a bridge for modernist writers to a mainstream market. Taking on innovative material required less risk for a magazine publisher than a novel did for a book publisher. It also required less of an investment from the reader: it was easier to read a plotless short story than a plotless novel, and readers were more willing to let go of narrative expectations and overlook the absence of familiar conventions to experience new forms of storytelling. (As an added incentive, 'modern' also carried the promise of frank depictions of sexuality.) In the case of Woolf's 'Kew Gardens' (1919), her fully fledged experimental style is shown here first, as if tried out on a smaller canvas before committing to a larger one. In most modernist short stories, frame tales are abandoned, little if any preamble or exposition is provided, and description is kept to a minimum. Stories rarely offer narrative closure, and the reader is left to interpret the significance of events. Unresolved endings, seen in the stories of Katherine Mansfield, Elizabeth Bowen, Woolf, and Joyce, were much in vogue at the time, and they were meant to linger in the reader's thoughts afterward, resisting easy, passive consumption for all their apparent insubstantiality. Two of the stories in *Dubliners* (1914), 'The Sisters' and 'Counterparts', actually end in a set of ellipses ('...'), but their enigmatic character refuses to leave the reader's mind, not unlike the haunting tales of Edgar Allen Poe, author of 'The Fall of the House of Usher' (1839) and 'The Tell-Tale Heart' (1843), one of the genre's early pioneers. Like poetry, stories were highly concentrated, distilled into key moments and impressions that could, with some effort, unfold into an array of possibilities. Taking their cue from Anton Chekhov, the stories of writers like Mansfield and Woolf generally relied on mood and character rather than plot for their effect. But while conventions were toned down, the majority of modernist short stories, responding in part to the demands of the market, still retained a minimum of character, plot, setting, and suspense.

The economy and precision of the short story form was well suited to the pared down aesthetic favoured by most modernists. Joyce described the style he employed in *Dubliners* as 'scrupulous meanness', a style of that required the reader to meet the author halfway. This style also suited Joyce's vision of Dublin as a culturally and intellectually impoverished city, a city caught in a state of moral paralysis. Death, and living death, are everywhere in the stories, beginning with mention of death and paralysis on the first page of 'The Sisters' and culminating in the closing words of the long short story 'The Dead', which are, in fact, 'the dead'. Joyce's free indirect style of narration, called the 'Uncle Charles Principle' by Hugh Kenner, meant that despite the third-person perspective stories were often told using the vocabulary and idioms of the characters themselves. Another shift, also seen in the novel, was the move away from moralizing tales to stories that presented sexual themes often simply as events, without passing judgement or digesting their meaning for the reader. In Hemingway's 'Hills Like White Elephants' (1927), a sketch of a couple sitting at a train station in the middle of nowhere, the subject of abortion is ever present but nowhere explicitly stated. The conversation hits a minor climax ('Would you please please please please please please please stop talking?') and then is cut off abruptly, leaving the reader to speculate about what just happened and what will happen next. American writers like Hemingway, Sherwood Anderson, William Faulkner, F. Scott Fitzgerald, and Katherine Anne Porter excelled in the form, building on the legacy of early masters of the genre including Mark Twain, Bret Harte, and Stephen Crane.

In Woolf's novel *The Waves* (1931), the character Bernard voices a complaint that rings true for her prose but is perhaps even more aptly applied to poetry. 'I begin to long for some little language such as lovers use,' he says, 'broken words, inarticulate words, like the shuffling of feet on the pavement.' Modernist poetry rejected the over-confident, moralizing tone and windy rhetoric that defined the worst excesses of the older generation, depicting instead the uncertainty that many felt especially after the war. The 'broken words' that Woolf describes can be seen in the collage technique favoured by artists and writers at the time: both *The Waste Land* and Pound's *Cantos*, as well as William Carlos Williams's *Spring and All* (1923), juxtapose fragmentary images, allusions, and bits of dialogue. At the same time, the modernist poets exhibited supreme confidence in conveying their radical new ideas of form. 'To break the pentameter, that was the first heave', Pound wrote in the *Pisan Cantos* in 1945, partly in recollection of his own imagist interventions. Modernist poetry aimed at being precise, compact, direct, and well crafted; it was impersonal and ironic in its treatment of subjects, to escape the trap of sentimentality. Like all modernist writing, it took difficulty as a virtue and demanded active readers. Perhaps even more than in the case of the novel or the short story, modernist poetry brought vitality to what had in the Edwardian period become a largely exhausted genre in Britain. Many poets including Yeats, Pound, Eliot, and H. D. were born outside Britain, and they drew much of their inspiration from the recent French avant-garde, captured in Arthur Symons's influential study *The Symbolist Movement in Literature* (1899). Aided by Pound, who was in Joyce's words 'a miracle of ebulliency, gusto, and help' (qtd in Carpenter, 1988, p. 374), Eliot, H. D., Richard Aldington, and others had their work packaged and promoted in Britain and in the United States as the epitome of the 'new'.

The entries chosen for this section represent important genres, themes, and movements of modernism. Aside from the novel, the short story, and poetry, all of which are discussed in general terms above and will be used as examples throughout the book, cinema, music, drama, and the manifesto will be considered in detail in this section. Visual art, architecture, photography, and dance were all integral parts of the modernist project; however, space does not allow for individual consideration of these forms in relation to modernist literature. That said, movements such as realism, naturalism, futurism, imagism, vorticism, dada, surrealism, the Bloomsbury Group, and the Harlem Renaissance – most of which produced works, in some cases the majority of their works, outside literature – will be represented here. Themes and stylistic devices that define modernist writing in various ways, including allusion, impersonality, epiphany, memory, violence, and stream of consciousness will also be covered.

Further Reading

Levenson, Michael, ed., *The Cambridge Companion to Modernism* (Cambridge and New York: Cambridge University Press, 1999).
Rainey, Lawrence, ed., *Modernism: An Anthology* (Oxford and Malden, MA: Blackwell, 2005).
Stevenson, Randall, *Modernist Fiction: An Introduction* (Lexington: University Press of Kentucky, 1992).

Aestheticism and Decadence

Aestheticism is the name given to the English variant of *l'art pour l'art*, or art for art's sake. It is one of a cluster of terms (decadence, symbolism, parnassianism) that describe a late nineteenth-century break with nature and new emphasis on style. Immanuel Kant's argument in the *Critique of Judgement* (1790) for aesthetic judgement independent of utilitarian concerns is one important precursor to aestheticism's ideal of artistic autonomy. In England, the term aestheticism can be traced back to the mid-century Pre-Raphaelite Brotherhood, but more commonly it is used to describe late Victorian writers and artists like Oscar Wilde, Aubrey Beardsley, James McNeill Whistler, Charles Algernon Swinburne, and William Morris. The 'Preface' to Wilde's *The Picture of Dorian Gray* (1891), with its declaration that 'All art is quite useless', captures aestheticism's protest against Victorian ideas of utility, progress, and rationality. Wilde's epigrams draw upon a much earlier statement of art for art's sake, Théophile Gautier's 'Preface' to *Mademoiselle de Maupin* (1835). Gautier states: 'Nothing is really beautiful unless it is useless; everything useful is ugly, for it expresses a need, and the needs of man are ignoble and disgusting, like his poor weak nature. The most useful place in a house is the lavatory.' The popular image of the aesthete as sensuous and effeminate was cultivated by George Du Maurier's satirical cartoons for *Punch* in the 1870s and 1880s, and in Gilbert and Sullivan's comic opera, *Patience: Or, Bunthorne's Bride* (1881). Wilde was chosen as the 'real-life' Bunthorne by the promoter Richard D'Oyly Carte to accompany *Patience* on its North American tour in 1882. Wearing the costume of the aesthete, complete with knee breeches and a sunflower, and drawing heavily on the ideas of Ruskin, Pater, and Morris, Wilde delivered lectures on topics such as 'The House Beautiful' and 'The Decorative Arts' in over two hundred cities across the United States and Canada.

Decadence is a term often used interchangeably with aestheticism, but it more accurately describes aestheticism's late, extreme phase. The artist James McNeill Whistler attempted to distinguish aestheticism from decadence in his 'Ten O'Clock' lecture, first delivered in London in 1885. With a nod to his former disciple Wilde, who was sitting in the audience, Whistler spoke of 'a weird *culte*' of the 'unlovely'. He cautioned: 'It is false, this teaching of decay.' Like aestheticism, which may simply describe the appreciation of beauty, 'decadence' also has a more general meaning. It has been used to describe various periods of literary and artistic decline, either in terms of the quality of the work itself or its moral standards. Now, however, it most commonly refers to movements in Paris, Vienna, London, and other European capitals at the *fin de siècle*. Not surprisingly, the self-styled 'decadents' of the 1880s and 1890s took inspiration from the earlier periods, especially ancient Greece, and Rome in its imperial decline. Though critics used it as a term of derision, to be labelled 'decadent' was considered an honour in some artistic circles, particularly in France. The decadent movement's 'morbid' obsessions with perversity, death, and decay can be seen as part of the wider secession of art from life. It represented a rejection of naturalism and moral didacticism, of bourgeois values like thrift and industry, and an embrace of everything opposite: boredom, exhaustion, and world-weary hedonism. The decadent cult of 'evil' was prefigured in earlier works, including Charles Baudelaire's *Les Fleurs du Mal* (1857) and Comte de Lautréamont's *Les Chants des Maldoror* (1869), and in Romantic literature generally.

The movement was represented in France by the magazine *Le Décadent* (1886–1889), whose counterpart in England was the *Yellow Book* (1894–1897) with its famous illustrations by Aubrey Beardsley. The title and appearance of the English magazine was significant: at the time, French novels were bound in yellow paper wrappers instead of cloth, and as France was generally seen in England as a source of corruption and sin, a decadent Francophile periodical could hardly choose a more evocative name. Wilde's novel *The Picture of Dorian Gray*, which despite its rather moralistic ending is the best-known example of the decadent movement in England, shows Dorian receiving a 'yellow book' as a gift from the aesthete Lord Henry Wotton. The book, like *Dorian Gray* as a whole, is modelled after Joris-Karl Huysmans's *A Rebours* ('Against Nature', 1884), a classic of the French decadence that features an effete, aristocratic protagonist, Des Esseintes, whose pursuit of ever more exotic pleasures (including a jewel-encrusted tortoise) only results in a growing sense of ennui. When Dorian reads the book, it 'poisons' him. As the narrator tells us, 'There were moments when he looked on evil simply as a mode through which he could realize his conception of the beautiful.' This description also suggests another model: Walter Pater's *Studies in the History of the Renaissance* (1873). Pater's influence on Wilde began at Oxford in the 1870s. The infamous 'Conclusion' to his book was withdrawn for a time over fears that, in Pater's words, 'it might possibly mislead some of those young men into whose hands it might fall' with its sermon on the pursuit of aesthetic pleasure. Excerpts from Wilde's novel and other works were examined at his trials in 1895, when he was convicted of 'gross indecency' and given two years' hard labour. Wilde's downfall effectively brought to a close aestheticism's long reign in art, and the first generation of modernists, including Wyndham Lewis and Ezra Pound, distanced themselves from the Romantic tendencies of aestheticism even as they pursued some of its other ideals.

See also: *Contexts*: Culture; *Texts*: Apocalypse, Bloomsbury, Imagism and vorticism, Irish literature.

Further Reading

Benjamin, Walter, *Charles Baudelaire: A Lyric Poet in the Era of High Capitalism*, trans. Harry Zohn (London: Verso, 1983).

Marshall, Gail, ed., *The Cambridge Companion to the Fin de Siècle* (Cambridge and New York: Cambridge University Press, 2007).

Weir, David, *Decadence and the Making of Modernism* (Amherst: University of Massachusetts Press, 1995).

Allusion

Generally speaking, an allusion is a reference made to anything outside the text. This could be another work of literature, or a contemporary or historical figure or event. T. S. Eliot's poem *The Waste Land* (1922) is famous not only for capturing the mood of the post-war period but also for including several pages of notes 'explaining' the poem's allusions. Some notes give particular sources ('Cf. *The Tempest*, I, ii.'), while others appear to clarify ambiguous lines ('Shantih. Repeated as here, a formal ending to an Upanishad.'). The idea of a poem that required notes was seen at the time, and is still seen by readers today, as representing a high-water mark in modernist difficulty. But how seriously should we take Eliot's explanations? And how much do they actually explain? It is the introduction to the notes that has exercised the strongest influence on the poem's reception over the decades. Eliot identifies Jessie Weston's book, *From Ritual to Romance* (1920), an anthropological study of the pre-Christian origins of Grail legends, as a key to 'the difficulties of the poem'. Near the end of his life, in 1956, Eliot suggested that he might have 'led critics into temptation' with his notes, which he said were intended merely to add bulk to the 'inconveniently short' poem for its publication in book form and to avoid accusations of plagiarism. He added: 'I regret having sent so many enquirers off on a wild goose chase after Tarot cards and the Holy Grail.' In his annotated edition of the poem, Lawrence Rainey uses these comments along with other evidence to argue that in fact there is only local coherence to the poem, and that tracking down all the allusions will not reveal a hidden plan or 'solve' the poem. Allusiveness of the kind seen in *The Waste Land* builds layers of complexity and ambiguity that encourage active reading but not the kind of active reading that necessarily leads to a sense of 'closure' or a satisfying end.

Literary allusion may be seen as a friendly game played between writer and reader, testing the limits of the reader's knowledge. It is also used to *form* a readership, or an ideal reader – someone who understands the references. If the reader catches references easily, allusions can be reassuring, making the reader feel knowledgeable and included. When allusions are difficult, however, they may frustrate or alienate the reader. Seen in a negative light, allusion becomes a form of gate keeping, an exercise in exclusivity. This has long been the accusation levelled against modernism: the bar is set too high, suggesting a desire on the author's part for an extremely select readership, or no readership at all. Modernist allusion has also been read as a rather cynical means for authors to market their own exclusivity, as an additional price of entry. A more generous reading of modernist difficulty is Vicki Mahaffey's *Modernist Literature: Challenging Fictions* (2007), which emphasizes the modernist text's resistance to easy consumption, and the reader's increased sense of shared adventure and 'interpretive responsibility'.

Modernist texts demand active readers, and this has long made modernism a favourite field of students and scholars. Joyce boasted of his last book, *Finnegans Wake* (1939): 'I've put in so many enigmas and puzzles that it will keep the professors busy for centuries.' In this context, Michael Hollington has referred to 'the allusions industry' to describe the plethora of guidebooks, dictionaries, and annotated editions catering to readers of modernist literature. Sticking only to Joyce, examples include Thornton's *Allusions in Ulysses* (1961), Gifford's *Ulysses Annotated* (1988), McHugh's *Annotations to Finnegans Wake* (1980), and Atherton's *The Books at the Wake: A Study of Literary Allusions in James Joyce's Finnegans Wake* (1959). Joyce encouraged this kind of reading, disseminating a 'schema' of *Ulysses* that revealed the corresponding episodes and characters from Homer's *Odyssey*, and overseeing a book of essays on the Work in Progress that would eventually become *Finnegans Wake*. This book, which contained as its lead essay the first piece of writing to be published by Joyce's protégé, Samuel Beckett, bore the suitably Joycean (and Joyce-penned) title *Our Exagmination Round His Factification for Incamination of Work in Progress* (1929). Beckett's essay answers in advance any complaints from the reader: 'if you don't understand it, Ladies and Gentlemen, it is because you are too decadent to receive it.'

See also: *Contexts*: Culture, Language, Market; *Texts*: Fragmentation, Impersonality; *Criticism*: Leavisite criticism, New criticism.

Further Reading

Diepeveen, Leonard, *The Difficulties of Modernism* (New York: Routledge, 2003).
Mafaffey, Vicki, *Modernist Literature: Challenging Fictions* (Oxford and Malden, MA: Blackwell, 2007).

Anti-Semitism

In the chilling and supremely ill-judged *Hitler* (1931), Wyndham Lewis refers to Nazi anti-Semitism as a 'racial red-herring' and advises his 'Anglo-Saxon' readers not to let the 'Jewish question' interfere with the 'blood-feeling' of an Anglo-German relationship. Without question, anti-Semitism and other types of prejudice represent a major stumbling block for readers of modernist literature. Reading after the Holocaust, even the most offhand anti-Semitic stereotype jumps out at us and demands that we re-evaluate the text in which it appears. A case in point is T. S. Eliot's 'Burbank with a Baedeker: Bleistein with a Cigar', included in *Poems* (1920). The poem concerns one of Eliot's most familiar themes, the decadence and decay of the present contrasted with the achievements of the past. But here this theme is troublingly personified in the figure of Bleistein, 'Chicago Semite Viennese', in other words an American Jew with European roots. The poem is set in Venice, shorthand in modernist geography for European culture and its decline (see, for example, Thomas Mann's *Death in Venice*). Some of its most famous lines, such as 'The rats are underneath the piles. / The Jew is underneath the lot', seem at first glance shocking and highly suspect. But we should not judge too quickly and easily such a complex and allusive poem, one that Eliot called 'intensely serious' and 'among the best that I have ever done'. The poem's setting in post-war Europe of 1919, the year of the 'failed' (in Eliot's view) Treaty of Versailles, its deeply surrealistic imagery, and its echoes of Shakespeare's *The Merchant of Venice* and Marlowe's *The Jew of Malta* are all elements worth examining. Critics at the time did not comment on the anti-Semitic stereotype, and it has been pointed out recently that Eliot's publishers and some of his chosen readers were part of the Anglo-Jewish community in London.

In recent decades Eliot's anti-Semitism has been the subject of much debate. 'Gerontion', also from *Poems*, features a stereotypical image of the Jewish slumlord, again a figure of decay. But his description – 'Spawned in some estaminet of Antwerp, / Blistered in Brussels, patched and peeled in London' – may not have been meant as disparaging. Rather, as Ronald Schuchard has argued, it may refer to the continuing forced exodus 'from nation to nation, ghetto to ghetto'. In the 1930s, with the publication of *After Strange Gods* (1934), based on a series of lectures delivered at the University of Virginia, Eliot attracted more serious accusations. In one lecture he declared:

> The population should be homogeneous; where two or more cultures exist in the same place they are likely either to be fiercely self-conscious or both to become adulterate. What is still more important is unity of religious background; and reasons of race and religion combine to make any large number of free-thinking Jews undesirable.

Most scholars have read these remarks as simple prejudice, which they may well be. Schuchard, however, has argued that the emphasis should fall on 'free-thinking': in the 1930s, it was the disintegration of religious culture in the face of secular humanism that concerned Eliot, a recent convert to Anglo-Catholicism. Whatever the intention, Eliot withdrew the book soon after publication and chose for the most part to remain silent regarding the allegations of anti-Semitism that continued to follow him throughout his career. However, responding to an accusation brought in

1947, Eliot replied, alluding to both 'Burbank' and 'Gerontion': 'There is no anti-semitism in my poetry whatever. You have probably noticed a Jewish character in a poem about Venice in which the reader is meant to infer some contrast between Venice of modern times and that depicted in Shakespeare's play. There is also a reference to a Jewish landlord in another poem' (qtd in Schuchard, 2003, p. 17).

Another of the so-called 'Men of 1914', Ezra Pound, stands apart even from Eliot and Lewis for his extreme remarks. While Lewis renounced anti-Semitism in the ironically titled treatise *The Jews, Are They Human?* (1939), and Eliot withdrew *After Strange Gods*, Pound's racist and fascist ideology came to dominate his writing in the 1930s and 1940s. A common problem for Pound and Lewis was the tendency to use a particular group – in Lewis's case homosexuals, Jews, and women in turn – to attack a perceived ill in society or the arts. Some modernists also used this technique to attack society at large, in the form of the 'mob' or the 'Philistine'. In this sense anti-Semitism can be seen as one extreme form of rhetorical violence among others. Pound was always prone to seeing things in polarized terms; nevertheless, his case is particularly disturbing. The early cantos are mostly free of anti-Semitism, but the thoroughly iconoclastic 'Salutation the Third', published in the first issue of Lewis's *Blast* (1914), contains the lines: 'Let us be done with Jews and Jobbery, / Let us SPIT upon those who fawn on the JEWS for their money.' Pound's anti-Semitism was always closely tied to his economic and political theories, and he truly believed that Jews were responsible for, among other things, the rise of communism. Pound was arrested in May 1945 by Italian partisans, a week after the death of Mussolini, for being pro-Fascist rather than anti-Semitic, which was judged merely offensive and not punishable by law. His arrest came as a result of more than a hundred broadcasts for Radio Rome during 1941–1943, in which he expressed repeatedly his support for fascism and warned of the threat of a global Jewish conspiracy. It is often noted by Pound's apologists that when Allen Ginsberg visited him in Venice in 1967, Pound reflected bitterly on his 'mistake'. He is reported to have said: 'My writing – stupidity and ignorance all the way through stupidity and ignorance . . . . But the worst mistake I made was that stupid, suburban prejudice of anti-Semitism. All along, that spoiled everything.' While his words ring true, it is hard to see that this statement, made by an 82-year-old man, excuses a lifetime of hate-filled prejudice.

In Europe, assimilation predated the era of modernism, and in fact Jews were often identified specifically as agents of modernity, and even scapegoated as such by those seeking a source of blame for the decline of civilization. Jews were linked to cosmopolitanism, a term that carried negative connotations for nationalists in particular. The 'cosmopolitan' label could be applied to most writers and artists of the period, but it became a euphemism for Jewishness in some (especially nationalist) circles. Immediately following the Second World War, for example, Joseph Stalin's anti-Semitic campaign (1949–1953) targeted 'rootless cosmopolitans', and in 1952, 13 prominent Jewish writers, actors, and artists were executed. France also had its problems with anti-Semitism in this period, most famously shown in the Dreyfus Affair that divided French politics and society at the turn of the century. Alfred Dreyfus, a French army officer of Jewish descent, was falsely accused of passing military secrets to Germany in 1894 and was only exonerated in 1906. (He went on to serve in the First World War and was awarded the Legion of Honour in 1918.) The case brought to the surface widespread anti-Semitic feelings in France. However, Dreyfus was also strongly defended: the most famous *Dreyfusard* was the novelist Émile Zola, whose open letter to the President of the French Republic, *J'accuse!* (1898), protested against Dreyfus's wrongful conviction. In the United States, assimilation mostly occurred after the Second World War, and the 1950s saw the rise of the 'Jewish intellectual' and the genre of the 'Jewish novel' identified with writers like Saul Bellow and Philip Roth.

Charges of anti-Semitism have for a long time tainted the reputations of Pound, Lewis, Eliot, Cummings, and other modernists. There were, of course, a significant number of modernists from Jewish backgrounds, including Marcel Proust, Franz Kafka, Italo Svevo, Mina Loy, Leonard Woolf, and the Americans Gertrude Stein (and Alice B. Toklas), Nathanael West, and Man Ray. Still, there are relatively few examples of non-stereotypical Jewish characters in the major works of modernism. Joyce's *Ulysses* (1922), with its half-Jewish protagonist Leopold Bloom, is one famous exception. Bloom is given Jewish heritage primarily to identify him as a wanderer and outsider, the same reason that Joyce himself identified with the Jews. Bloom is humanistic, rational, and urban, all features Joyce associated with post-Enlightenment European Jews. Like Joyce, he occupies an ambiguous and often ambivalent position in relation to his birthplace of Ireland. In the 'Cyclops' episode of *Ulysses*, Bloom is confronted in Barney Kiernan's pub by the bigoted nationalist known as the Citizen, modelled on Michael 'Citizen' Cusack, the founder of the Gaelic Athletic Association. The Citizen, who is figuratively monocular because he can see only his own narrowly nationalistic view, runs through Ireland's troubled history, blaming 'strangers' for Ireland's problems. Bloom concurs that persecution and 'hatred among nations' is an age-old problem. When the Citizen challenges Bloom's own nationality (as Stephen Dedalus was challenged in *A Portrait*), Bloom answers that he is Irish, but adds: 'I belong to a race too...that is hated and persecuted. Also now. This very moment.' Though he begins by ignoring the Citizen's taunts, Bloom eventually rises to the occasion, giving a speech about love and tolerance. After he departs, animosity slowly builds over a mistaken suspicion that Bloom has selfishly kept a sure bet on the day's Gold Cup horse race and neglected to buy a round of drinks with his winnings. 'We know those canters', remarks the Citizen, 'preaching and picking your pocket'. Bloom returns only to be rushed out again by his friends who fear for his safety, but as he is leaving he shouts at the Citizen: 'Mendelssohn was a jew and Karl Marx and Mercadante and Spinoza. And the Saviour was a jew and his father was a jew. Your God.' At which point the Citizen hurls a biscuit tin at him and Bloom escapes in a jaunting car, described in biblical language as Elijah's ascent to heaven in his chariot ('And they beheld Him even Him, ben Bloom Elijah, amid clouds of angels ascend to the glory of the brightness').

See also: *Contexts*: Fascism, Nationalism, Race, Religion; *Texts*: Violence.

Further Reading

Julius, Anthony, *T. S. Eliot, Anti-Semitism, and Literary Form* (Cambridge and New York: Cambridge University Press, 1995).
Nadel, Ira B., *Joyce and the Jews* (Iowa City: University of Iowa Press, 1989).
Schuchard, Ronald, 'Burbank with a Baedeker, Eliot with a Cigar: American Intellectuals, Anti-Semitism, and the Idea of Culture', *Modernism/Modernity* 10.1 (2003), pp. 1–26.
Surette, Leon, *Pound in Purgatory: From Economic Radicalism to Anti-Semitism* (Urbana: University of Illinois Press, 1999).

Apocalypse

The opening stanza of Yeats's 'The Second Coming' (1920) contains a series of apocalyptic images that have come to represent the political turmoil of the early twentieth century.

> Turning and turning in the widening gyre
> The falcon cannot hear the falconer;
> Things fall apart; the centre cannot hold;
> Mere anarchy is loosed upon the world,
> The blood-dimmed tide is loosed, and everywhere
> The ceremony of innocence is drowned;
> The best lack all conviction, while the worst
> Are full of passionate intensity.

The second stanza begins with the assertion, 'Surely some revelation is at hand; / Surely the Second Coming is at hand.' From there proceeds a disturbing vision of the future, embodied in the 'rough beast' that 'Slouches towards Bethlehem to be born'. Like Eliot's *The Waste Land* (1922), Yeats's poem conveys a sense of crisis, chaos, and destruction that rang true for contemporary readers, even if they did not apprehend the subtler meaning of the lines. The poem was responding on a local level to the upheavals in Irish politics after the 1916 Easter Rising. More broadly, it was responding to the revolutions and chaos that swept Europe during the First World War and Russia after 1917, feeding into a general sense of apocalypse on a historical scale. Falconry, an aristocratic sport, opens the poem, and with the contrasting image of a 'blood-dimmed tide' it suggests anxiety sparked by the overthrow of the old aristocracy and the new mass democracy taking its place. When Yeats began writing the poem, in 1919, his interest in historical cycles or 'gyres', which culminated in *A Vision* (1925), was becoming more prominent, encouraged by marathon automatic-writing sessions with his wife, Georgie Hyde Lees. Yeats believed that a 2000-year cycle (coinciding with the rise of Christianity) was coming to an end, and a new one was about to begin. The state of the world occupied the thoughts of many writers at the time, understandably given the political chaos and other events, like the influenza pandemic of 1919, that engulfed Europe and showed little sign of letting up, even after the welcome Armistice.

'Apocalypse' is of course a religious term, coming from the ancient Greek word for 'revelation' and usually denoting the destruction of the world as described in the Book of Revelation. One of D. H. Lawrence's last projects was a commentary on the Book of Revelation entitled *Apocalypse* (1931), which, like most of Lawrence's essays, also served as a wider platform for his views on humanity. Christianity is the main target of his Nietzschean attack on the triumph of weakness and mediocrity over a more vital pre-Christian culture. The condemnation of modernity also takes in scientific materialism and mass democracy. Nietzsche, along with William Blake, offered the template for the apocalyptic-prophetic tone of many modernist writers, including Lawrence and Yeats. For these writers, Western society had become so stagnant and corrupt that democratic reform was no longer enough. Instead, a catastrophic end – the First World War, perhaps – would have to be followed by a dramatic new beginning and a new order. Epochal thinking is also a central element of *The Cantos*; Pound and Yeats worked closely together during the winters of 1913–1916 at Stone Cottage, Sussex, where they read deeply in the occult. 'Make it new', his most famous slogan, applied to life as well as to art: both were seen as moribund and in need of complete overhaul. Theories of racial, social, and cultural decline, from Max Nordau's *Degeneration* (1892) to Oswald Spengler's *The Decline of the West* (1918–1922), argued that the West had been on a downward spiral for decades. Some even welcomed the First World War as a chance to 'cleanse' Europe of its decadence. (The futurists famously championed war as 'the world's only hygiene' in 1909.) Apocalyptic themes run through much of Lawrence's work, particularly dating from the war years. It was during this time, against the already terrifying backdrop of the war, that the authorities subjected him to traumatic physical exams and closely controlled his movements, expelling him from Cornwall on suspicion of spying and refusing him permission to leave England. Worse yet, a ban imposed on *The Rainbow* (1915) left him impoverished for the duration of the war. *Women in Love*, completed in 1916, reflects this apocalyptic turn of mind; tellingly, *Dies Irae* (Day of Wrath) and *The Latter Days* were two of the alternate titles Lawrence considered.

The sense of an impending apocalypse was difficult to avoid in a period bookended by two world wars. Modernist literature is often, and accurately, described as a 'literature of crisis', one that thrives on ideas of destruction and disintegration. Indeed, it is hard to think of modernist literature as existing without this key aspect of its character. Jane Goldman's *Modernism, 1910–1945: Image to Apocalypse* (2004) ends with a chapter on the group of British poets called The New Apocalypse, or simply Apocalypse, who formed during the Second World War. The group published three anthologies: *The New Apocalypse* (1939), *The White Horseman* (1941), and *The Crown and the Sickle* (1943). Members included Henry Treece, J. F. Hendry, and Dorian Cooke, along with Nicholas Moore, Norman MacCaig, G. S. Fraser, and – most famously, though perhaps unwillingly – Dylan Thomas. The group was strongly influenced by surrealism, and by the new Romanticism of the *transition* circle in Paris between the wars. These poets were united by, among other things, a love of the prophetic Blake, a dislike of machines and mechanization, and a rejection of the classicism of the Auden circle. An apocalyptic trend of a very different sort, also occurring in the late modernist period, was the hard-boiled American crime novel and its cinematic counterpart, film noir. Some of the best examples of this nihilistic pair include the detective fiction of Raymond Chandler, James M. Cain, and Dashiell Hammett, as well as *Brighton Rock* (1938), written and later adapted to film (1947) by Graham Greene, who also wrote the screenplay for Carol Reed's classic British film noir *The Third Man* (1949). Film noir in particular has often been read as an expression of post-war disillusionment, akin to the modernist reaction to the trauma of the First World War.

See also: *Contexts*: Culture, Psychology, Race, Religion, Science and technology, War; *Texts*: Aestheticism and decadence, Dada and surrealism, Fragmentation, Violence.

Further Reading

Goldman, Jane, *Modernism, 1910–1945: Image to Apocalypse* (Basingstoke and New York: Palgrave Macmillan, 2004).

Kermode, Frank, *The Sense of an Ending: Studies in the Theory of Fiction* (Oxford and New York: Oxford University Press, 1968).

Avant-Garde

Like the term 'manifesto' – which once signified a declaration of war – 'avant-garde' (advance guard) was first used as a military term. In France, at the end of the nineteenth century, 'avant-garde' denoted the radical left. In 1878, for example, the anarchist Mikhail Bakunin founded a journal called *L'Avant-garde*, which was devoted to political agitation. The term also became associated with cutting-edge movements in art and literature, and gradually it became more common in the cultural than the political sphere. But the link to politics and war never entirely disappeared: the early twentieth-century avant-gardes were militant in their actions, often behaving like the 'shock troops' from which their name derived. The Italian futurists, for example, taunted their audience during performances, sometimes resulting in violent clashes between actors and spectators. Futurist manifestos are full of verbal violence, glorifying war and calling for the destruction of libraries, museums, and other venerable institutions. The movement was innovative in the extreme, even prophetic: the experiments it conducted in music, poetry, painting, sculpture, theatre, clothing, and architecture – not to mention cooking – still strike us as startlingly modern. In 1914, for example, one manifesto, anticipating cybernetics, declared: 'there is no essential difference between a human brain and a machine. It is mechanically more complicated, that is all'. In Britain, the vorticists and their magazine *Blast* (1914–1915) borrowed some of their most striking avant-garde tactics from futurism, whose leader Marinetti visited London several times before the War. In contrast to the 'high' modernism of the 1920s, *Blast* addressed the general public directly, if scornfully, and made reference to current politics and popular culture in its columns of 'blasts' and 'blesses'. (These, in turn, were modelled on Apollinaire's manifesto of 1913, 'L'Antitradition futurist', which declared 'Merde aux' some things and 'Rose aux' others.) The bold pink cover of the first issue, with its manifestos set in tabloid-headline typeface, was dynamic, shocking, and overtly theatrical, a vorticist creation in itself and a far cry from the calm cerebrality of Eliot's post-war *Criterion* magazine.

The dividing line between modernism and the avant-garde is often blurred at best. In an Anglo-American context, the two terms are sometimes used interchangeably. 'Avant-garde' may also simply refer to the more extreme end of modernism, the side that is more prone to disruption and conflict. *Blast*, for example, would be labelled avant-garde because it was more aggressively confrontational than, say, Woolf's novel *The Waves* (1931). (But what of *Three Guineas* [1938], with its cry of ' "Take this guinea and with it burn the college to the ground. Set fire to the old hypocrisies"?') In Britain, the avant-garde was so short-lived that it has usually been treated as an early, pre-war phase of modernism, or an anomalous occurrence under futurism's foreign sway. Imagism and vorticism, the two major avant-garde movements in England, were both largely the creations of Ezra Pound, in partnership with a few others including Wyndham Lewis (vorticism), Richard Aldington, F. S. Flint, and H. D. (imagism).

However, some critics draw a clearer line between the two categories. Modernism, they argue, prefers to see itself as a separate, autonomous sphere, while the avant-garde, rebelling against modernist exclusivity, seeks to re-engage with society and politics. Peter Bürger made this case in his landmark book, *Theory of the Avant-Garde* (1974, translated 1984). Bürger, focussing on the institutional aspects of art in the late nineteenth and early twentieth century, saw the European avant-garde as a reaction against the increasingly professional, bourgeois character of modern art. In this distinction, the avant-garde reveals its ties to radical politics, and it attempts to overcome the separation of art and life that began with *l'art pour l'art*. Modernism, meanwhile, continues in the aestheticist line, apart from life and engaged only with the concerns of style and form, or with language in the case of literature. In geo-linguistic terms, 'modernism' is strictly speaking an Anglo-American concept, with no exact equivalent in French; it speaks directly to the modern Anglo-American tradition of experimental literature and art. The concept of the avant-garde, in contrast, originates in continental Europe, and it best describes the innovations and movements that took place there: futurism, dada, surrealism, expressionism, and so forth. In this view, vorticism would be seen as a product of (or response to) European influence. Finally, the meaning of these terms has shifted significantly over the decades, especially after the 'second wave' avant-garde of the 1960s, with its even closer ties to radical politics.

Whether 'avant-garde' or 'modernist', this period saw a veritable explosion of movements, manifestos, and little magazines. Many of these were in fierce competition with each other. As Malcolm Bradbury has noted, 'ism tended toward schism'. Beginning with the competing forces of naturalism (which may be found in the novels of Zola, Gissing, and Dreiser, or the plays of Strindberg, Ibsen, Chekhov, and Hauptmann) and symbolism (seen in the poetry of Baudelaire, Rimbaud, Verlaine, Mallarmé, and Valéry), there opened up a broad field of competing movements, many of which were interdisciplinary and international in scope. Italian futurism burst onto the scene in 1909 with 'The Founding and Manifesto of Futurism', published in *Le Figaro*. Although this was neither the first avant-garde movement nor the first manifesto, its impact was felt across Europe, and it set the tone of crisis and immediacy that many others would follow. Unlike the more cohesive Italian futurism, Russian futurism emerged as a series of smaller groups with their own manifestos and anthologies, including Hylaea, the Mezzanine of Poetry, ego-futurism, cubo-futurism, rayonism, and Zaoum. Dada followed, beginning in Zurich in 1916 and establishing branches in Berlin, Paris, New York, and other cities. Surrealism, led by André Breton, developed out of dada in the 1920s and continued as a worldwide movement for much of the twentieth century. Expressionism was confined primarily to Germany and the visual arts, as seen in two groups: Die Brücke (The Bridge), founded in 1905, and Der Blaue Reiter (The Blue Rider), founded in 1912. In literature, the influence of expressionist theatre, with its strong depiction of psychological states, can be seen in the plays of Eugene O'Neill, Elmer Rice, and other American playwrights. Some efforts were made to translate impressionist theories into literature (see Ford Madox Ford, 'On Impressionism', 1914); more successful, however, was cubism's revolution in representation, seen in the fragmented perspectives of modernist novels by Woolf, Joyce, Faulkner, and Stein, who acknowledged the debt to her friend Picasso and his major influence, Cézanne. Stein's Paris apartment was just one of many important gathering points for artists and writers of the avant-garde: in London, before the war, there was the Rebel Art Centre, presided over by Wyndham Lewis but funded by a woman, Kate Lechmere, as many such ventures were; Harold Monro's Poetry Bookshop; Roger Fry's pre-Bloomsbury Omega Workshops; T. E. Hulme's Frith Street salon; and the Cave of the Golden Calf, a Soho cabaret-style nightclub decorated by Lewis and others.

See also: *Contexts*: Culture, Fascism, Language, Market; *Texts*: Aestheticism and decadence, Dada and surrealism, Futurism, Imagism and vorticism, Manifesto, Primitivism, Violence.

Further Reading

Bürger, Peter, *Theory of the Avant-Garde,* trans. Michael Shaw (Minneapolis: University of Minnesota Press, 1984).

Calinescu, Matei, *Five Faces of Modernity: Modernism, Avant-Garde, Decadence, Kitsch, Postmodernism* (Durham, NC: Duke University Press, 1987).

Webber, Andrew, *The European Avant-Garde 1900–1940* (Cambridge: Polity Press, 2004).

Bloomsbury

The Bloomsbury Group, or simply Bloomsbury, came into being in the first decade of the twentieth century and lasted as long as, and in many ways defined, British modernism. Included in the group were the writers Virginia Woolf, Lytton Strachey, and E. M. Forster; the art critics Roger Fry and Clive Bell; the economist John Maynard Keynes; the philosopher Bertrand Russell; and the painters Vanessa Bell and Duncan Grant, among others. Bloomsbury was a fashionable neighbourhood at the time, but it was also an intellectual one, being home to the British Library (housed within the British Museum until 1997) and University College London. Most members came from an upper-middle class background, which sometimes meant a private income, and some were related to each other: Virginia Woolf and Vanessa Bell were sisters, while Strachey and Grant were cousins. In 1917, the Woolfs started the Hogarth Press, initially intended to be a diversion for Virginia. It soon became much more, however, publishing books by Bloomsbury authors, as well as T. S. Eliot (including a limited edition of *The Waste Land*), Katherine Mansfield, Robert Graves, Christopher Isherwood, H. G. Wells, Cecil Day Lewis, and Henry Green, along with translations of modern Russian and European authors including Freud (translated by James Strachey), Chekhov, Tolstoy, Gorky, Dostoevsky, and Svevo. The press began life at Hogarth House in Richmond but moved to Tavistock Square, Bloomsbury, in 1924.

Another of the important cultural contributions from the group was Roger Fry's Omega Workshops, a decorative-arts collective with headquarters in Bloomsbury's Fitzroy Square. Wyndham Lewis and other future vorticists were among the original members in 1913, but Lewis fell out with Fry and left the group after a few months, taking with him Frederick Etchells, Edward Wadsworth, and Cuthbert Hamilton. (This was the first and perhaps formative incident of Lewis's long-running feud with Bloomsbury.) When Fry started Omega he had already laid the theoretical groundwork of his aesthetic philosophy in 'An Essay on Aesthetics' (1909). His early résumé also featured several years' work at the Metropolitan Museum of Art in New York (1905–1910) and contributions to the *Athenaeum* magazine (as art critic) and the *Burlington Magazine* (as co-founder). Most significantly, he put together the hugely influential post-impressionist exhibitions of 1910 and 1912 at the Grafton Galleries in London. The first of these exhibitions, *Manet and the Post-Impressionists*, included numerous works by Cézanne, Gauguin, van Gogh, and other modern French artists whose work had rarely, if ever, been seen in Britain. The exhibition (and its successor) excited a strong public reaction consisting mostly of shock and outrage. Woolf spoke to the dramatic effect the exhibition had on artists and writers, and to the sense of rupture it created, when she famously stated that 'on or about December 1910 human character changed'.

Aside from Woolf's novels and Fry's exhibitions, the group is known mainly for the unconventional lifestyles of its members and its progressive stance on social and cultural issues. In a posthumously published account of 'Old Bloomsbury' ('1904–1919'), Woolf memorably recalled the word 'semen' being mentioned by Lytton Strachey in mixed company in 1908, and the liberating effect it had:

> With that one word all barriers of reticence and reserve went down. A flood of the sacred fluid seemed to overwhelm us. Sex permeated our conversation. The word bugger was never far from our lips. We discussed copulation with the same excitement and openness that we had discussed the nature of the good.

Sex aside, the group's early philosophy and values were strongly indebted to the Cambridge philosopher G. E. Moore, whose groundbreaking *Principia Ethica* (1903) was the likely source of this discussion of 'the nature of the good'. Moore's book concludes by affirming the value of close friendship and art: 'the most valuable things which we know or can imagine', he wrote, 'are certain states of consciousness which may be roughly described as the pleasures of human intercourse and the enjoyment of beautiful objects'. Moore was a member of the Cambridge Conversazione Society, the university discussion and friendship society more commonly known as the Cambridge Apostles. His fellow Apostles at the turn of the century included Leonard Woolf, Lytton Strachey, E. M. Forster, Bertrand Russell, and John Maynard Keynes. This close circle of friends, minus Moore and with the addition of the Stephen sisters Virginia and Vanessa, who moved into a house in Bloomsbury in 1904, formed the nucleus of the group. If Bloomsbury's ethics came from Moore (and the pacifist Russell), its aesthetics came from Fry and Bell, both of whom advocated strongly for a formalist view of art. The art these critics championed, as the post-impressionist exhibitions show, was overwhelmingly French; in the pre-war period, it was left to Ezra Pound and T. E. Hulme to promote English abstract art in the form of London-based avant-garde artists like Jacob Epstein, Wyndham Lewis, and Henri Gaudier-Brzeska.

In the 1930s, the modernist writer Mary Butts began a piece on Blooms-bury with a summary of the usual responses the group's name evoked: 'Say "Bloomsbury" and...only too often a string of words will follow, varying with the player: "The Intelligentsia in excelsis." "Oh, that lot," "those barren leaves." "N. B. G." [No Bloody Good], *"faisandés,"* "awful warnings," "mental hermaphrodites," "brittle intellectuals," *"that* bunch" ' (Butts, 1998, p. 32). From the point of view of E. M. Forster, it was 'the only genuine *movement* in English civilization' (Forster, 1985, p. 48). Forster's hyperbolic statement exhibits precisely the kind of self-regard that outsiders to Bloomsbury found so irritating. Its most notorious enemy, Wyndham Lewis, and later the influential critic Hugh Kenner, regarded its literature and its members as precious and effete, mired in snobbery, and essentially Victorian in their outlook with only a veneer of innovation. Some of the criticism the group attracted was itself infected by class-consciousness and other forms of prejudice. D. H. Lawrence expressed a very strong and seemingly homophobic hatred of Keynes, Strachey, Grant, and Francis Birrell, whom he said gave him nightmares of 'black beetles'. It has been suggested that the response was partly a reaction to his own latent homosexuality; in any case, he grew to asso-ciate homosexuality with a kind of Bloomsbury intellectualism that was repugnant to him, though he insisted that his reaction was 'not from any moral disapprobation'. Lewis's many public diatribes against the group were also tainted by homophobic language, for example in the closing part of his post-war manifesto, *The Caliph's Design* (1919). Lewis also caricatured Bloomsbury figures such as Lytton Strachey (as Matthew Plunket) in his epic satire *The Apes of God* (1930), and Bloomsbury figured centrally in Lewis's idea of the 'child-cult', represented by Joyce, Stein, Charles Chaplin, and others, which he believed bred passivity and ele-vated an irresponsible naivety. Lewis's caustic attacks notwithstanding, it is fair to say that Bloomsbury members were often dismissed solely on the basis of the group's reputation. Looking at the period now, especially with regard to literary modernism, the truly daring nature of Virginia Woolf's fiction and essays comes through, as does the group's dedication to challenging contemporary social norms. Unlike the many 'isms' that existed at the time, Bloomsbury never issued a collective statement of principles, although Clive Bell's *Art* (1914) and Woolf's 'A Room of One's Own' (1929) and *Three Guineas* (1938) are manifestos of a kind.

See also: *Contexts*: Class, Culture, Sex and sexuality, Women and gender; *Texts*: Aestheticism and decadence, Consciousness, Stream of, Epiphany, Imagism and vorticism; *Criticism*:
Feminist and gender criticism.

Further Reading

Bell, Quentin, *Bloomsbury* (London: Weidenfeld and Nicholson, 1968).

Lee, Hermione, *Virginia Woolf* (London: Chatto and Windus, 1996).

Rosenbaum, S. P., ed., *A Bloomsbury Group Reader* (Oxford and Malden, MA: Blackwell,
1993).

Stansky, Peter, *On or About December 1910: Early Bloomsbury and its Intimate World*
(Cambridge, MA: Harvard University Press, 1996).

Cinema, Influence of

The influence of the cinema on modernist literature was varied and pervasive. Film was in many ways the quintessential modernist medium.
It attracted avant-gardists like Marcel Duchamp, Man Ray, René Clair,
László Moholy-Nagy, and the surrealist Luis Buñuel, whose collabora-
tions with Salvador Dali, including *Un Chien andalou* (1928) and *L'Age
d'or* (1930), are among the most lasting contributions to modernist cinema. Futurism and other movements issued manifestos addressing the
possibilities of the new medium. The popular cinema of Hollywood,
meanwhile, represented the growing threat of mechanized mass culture
but also new possibilities in mainstream features from D. W. Griffiths's
Broken Blossoms (1919) to the Marx Brothers' *Duck Soup* (1933). There
were personal exchanges: the meeting between James Joyce and the
Russian film pioneer Sergei Eisenstein in 1930 to discuss interior monologue and cinematic montage in relation to *Ulysses*; the meeting between
Gertrude Stein and Charles Chaplin in Paris in 1931; or the collaboration of Samuel Beckett and Buster Keaton on the much later work, *Film*
(1965). Tributes to Chaplin, the era's biggest star, came from all quar-
ters of modernism. Chaplin's first international success was his feature
film *The Kid* (1921). The American modernist poet Hart Crane, inspired
by Chaplin's film, responded the same year with 'Chaplinesque' ('For we
can still love the world, who find / A famished kitten on the step, and
know / Recesses for it from the fury of the street'). Later films included
The Gold Rush (1925), *City Lights* (1931), *Modern Times* (1936), and his
first dialogue film, *The Great Dictator* (1940). Joyce refers to Chaplin several times in *Finnegans Wake* (1939), and the Chaplinesque qualities and
appearance of Leopold Bloom in *Ulysses* (1922) have often been noted.
In 1927, the surrealists even rose to Chaplin's defense when his young

wife, Lita Grey, accused him of 'indecent acts' in a high-profile divorce suit. The manifesto, 'Hands Off Love', published in *transition* magazine, claimed that Chaplin was the personification of love and therefore beyond reproach.

Perhaps no modernist author followed the development of cinema more closely than Joyce. Still in his twenties, he broke his self-imposed exile in Trieste long enough to return to Dublin with a scheme to open the city's first cinema, Cinematograph Volta, with the help of Italian backers. (There were also similar plans for ventures in Belfast and Cork.) The Volta opened in December 1909 but failed after six months and was sold at a loss. Nevertheless, the venture set the tone for Joyce's lasting interest in the medium. *Ulysses*, especially its central episode, 'Wandering Rocks', with its series of short scenes and many interpolated mini-scenes, has long been recognized for its cinematic qualities. These include rapid shifts in perspective, including cuts from wide panoramas (even aerial views) to close-ups, quick jumps, simultaneity, flashbacks, and flash-forwards. According to Richard Ellmann, Joyce initially 'thought...that the book could not be translated into another language, but might be translated into another medium, that of the film'. In the 1930s, Warner Brothers wrote to Joyce, and casting possibilities were discussed. But it was not until 1967 that the first major movie adaptation appeared, directed by Joseph Strick and starring Milo O'Shea as Leopold Bloom and Barbara Jefford as Molly Bloom. Strick's version includes some evocative scenes, but overall the book has been judged resistant to cinematic treatment – a judgement largely unaffected by the recent Irish adaptation, *Bloom*, that debuted in Dublin on 16 June 2004, the centenary of the day on which *Ulysses* takes place.

Another modernist writer who took a strong interest in film was Virginia Woolf. In her essay, 'The Cinema' (1926), she notes some of the possibilities of the 'savage' new medium, but also the pitfalls, especially the passivity it engenders: 'The eye licks it all up instantaneously, and the brain, agreeably titillated, settles down to watch things happening without bestirring itself to think.' The Hogarth Press, which was run by the Woolfs, also published books on film. In its early history, the cinema was often gendered as female – partly as a result of its association with mass culture – and it was seen as catering to a predominantly female audience. A number of modernists, women in particular, wrote on film in the 1920s and 1930s. Iris Barry, for example, was a founder of both the London Film Society and the MOMA Film Library in New York. The poet H. D. and the novelist Dorothy Richardson helped to establish the British film journal *Close Up* (1927–1933), which in one of its cover slogans declared: 'Theory and Analysis – No Gossip.' H. D. also acted alongside Paul Robeson in the silent film *Borderline* (1930), an experimental melodrama. The film explores racial and sexual politics, as it follows the main characters through a series of relationships, portrayed in a suitably dizzying style of quick cuts and set to a jazz score.

See also: *Contexts*: Cities and urbanization, Culture, Science and technology; *Texts*: Avant-garde, Dada and surrealism, Fragmentation, Music.

Further Reading

Burkdall, Thomas L., *Joycean Frames: Film and the Fiction of James Joyce* (New York and London: Routledge, 2001).

McCabe, Susan, *Cinematic Modernism: Modernist Poetry and Film* (Cambridge and New York: Cambridge University Press, 2005).

Trotter, David, *Cinema and Modernism* (Oxford and Malden, MA: Blackwell, 2007).

Wood, Michael, 'Modernism and Cinema', in Michael Levenson, ed., *The Cambridge Companion to Modernism* (Cambridge and New York: Cambridge University Press, 1999), pp. 217–32.

Consciousness, Stream of

'Illumine the mind within rather than the world without', Virginia Woolf proclaimed in 'Phases of Fiction' (1929). In their fiction, Woolf, Joyce, Faulkner, Richardson, Proust, and other writers used the 'stream of consciousness' narrative style to give expression to this new interest in interiority. The American psychologist William James (Henry James's brother and Gertrude Stein's professor at Radcliffe) coined the term in his *Principles of Psychology* (1890). May Sinclair was the first person to describe literature using the term almost three decades later, in 1918, in an essay on Dorothy Richardson. Stream of consciousness is a literary rendering of the thoughts that flow through a character's mind at any given time. It is often used interchangeably with 'interior monologue', although by some definitions interior monologue is the broader term, referring to any representation of a character's inner thoughts. Stream of consciousness would in this case refer to the more experimental style of representing consciousness in an apparently raw or unedited form, sometimes sacrificing intelligibility and conventional grammar in the process. A good example of this purer sort of stream of consciousness is the closing 'Penelope' episode of Joyce's *Ulysses* (1922), which conveys the mind of Molly Bloom as an uninterrupted, free-associating, and unpunctuated flow of language. (Joyce claimed to have borrowed the stream of consciousness technique from the French novelist Edouard

Dujardin.) The novel concludes with Molly's memory of her husband's proposal on Dublin's Howth Head, and her answer:

> and I thought well as well him as another and then I asked him with my eyes to ask again yes and then he asked me would I yes to say yes my mountain flower and first I put my arms around him yes and drew him down to me so he could feel my breasts all perfume yes and his heart was going like mad and yes I said yes I will Yes.

Thoughts expressed in this form are given to rapidly shifting from reveries of the past to concerns about the present and from brief observations or digressions to longer flights of fancy. Without conventional 'sign-posting' this can be disorienting, as the reader is left to interpret and judge the significance of fleeting thoughts and allusions to people and places. Joyce's stream of consciousness suggests the influence of the French philosopher Henri Bergson's concept of *durée*, or duration. In Bergson's 'time-philosophy', memory holds a crucial place in consciousness. Bergson used the metaphor of a single, unbroken sentence to convey his idea of consciousness: 'This single sentence that was begun at the first awakening of consciousness, a sentence strewn with commas but in no place cut by a period.' The present is formed by and intimately bound up with the past in the individual consciousness.

The year after *Ulysses* finally appeared in book form after several years' serialization, Woolf completed 'Mrs. Dalloway in Bond Street' (1923), the short story that was the germ of one of her most successful novels. The following description is another good example of stream-of-consciousness style, but this time it is choppier, and replete with punctuation. This start-stop form conveys what Woolf described in her essay 'Modern Fiction' (1919/1925) as the 'myriad impressions' that fell like 'an incessant shower of innumerable atoms' upon 'an ordinary mind on an ordinary day'. The voice of an omniscient narrator fuses with Clarissa Dalloway's own fleeting thoughts as she walks through central London:

> she was in Picadilly, passing the house with the slender green columns, and the balconies; passing club windows full of newspapers...and Claridge's, where she must remember Dick wanted her to leave a card on Mrs. Jepson or she would be gone. Rich Americans can be very charming. There was St. James's Palace; like a child's game with bricks; and now – she had passed Bond Street – she was by Hatchard's book shop. The stream was endless – endless – endless. Lords, Ascot, Hurlingham – what was it? What a duck, she thought, looking at the frontispiece of some book of memoirs spread wide in

the bow window, Sir Joshua perhaps or Romney; arch, bright, demure; the sort of girl – like her own Elizabeth – the only real sort of girl. And there was that absurd book, Soapy Sponge, which Jim used to quote by the yard; and Shakespeare's Sonnets. She knew them by heart.

As the passage demonstrates, flights of memory are often triggered by the senses, whether it is the sight of a book in a window, or something felt, or a smell, or a sound, or (most famously) the taste of a tea-soaked madeleine biscuit that carries Marcel back to the Combray of his childhood in the first volume of Proust's *In Search of Lost Time* (1913–1927).

One of the defining characteristics of the modernist narrative is the so-called inward turn. In the second half of the nineteenth century, writers like Conrad, James, Flaubert, and Dostoevsky brought an increased self-consciousness and a new interest in subjectivity to their novels, privileging the private and personal – and especially the personal crisis – over the public and social. The representation of new states of consciousness in literature was aided significantly by new theories that began to appear in psychology and philosophy at this time. The Hogarth Press, run by Leonard and Virginia Woolf, was the authorized publisher of the International Psycho-Analytical Institute from 1924 and began to publish the Standard Edition of Freud's works the same year. The Woolfs were, therefore, largely responsible for introducing English readers to psychoanalytic theory, and indeed for making it to some extent fashionable. D. H. Lawrence's novels *The Rainbow* (1915) and *Women in Love* (1920) testify to the growing sense of a new, modern consciousness awakening out of the old Victorian frame of mind. This shift in consciousness is often described in terms of a generational divide. Although Lawrence harboured deep reservations about the growing trend of 'Freudianism', he published two books after the war, *Psychoanalysis and the Unconscious* (1921) and *Fantasia of the Unconscious* (1922), which not only offered criticisms of Freudian psychoanalysis and resistance to psychoanalytic interpretations of his work but also put forward his own theories of the unconscious. Lawrence disliked what he took to be Freud's view of the unconscious as a repository of 'bad' or anti-social urges, and Freud's desire to 'cure' individuals so that they could reintegrate with society. For Lawrence, ever the dissenting romantic, it was society that was sick, and the unconscious remained a positive source of creativity and potential liberation. The individual consciousness must awake and free itself from the deadening conformity and corruption of mass-consciousness.

There was another change in consciousness taking place, however, which was anything but optimistic. Even while the revolution in perception and the sense of self was taking place, the specter of what

D. H. Lawrence called 'the end of consciousness' loomed large over those who were caught up in the First World War. In Lawrence's story 'England, My England' (1922), the moment of death, preceded by 'the awful faint whistling of a shell', comes almost as a relief to his protagonist: 'To forget! To forget! Utterly, utterly to forget, in the great forgetting of death. To break the core and the unit of life, and to lapse out on the great darkness.' For many who fought and survived, like Septimus Smith in Woolf's *Mrs. Dalloway* (1925), there was the shattered consciousness of shell shock, the survivor's guilt, and the altered perception of the world after war. Septimus, who had gone to war as an idealistic young poet, came back believing 'human beings have neither kindness, nor faith, nor charity.... They hunt in packs.... They desert the fallen.' His mind resembles in some ways the other minds we meet in the novel, but his works at a more anxious, fevered pitch, and the free association that in others takes the form of a gently meandering stream resembles in him a torrent of nightmarish visions. Shortly before his death, Septimus struggles to separate his hallucinations from the hard, banal objects in the room:

> He was alone, exposed on this bleak eminence, stretched out – but not on a hill-top; not on a crag; on Mrs. Filmer's sitting-room sofa. As for the visions, the faces, the voices of the dead, where were they? There was a screen in front of him, with black bulrushes and blue swallows. Where he had once seen mountains, where he had seen faces, where he had seen beauty, there was a screen.

> 'Evans!' he cried. There was no answer. A mouse had squeaked, or a curtain rustled. Those were the voices of the dead. The screen, the coal-scuttle, the side-board remained to him.

The explanation and dating of the change in consciousness may have varied, but what remained constant in this period was the acknowledgment that an irrevocable rupture had taken place, and consciousness could never be seen, or depicted, the same way again.

See also: *Contexts*: Psychology, War; *Texts*: Bloomsbury, Epiphany, Fragmentation, Irish literature; *Criticism*: Psychoanalytic criticism.

Further Reading

Humphrey, Robert, *Stream of Consciousness in the Modern Novel* (Berkeley: University of California Press, 1954).

Kumar, Shiv K., *Bergson and the Stream of Consciousness Novel* (London: Blackie, 1962).

Dada and Surrealism

'If you have serious ideas about life, if you make artistic discoveries, and if all of a sudden your head begins to crackle with laughter, if you find all your ideas useless and ridiculous, know that IT IS DADA BEGINNING TO SPEAK TO YOU.' So declared the 1921 manifesto, 'Dada Excites Everything'. Published in Paris, its signatories, including Tristan Tzara, Man Ray, Francis Picabia, Max Ernst, André Breton, Louis Aragon, Marcel Duchamp, and many others, are said to 'live in France, America, Spain, Germany, Italy, Switzerland, Belgium, etc., but have no nationality'. This was dada at its height, and just on the brink of implosion; Breton and Tzara would soon split the group in two, and it would be 'dead' by early 1922. But what was dada? Dada was born in the Cabaret Voltaire in Zurich in 1916, a small vortex of artistic energy in the centre of war-torn Europe. Its original members included Richard Huelsenbeck, Hugo Ball, and Emmy Hennings, all of whom were German, and two Romanians, Tzara and Marcel Janco. Jean (or Hans) Arp, from Alsace, joined the group shortly thereafter. Their first performances, made up of manifestos, poetry, stories, and songs, were plainly inspired by futurism, a movement whose influence was felt across the European avant-garde at the time. By the summer of 1916, when the journal *Dada* was issued (succeeding the single-issue *Cabaret Voltaire*), Tzara had taken control of the group, and from this point its nihilistic character came to the fore.

The origin of the name 'dada' has been variously 'explained' as the randomly chosen French word for hobbyhorse, the Romanian for 'yes, yes', and a popular brand of hair lotion. Importantly, it was nonsensical, infantile, and international. The main centres of dada activity were the cities of Zurich, Berlin, Paris, and New York. Dada arrived in America in 1916, shortly after its inception in Zurich – although this chronology has been a subject of dispute – when New York became another refuge for artists fleeing the war. French expatriates Duchamp and Picabia settled in New York until the war ended and there met American artists like Man Ray and Beatrice Wood, and the patrons Walter and Louise Arensberg. After the war, dada travelled 'home' with some of its participants to Paris, Berlin, Cologne, and other cities.

Like futurism, dada was a movement across the arts. Some of its innovations include found art, collage, and sound poetry. Its more famous visual works include Duchamp 'readymades' such as the urinal signed 'R. Mutt' and entitled *Fountain* (1917), and *L. H. O. O. Q* (1919), a reproduction of the *Mona Lisa* with a moustache drawn on and a title that sounds like *elle a chaud au cul*, which translates roughly as 'she's got hot pants'. Dada was in one sense a product of the war and impossible to imagine apart from that context; in another, however, it was a heroic continuation and culmination of the pre-war avant-garde that had largely been killed off by the war. (For example, Duchamp's earliest 'readymade', the *Bicycle Wheel* of 1913, and the 1912 painting *Nude Descending a Staircase, No. 2*, predate dada and the war.) Dada presented itself as the 'ism' to end all 'isms'. The manifesto quoted above runs through a list of movements – cubism, expressionism, simultaneism, futurism, unanism, ultraism, vorticism, and imagism – and dismisses each in turn, attacking their pretense and preachiness. 'Dada is never right', it proclaims; 'Dada has no fixed idea.' Yet 'Dada has always existed' and 'Dada knows everything'. It is all movements and not a movement; it is everything and nothing. Contrary, primitivist, volatile, anti-art, and intensely nihilistic, especially under Tzara's leadership, 'Dada spits everything out'.

Dada and surrealism are best understood as sequential and interrelated. Surrealism, which survived the Second World War and lived on for several decades, rose from the ashes of the much briefer dada movement in the early 1920s. Although the transition was not entirely peaceful, the two movements shared members, ideas, and approaches. The main development of surrealism from dada was, in a sense, the idea of development; where dada was aggressively nihilistic and anarchistic, having been born in the middle of the war, surrealism proposed a constructive, if rather fantastic, alternative to post-war social and cultural *malaise*. The surrealist solution lay primarily in the liberation of consciousness. It borrowed many of its ideas from psychology, especially Freud, and its experiments took the form of dream analysis, automatic writing, hypnosis, and other techniques. There was also an interest in eroticism, psychotic states, and hallucinatory visions, and a desire to bypass the logical mind to discover in the subconscious new energies and new ways of seeing. Like dada, surrealists were attracted to found objects and 'primitive' art and artifacts, seeking in these objects what they also sought in the subconscious mind, that is, hidden energies. Automatism, of which automatic writing was just one outlet, was a central feature of surrealist theory. The movement's central text is Breton's 'Manifesto of Surrealism', published in 1924.

Surrealism heralded a return to Romanticism from the classical tendencies of some earlier modernisms. It was also linked to communism, especially through Breton, who was a member of the Communist Party from 1927 to 1935. He left, as many artists did, out of disgust for Stalinism. (In 1938 he met Leon Trotsky in Mexico, and they co-authored a manifesto together.) None of this had a particularly strong impact on modernism in Britain until the mid-1930s, when surrealism briefly took hold in London. The 19-year-old poet David Gascoyne's *A Short Survey of Surrealism* was published in 1935, followed by *Surrealism*, edited by Herbert Read, which accompanied the London International Surrealist Exhibition of 1936. Gascoyne was one of a number of young British writers who were influenced by surrealism at this time, including Charles Madge, Dylan Thomas, and Lawrence Durrell. In 1937 Madge, together with Humphrey Jennings and Tom Harrisson, founded Mass Observation, a sociological survey group whose early experiments were indebted to surrealist theory. Dada and surrealism also influenced expatriate writers living in Paris and Zurich, including Joyce, Pound, and the circle of Americans that gathered around Gertrude Stein and later *transition* magazine.

See also: *Contexts*: Anthropology, Psychology, War; *Texts*: Futurism, Manifesto, Primitivism.

Further Reading

Ades, Dawn, *The Dada Reader: A Critical Anthology* (London: Tate Publishing, 2006).
Ball, Hugo, *Flight Out of Time* (Berkeley: University of California Press, 1996).
Breton, André, *Manifestos of Surrealism*, trans. Richard Weaver and Helen Lane (Ann Arbor: University of Michigan Press, 1969).
Dachy, Marc, *The Dada Movement 1915–1923* (New York: Rizzoli, 1990).
Durozoi, Gérard, *History of the Surrealist Movement*, trans. Alison Anderson (Chicago: University of Chicago Press, 2002).
Foster, Hal, *Compulsive Beauty* (Cambridge, MA: MIT Press, 1993).
Huelsenbeck, Richard, *Memoirs of a Dada Drummer* (Berkeley: University of California Press, 1991).
Richter, Hans, *Dada: Art and Anti-Art* (London: Thames and Hudson, 1978).
Tzara, Tristan, *Seven Dada Manifestos and Lampisteries*, trans. Barbara Wright (London: Calder, 1992).

Drama

Despite the vitality of avant-garde theatre, from Ibsen to Brecht, in continental Europe, Anglo-American modernism produced little in the way of major drama. The Irish Literary Theatre, co-founded in 1899 by William Butler Yeats, Lady Gregory, and Edward Martyn (who became the first president of Sinn Féin in 1905), is the notable exception. The ILT produced its first play, Yeats's *The Countess Cathleen*, in 1899. The group found its home in Dublin's Abbey Theatre in 1904. As well as producing their own works, Yeats and Lady Gregory helped to launch the careers of J. M. Synge, Sean O'Casey, and others. However, it is Yeats's plays, particularly those written after 1916, which stand apart as being formally innovative. Inspired by his close collaboration with Ezra Pound during the winters of 1913–1916, Yeats borrowed from the Japanese Noh tradition to create an intimate, literary drama. Eschewing the Ibsen-inspired naturalism that was popular in European drama at the time, *At the Hawk's Well* (1916) and *Four Plays for Dancers* (1921) are static and heavily symbolic, and they make extensive use of stylized gestures and masks. These 'aristocratic' plays were intended more for small private audiences than large public ones. If 'British' modernist drama was chiefly an Irish affair, the same could be said of mainstream drama, where George Bernard Shaw, like Oscar Wilde before him, made highly successful plays with a strong undercurrent of social criticism, including *Man and Superman* (1903), *Major Barbara* (1905), *The Shewing-up Of Blanco Posnet* (1909), and *Saint Joan* (1923). Samuel Beckett turned to drama fairly late in his career, with *Waiting for Godot* having its London debut in 1955.

Aside from Yeats, modernist drama written in English tended to be rather marginal, coming from writers who found greater success in other genres. Joyce's *Exiles* (1918), which was rejected by the Abbey Theatre and first produced in a German translation in Munich in 1919, is one case in point. Another is Wyndham Lewis's challenging vorticist drama *Enemy of the Stars*, published in the first issue of *Blast* (1914), which was written for the most part in narrative prose and suggests little desire for actual staging. D. H. Lawrence wrote ten plays, beginning with *A Collier's Friday Night* in 1909. Most were published posthumously, and only one, *The Widowing of Mrs Holroyd* (1914), achieved any recognition during his lifetime. After decades of neglect, however, Lawrence's plays experienced a revival beginning in the late 1960s. T. S. Eliot turned from poetry to verse plays in the 1930s with some success. The most famous of these is *Murder in the Cathedral* (1935), based on the martyrdom of Archbishop Thomas Becket in Canterbury Cathedral, where Eliot's play was first performed. Subsequent plays, including *The Family Reunion* (1939) and *The Cocktail Party* (1949), are lighter entertainments but still reflect the author's interest in questions of religious faith.

British theatre of the 1920s and 1930s was dominated by Noel Coward's sometimes risqué but nevertheless popular confections. These included *The Vortex* (1924), which caused a stir with its veiled references to homosexuality and drug use, along with *Private Lives* (1929), *Design for Living* (1932), and the patriotic extravaganza *Cavalcade* (1931). Success for cutting-edge British theatre came later, finally arriving in the 1950s with the gritty realism of 'kitchen sink' dramas like John Osbourne's *Look Back in Anger* (1956) and Shelagh Delaney's *A Taste of Honey* (1958), or the politically charged productions of Joan Littlewood's Theatre Workshop, such as *Oh! What a Lovely War* (1963). In the United States, meanwhile, homegrown modernist drama can hardly be said to have existed in any significant way in the early twentieth century. As in Britain, the era of the great American dramatists – Tennessee Williams, Thornton Wilder, Arthur Miller, Edward Albee – happened in the 1940s and 1950s. Eugene O'Neill is the notable exception: the Pulitzer Prize-winning *Strange Interlude* (1928), which employs masks and soliloquies, and *Mourning Becomes Electra* (1931), an updating of the *Oresteia* trilogy by Aeschylus to the American Civil War, display O'Neill's experimental tendencies. O'Neill's plays of this period also reflect the growing influence of Freud and Jung in their depiction of new models of subjectivity and desire.

The impact of European modernist drama on Anglo-American modernism was not limited to the theatre. The groundbreaking early modernist plays of Henrik Ibsen and August Strindberg were strongly influential across the genres for their naturalism and depiction of interior states. Rebecca West, born Cicily Fairfield, took her name from the 'New Woman' heroine of Ibsen's *Rosmersholm* (1886) when she began writing for the *New Freewoman* in 1912. In 1900, the 18-year-old Joyce, having studied Norwegian in order to read Ibsen's plays in the original, reviewed Ibsen in the *Fortnightly Review*, and the playwright sent a note (in Norwegian) thanking Joyce for his generous appraisal. Ibsen's most direct influence on modern drama in English was on Shaw, who saw in Ibsen's work a liberating alternative to Victorian orthodoxies of all kinds. Although this account focuses on Anglo-American authors, it is impossible to discuss modernism and drama without mentioning two key figures of the European theatre, Antonin Artaud and Bertold Brecht. As a playwright and director, Brecht is best known for his development of 'epic theatre' (as opposed to dramatic theatre), which attempted to put socialist theories and aesthetics into practice. Brecht's concept of the theatre built on the earlier innovations of Vsevolod Meyerhold and Erwin Piscator, and he shared ideas with his friend the critic and philosopher Walter Benjamin. The new theatre demanded a more dynamic relationship between actors and audiences. Brecht wanted to replace audience passivity with active engagement; he wanted audiences to think and make decisions during the course of a play and to have their ideas challenged rather than simply reinforced. The play would present an argument, and the audience would be asked to make a judgement. Epic theatre was anti-illusionistic and called not for a suspension of disbelief but a distanced or 'alienated' view of the action on stage. Unlike the earlier avant-garde of futurism, which sought engagement in the form of a strong audience reaction, Brecht's theatre went further, fully embracing the didacticism that had been chased out of art by 'art for art's sake'. In this case, however, narrative art would be used to convey revolutionary political ideas. Good examples of Brecht's epic theatre include *The Threepenny Opera* (1928), freely adapted from John Gay's *The Beggar's Opera* (1728), and *Mother Courage and Her Children* (1939).

The 'theatre of cruelty', meanwhile, pioneered by the ex-surrealist Artaud, plotted a very different course for the theatre. Artaud's principles for the new theatre, formulated in *The Theatre and Its Double* (1938), also sought to rid audiences of their complacency but with different methods and objectives. Artaud wanted to strike at the core of his audiences' psyches, to make people see life as it really is: irrational, violent, and cruel. Techniques used to achieve this cathartic effect were to include gesture and spectacle (partly derived from Balinese theatre), with a lesser emphasis on words. Artaud failed to realize his theories in his own work, but later plays including Peter Weiss's *Marat/Sade* (1963), directed by Peter Brook for both stage (1964) and screen (1967), showed his strong influence. Finally, one other key figure of modernist drama must be mentioned: Edward Gordon Craig. The English dramatist and theoretician provided a rare link between the modernist theatres of Britain, Ireland, continental Europe, and Russia. Craig was part of the theatrical Terry family, and his mother was the renowned Shakespearean actress Ellen Terry. He toured with Henry Irving's acting company in the 1890s and later worked on set designs for Stanislavsky at the Moscow Art Theatre and Yeats at the Abbey Theatre in Dublin. He moved to Italy in 1908, and from there published a journal, the *Mask* (1908–1929), which was strongly influential in the development of avant-garde theatrical techniques across Europe. One innovation, intended to break the illusion of the theatre and the egotism of the actor, proposed the casting of marionettes in place of human actors. Craig published several books during his long and varied career, including *The Art of the Theatre* (1905) and *On the Art of the Theatre* (1911).

See also: *Contexts*: Culture; *Texts*: Aestheticism and decadence, Dada and surrealism, Irish literature; *Criticism*: Cultural materialism/New Historicism, Marxist criticism.

Further Reading

Innes, Christopher, *Avant Garde Theatre, 1892–1992* (London: Routledge, 1993).
——, *Modern British Drama: The Twentieth Century* (Cambridge and New York: Cambridge University Press, 2002).
Puchner, Martin, *Stage Fright: Modernism, Anti-Theatricality, and Drama* (Baltimore: Johns Hopkins University Press, 2002).
Taxidou, Olga, *Modernism and Performance: Jarry to Brecht* (Basingstoke and New York: Palgrave Macmillan, 2007).

Epiphany

Epiphany is a Christian term for the manifestation of the divine in the human or everyday. The term became associated with modernist literature through Joyce, who adapted it for secular literary use near the start of his writing career (*c.* 1901–1904), at first as a sort of writing exercise. He employed it later especially in *Dubliners* (1914) and *A Portrait of the Artist as a Young Man* (1916). In *Dubliners*, Joyce drew upon two major influences of the turn of the century, naturalism and symbolism. Both these influences come into play in the Joycean epiphany, which is defined by Stephen Dedalus in the manuscript of *Stephen Hero* (1944), the novel that Joyce would later rewrite as *A Portrait*. Stephen confides to his friend Cranly: 'By an epiphany he meant a sudden spiritual manifestation, whether in the vulgarity of speech or of gesture or in a memorable phase of the mind itself . . . the most delicate and evanescent of moments.' Only the artist, in Joyce's view, is able to capture effectively the moment of epiphany, of revelation. Such moments are present in the climactic closing scenes of many of the short stories in *Dubliners*, as well as at the end of each of the five chapters in *A Portrait*.

In 'Araby', the third story in *Dubliners*, for example, the first-person narrator conveys in the final sentence a moment of terrible self-knowledge. 'Gazing up into the darkness I saw myself as a creature driven and derided by vanity; and my eyes burned with anguish and anger.' Up to this point, the young narrator has been consumed with a quasi-religious romantic fervour and has embarked upon a quest for a prize fit to present to his beloved, identified only as Mangan's sister. He hopes to find at Araby, the bazaar Mangan's sister told him about, a present that will win her affection. Instead, as the hall darkens and he overhears a flirtatious conversation in English accents between a shop-girl and two young men, he experiences a moment of bitter insight into his own vanity and wasted ardour. In *A Portrait*, the epiphanies that close each chapter are followed immediately at the beginning of the next chapter by a contrastingly sober and mundane image; a 'hangover' to the wild euphoria of the night before. Thus, for example, the second chapter ends with the adolescent Stephen losing his virginity to a prostitute: 'He closed his eyes, surrendering himself to her, body and mind, conscious of nothing in the world but the dark pressure of her softly parting lips.' This transcendent moment of release is followed by the more pedestrian image in the next chapter of Stephen with a dull hunger in his belly, thinking of mutton stew and his visit that night to 'the squalid quarter of the brothels'. He has become a regular sinner and thinks constantly of 'eternal damnation'. By chapter's end, however, he reaches another temporary peak by confessing his sins and receiving communion: 'A life of grace and virtue and hap-piness! It was true. It was not a dream from which he would wake. The past was past.'

The examples from *A Portrait* should suggest not only the (apparently) transcendent nature of the epiphany but also its complex and equivocal nature. Epiphanies in Joyce should not necessarily be taken at face value. We must keep in mind that in Joyce, as in most modernist literature, indeterminacy and instability rule. An epiphany does not provide a neat solution to an otherwise ambiguous tale. Where insights are gained, they are often negative (as in 'Araby'), and their interpretation is left open and uncertain. They are climactic, perhaps, but far from conclusive, opening up a range of possibilities as the curtain falls on the action. One compli-cating factor in how we read moments of epiphany in Joyce is his use of free indirect discourse, what Hugh Kenner called (in Joyce's *Voices*) the 'Uncle Charles Principle'. In this narrative technique, the thoughts and vocabulary of character and narrator merge so that, for example, a third-person narrative uses words peculiar to the main character in a scene. (An example used by Kenner is the opening line of 'The Dead': 'Lily, the caretaker's daughter, was literally run off her feet.' Here the word 'lit-erally' is Lily's own idiom.) Free indirect discourse sometimes produces an ironic gap, or the possibility of such a gap, leaving us unsure of the sincerity of a character's feelings or motives. Is a character's moment of insight authentic? Are we seeing them clearly? In the ending of 'A Painful Case', for example, Duffy experiences profound feelings of regret, lone-liness, and a sense of his own mortality. Or does he? 'No one wanted him; he was an outcast from life's feast.' On one reading, this is a gen-uine moment of insight. On another, however, this is merely Duffy – a highly self-conscious character 'with an odd autobiographical habit' (as we learn earlier) 'which led him to compose in his mind from time to time a short sentence about himself containing a subject in the third per-son and a predicate in the past tense' – narrating his own misery in a romantic and rather maudlin, self-pitying fashion.

Although the term epiphany is most commonly associated with Joyce, similar moments of radiant insight can be found elsewhere in modernist fiction. Indeed the debt to symbolism and the tendency towards densely suggestive imagery, along with the desire to find the exceptional in the everyday, make the epiphany an ideal modernist device. (If the defini-tion is allowed too much latitude, however, it may seem to include, for example, all lyric poetry, which is built upon such isolated moments of revelation, usually deriving from the contemplation of everyday scenes or objects.) William Wordsworth, who wrote of 'spots in time' in *The Pre-lude* (1850), is an important precursor, as is Walter Pater. In Proust's *In*

dialect [margin annotation]

Search of Lost Time (1913–1927), Marcel experiences sudden, intense flights of memory that are triggered by his senses, the most famous trigger being the taste of a tea-soaked madeleine biscuit. Virginia Woolf, Katherine Mansfield, and other modernist contemporaries of Joyce also developed the technique. As examples by Joyce, Woolf, and Mansfield make clear, the epiphany is particularly well suited to the rich allusiveness and compression of the open-ended modernist short story.

See also: *Contexts:* Psychology, Religion; *Texts:* Aestheticism and decadence, Allusion, Bloomsbury, Consciousness, Stream of, Irish literature, Memory.

Further Reading

Beja, Morris, *Epiphany in the Modern Novel* (London: Owen, 1971).

Tigges, Wim, ed., *Moments of Moment: Aspects of the Literary Epiphany* (Amsterdam: Rodopi, 1999).

Fragmentation

'These fragments I have shored against my ruins' is certainly one of the most famous lines of modernist literature, and it is also one of the most telling. *The Waste Land* (1922) is T. S. Eliot's nightmarish vision of modern, alienated, post-war London, conveyed in a narrative of fragments. The haunting line, which appears at the end of the poem, is wedged between two fragments of literary texts: preceding it, in the original French, is (as Eliot's own notes to the poem explain) a line from the sonnet 'El Desdichado' (1853) by Gérard de Nerval. The line that follows is from Thomas Kyd's *The Spanish Tragedy* (1592), subtitled *Hieronymo Is Mad Againe.* 'These fragments . . .' is at once an example of the kind of fragmentary, allusive utterance that makes up the poem, and a broader symbolic description of the effort to rebuild post-war Europe – in every sense: physically, spiritually, culturally, and psychologically. Furthermore, it performs a kind of unification, bringing the poem to a satisfying, if not conclusive, end. Far from celebrating the fragmentation his poem describes, Eliot wanted only to renew the literature and society of the present using the traditions and achievements of the past, just as the Fisher King of the poem seeks to heal his wounds and return life to his barren lands. That is not to say that the author succeeds in building a perfect whole out of these fragments, but he does manage to construct a series of smaller unities. As Michael Levenson has stated, 'Fragments of the Buddha and Augustine combine to make a new literary reality which is neither the Buddha nor Augustine but which includes them both'

(Levenson, 1984, p. 190). The same poetic technique is employed by Ezra Pound in *The Cantos*. Pound attempted to 'make it new' using fragments of the past, which were channelled, assembled, translated, parodied, and performed in different ways. (Eliot's poem, famously edited by Pound, was given the odd provisional title 'He do the police in different voices', suggesting the act of mimicry.) The confusion faced by readers of the poem is represented in the lines: 'You cannot say, or guess, for you know only / A heap of broken images.' The 'broken images', which may refer to the images of false idols destroyed by God, also represent the desert landscape of the secular and materialist present, its inhabitants alienated from meaning and from the rich traditions of the past.

Other modernists, including James Joyce and Virginia Woolf, used fragmented prose in their novels to suggest various aspects of the modern consciousness. Time and space, memory and perception were all touched by a new epistemological uncertainty. *A Portrait of the Artist as a Young Man* (1916) opens with fragments of memories from childhood, the narrative inflected with a child's consciousness. ('He was baby tuckoo. The moocow came down the road where Betty Byrne lived: she sold lemon platt.') It also closes with fragments, this time snippets of journal entries that record Stephen Dedalus's planned escape from Dublin to Paris and the wider world ('16 *April*: Away! Away!'). Another kind of fragmented subjectivity appears in Woolf's *Mrs. Dalloway* (1925) in the mind of Septimus Smith, a veteran of the war and victim of shell shock. His fragmented, tortured thoughts are like the shell fragments that were a constant threat to soldiers in the trenches. But Septimus is not the only character whose mind and personality fall short of the Victorian ideal of wholeness and consistency: Clarissa Dalloway, too, 'had tried to be the same always, never showing a sign of all the other sides of her', but the reader sees how she 'drew the parts together' only with effort, showing a unified self to the world. An earlier effort, *Jacob's Room* (1922), built a portrait of the absent figure at the centre of the novel, Jacob Flanders, one of the war dead, out of fragments – none of which is given more importance than any other and without transitions or connections between them. In *To the Lighthouse* (1927), the artist-figure Lily Briscoe struggles to piece together, in her painting, the fragments of life after the First World War. She attempts to bring about a thematic unity but also a formal balance of 'masses' in the picture. Returning to a canvas she had started before the war, she thinks: 'Going to the Lighthouse. But what does one send to the Lighthouse? Perished. Alone. The grey-green light on the wall opposite. The empty spaces. Such were some of the parts, but how bring them together?' Lily's task mirrors Woolf's efforts to structure the novel in a unique and modern way, not through the standard conventions of rising and falling action but through the balance of 'masses' and by techniques such as pattern and repetition. Modernist writing, whether poetry or prose, often resembles fragments of film spliced together in a montage; quick cuts are made to other points of view and other positions in time or space, and (as in montage) the meaning can be seen not in the individual parts but only in the resulting whole, and even this greater picture may be open and uncertain.

According to Pound, *The Waste Land* has 'emotional unity', whether or not it can be described as unified in other ways. In the broadest possible terms, what separates modernism from postmodernism is the desire for some degree of formal unity, and the belief that art can achieve it – even, perhaps, that art can serve a 'higher' purpose fulfilling a quasi-religious role with the promise of salvation and redemption or, at least, as the glue that can hold society together and provide meaning after a catastrophe like the First World War. The contemporary criticism of F. R. Leavis and the American New Critics was built upon the assumption that while modernist writers often depicted a fragmented modernity, poems like *The Waste Land* were themselves ultimately coherent and unified. In their view, readers needed to look no further than the works themselves to find meaning, and the more successful the works, the more perfect the 'wholeness' they achieved. Art would provide the perfection and unity that the world so obviously lacked, an idea that has roots in the aestheticism of Pater and Whistler; it is in the work of art, rather than nature, that perfection is to be found. Although the New Critics themselves were reluctant to take it on, Joyce's *Finnegans Wake* (1939), that colossal book of fragments, similarly achieves what meaning and coherence it possesses not through its resemblance to the outside world, which is minimal by any measure, but through repetition, sound, pattern, and tone.

See also: *Contexts*: Language, Psychology, War; *Texts*: Aestheticism and decadence, Allusion, Consciousness, Stream of, Impersonality, Memory; *Criticism*: Leavisite criticism, New Criticism.

Further Reading

Eliot, T. S., *The Annotated Waste Land with Eliot's Contemporary Prose*, ed. Lawrence Rainey (New Haven and London: Yale University Press, 2005).

Futurism

The name futurism has stood for two major movements in the European avant-garde: Italian and Russian. It was also used as a generic term for experimental art before the war, in the English press for example, owing to the notoriety of Italian futurism after the release of its first manifesto in 1909. Based in Milan, Italian futurism, under the charismatic leadership of the poet and promoter F. T. Marinetti, was a more or less corporate entity with a coherent platform and aesthetic. Its members were mainly artists and musicians, including Umberto Boccioni, Carlo Carrà, Giacomo Balla, Luigi Russolo, and Gino Severini, with Marinetti handling the movement's literary output. Although it was styled as a national movement, Italian futurism held close ties with Paris, then the centre of the artistic avant-garde, and published its first manifesto in the daily newspaper *Le Figaro*. Italian futurism differs from its Russian rival in one crucial respect, which also separates it from other futurist-inspired movements, including vorticism. The majority of avant-gardes outside Italy, even those that accept the label 'futurist', display a central ambivalence about modernity and its effects. Only Marinetti's futurism proclaims total allegiance to all things modern, including technological warfare, heavy industry, and the destruction of monuments and objects associated with the past. While Russian futurism called for a renovation of language, Italian futurism allied itself with all things modern – in a sense, modernism for modernism's sake.

Italian futurism inspired many similar movements across Europe. There were futurisms of various kinds not only in England and Russia but also in Poland, Hungary, France, and Serbia. Russian futurism comprised a number of factions: cubo-futurism, ego-futurism, the Mezzanine of Poetry, Company 41°, the Left Front of the Arts (LEF), and Centrifuge were the largest. The main division, however, was between a small minority who supported Marinetti and a majority who did not. (Marinetti visited Moscow in 1914 but did not receive a friendly reception.) Cubo-futurism, whose members included David Burliuk, Vladimir Mayakovsky, and Victor Khlebnikov, had close ties with the Russian formalist movement led by influential linguists and literary critics like Roman Jakobson and Victor Shklovsky. Russian formalism was a primary influence on much twentieth-century literary theory, in particular French structuralism and its offshoots. The issue of whether Russian or Italian futurism came first was, oddly enough, a contentious one. Although it is clear that Italian futurism made the first move, some Russian futurists denied and even attempted to reverse the order of influence. Marinetti toured Europe constantly during the pre-war years – what Marjorie Perloff has called the 'Futurist moment' – but despite his undeniable impact, he was a figure that artists, critics, and the public all loved to hate. This hostile reception was smoothly incorporated into Marinetti's platform: one of his early theatre manifestos was even subtitled *The Pleasures of Being Booed* (1911).

One of Italian futurism's most remarkable influences was the nineteenth-century American poet Walt Whitman. Whitman's ecstatic depiction of modern machinery and industrial life anticipated the futurist vision, first given expression in the preamble to 'The Founding and Manifesto of Futurism' (1909). The London *Daily Telegraph*, critical of the futurists' tendency to promise more than they produced, wrote in 1910, on the occasion of Marinetti's first visit to England:

> M. Marinetti writes like Walt Whitman gone mad. But Whitman sang, instead of telling us what he was going to sing. Why do not the futurists write their poems about railway trains and aeroplanes, their sermons in steam-engines, and books in racing motor-cars, instead of telling us they mean to write them?

More important than Whitman, however, was the philosopher Friedrich Nietzsche, whose influence can be seen in the violent attacks on weakness and sentimentality, and in the aggressive, hyperbolic tone of the manifestos. Indeed, Marinetti once stated that the key ingredients of the manifesto were 'violence and precision'. Italian futurism in turn served as the template for avant-garde movements throughout the twentieth century, including vorticism, dada, and surrealism; situationism in the 1960s; and punk rock (notably the Sex Pistols) in the 1970s. There is a certain amount of truth to the claim that futurism started it all: undeniably, it set the standard for an avant-garde aesthetic, and for the avant-garde's most distinct genre, the manifesto. It has even been argued that Marinetti's futurism anticipated – as opposed to merely endorsing, at its inception in 1919 – the ideology and tactics of Mussolini's Fascism. In 1924, the Italian philosopher Benedetto Croce compared futurism and fascism for their similar cult of personality, aggressive and provocative style, 'exaltation of youth', and 'eagerness to break with all traditions'.

Italian futurism left a significant imprint on British modernism. Marinetti's visits between 1910 and 1914 received substantial media coverage, from *The Times* to the tabloids. Imagism and vorticism have both been widely interpreted as reactions to futurism, although Ezra Pound and Wyndham Lewis did their best to downplay the importance of Marinetti's ideas and emphasize the differences between his movement and their own. (Pound called futurism 'a sort of accelerated impressionism'.) It is hard to imagine the audacity of *Blast* (1914), the vorticist magazine, which devoted considerable space to attacking futurism in its pages, without the influence of Marinetti. Indeed, although it was Pound who first described the London 'vortex', the term was already part of the futurist vocabulary. Lawrence Rainey and others have emphasized the competition for publicity and audience that Marinetti's movement generated and the specifically English character of the response that came in the form of vorticism, which was reactionary, satirical, and individualistic. D. H. Lawrence was also briefly intrigued by the possibilities of futurism, having first read one of Marinetti's manifestos in Harold Monro's *Poetry and Drama* in September 1913. The following year, Lawrence saw a book of 'futurist pictures' and read futurist poetry in the original Italian. He admired the force of their expression but disliked what he called their 'pseudo scientific' approach.

See also: *Contexts*: Fascism, Language, Science and technology; *Texts*: Avant-garde, Dada and surrealism, Imagism and vorticism, Manifesto, Primitivism, Violence.

Further Reading

Apollonio, Umbro, ed., *Futurist Manifestos* (New York: Viking, 1973).
Lawton, Anna, and Herbert Eagle, eds, *Russian Futurism Through Its Manifestoes, 1912–1928* (Ithaca, NY: Cornell University Press, 1988).
Marinetti, F. T., *Critical Writings*, ed. Günter Berghaus, trans. Doug Thompson (New York: Farrar, Straus and Giroux, 2006).
Perloff, Marjorie, *The Futurist Moment: Avant-Garde, Avant-Guerre, and the Language of Rupture* (Chicago: Chicago University Press, 1986).

Harlem Renaissance

For much of the twentieth century, accounts of Anglo-American modernism overlooked the Harlem Renaissance. Since the 1980s, however, surveys and anthologies have begun to recognize the importance of this vibrant literary and cultural movement of the 1920s and 1930s. Exactly how such an important adjustment to the modernist canon should be made, however, remains a daunting question: one editor of a recent modernist anthology threw up his hands and decided to make no change whatsoever, claiming that 'any attempt to include them in an anthology containing Joyce, Eliot, Woolf, and Stein would inevitably smack of tokenism' (Rainey, 2005, p. xxxi). Rewriting the story of literary modernism, whether to include women writers, writers of colour, or writers from countries outside Europe and North America, has proved difficult enough that consensus about what constitutes modernism is becoming harder to achieve. Increasingly, however, the Harlem Renaissance is being seen not as an isolated pocket of the avant-garde but as connected on many levels – social, thematic, and stylistic – to other modernisms.

One argument about literary modernism sees it partly as a social phenomenon, a sort of clique. The 'Men of 1914' (Pound, Joyce, Eliot, and Lewis), for example, knew and collaborated with each other or promoted each other's work. Even in this very conservative sense, however, Harlem Renaissance writers were part of the transatlantic social network of modernism. They were linked to circles in Paris and London by figures like Nancy Cunard, who compiled the massive and wide-ranging *Negro: An Anthology* (1934), and Carl Van Vechten, author of *Nigger Heaven* (1926), who was another important (if controversial) bridge between black and white literary worlds. Cunard's anthology gathered an eclectic assortment of documents from across the black diaspora: fiction, poetry, music, ethnography, African art, articles on colonialism, and much else. There were essays on folklore by Zora Neale Hurston, who trained in anthropology under Franz Boas. The work of canonical modernists like Pound, Beckett, and William Carlos Williams also featured in the anthology. By any definition, the writing of Hurston, Langston Hughes, Countée Cullen, Claude McKay, Jean Toomer, Nella Larsen, and others, merits full membership in the larger 'club' of modernism. The movement's short-lived magazine, *Fire!!*, founded in 1926 by Hurston, Hughes, and others, was part of the culture of modernist little magazines that reached its peak in the 1920s and 1930s. Not only did these writers emphasize stylistic innovation and promote revolutionary artistic and social ideas, they were also immersed in the same post-war modernist milieu, with its fluid exchange of aesthetics and ideas.

The Harlem Renaissance shared similarities with other cultural-political movements of the modernist period: the twin revivals in Scotland and Ireland, for example, led by Hugh MacDiarmid and W. B. Yeats, respectively. All these movements linked artistic innovation to social progress. They expanded the modernist vocabulary of the 'new' to include the rhetoric of self-determination. The Harlem Renaissance was buoyed up on a wave of race consciousness that included on the one hand the 'back to Africa' movement led by Marcus Garvey and a surge in popularity among black and white audiences and writers alike of depictions of the African American experience on the other. This was the period that saw the immensely popular *Shuffle Along* (1921), the first successful musical revue to be written and performed by African Americans (including Josephine Baker), open on Broadway. Alain Locke drew a parallel between the Harlem Renaissance and other movements of self-determination in his foreword to *The New Negro: An Interpretation* (1925), the most important anthology of Harlem Renaissance writing. 'As in

India, in China, in Egypt, Ireland, Russia, Bohemia, Palestine and Mexico', Locke declared, 'we are witnessing the resurgence of a people'. *The New Negro* featured poetry by Cullen, McKay, Toomer, and Hughes; fiction by Toomer and Hurston; and essays on music, drama, black history, and pan-Africanism by Jessie Redmond Fauset (who also wrote perhaps the first novel of the Harlem Renaissance, *There is Confusion*, published in 1924), James Weldon Johnson (first secretary of the National Association for the Advancement of Colored People), and W. E. B. DuBois (who had organized the first Pan-African Congress, in Paris, in 1919). Locke himself was the first African American Rhodes Scholar, and studied at Harvard and Oxford, the University of Berlin, and the Collège de France before becoming Chair of the Department of Philosophy at Howard University in Washington, DC.

See also: *Contexts*: Anthropology, Race; *Texts*: Music, Primitivism; *Criticism*: Cultural materialism/New Historicism, Postcolonialism.

Further Reading

Baker, Houston A., *Modernism and the Harlem Renaissance* (Chicago and London: University of Chicago Press, 1987).

Lewis, David L., ed., *The Portable Harlem Renaissance Reader* (New York: Viking, 1994).

Locke, Alain, ed., *The New Negro: An Interpretation* (New York: Albert and Charles Boni, 1925).

Imagism and Vorticism

Pre-war avant-gardism, embraced with such enthusiasm by artists in Paris and Milan, was a smaller if not exactly quieter affair in London. Two movements of note were launched in Britain before the war: imagism (1912–1917) and vorticism (1914–1915). Both began in London, and both bore the imprint of the poet and impresario Ezra Pound, who coined both 'isms'. Imagism, at least as far as Pound and his involvement were concerned, was a short-lived movement that was formally launched in 1912, though its history went back further, and ended in 1914. In Pound's view, imagism largely gave way to the next phase of the London avant-garde – vorticism. However, imagism also went on to become a larger phenomenon, especially with the support of the American poet and heiress Amy Lowell. Imagist propaganda began to appear in the press in 1912. *Des Imagistes*, the first imagist anthology, was put together by Pound and published by Harold Monro's Poetry Bookshop in 1914. It featured 11 'imagistes' from both sides of the Atlantic, including Pound,

Lowell, Richard Aldington, H. D., William Carlos Williams, F. S. Flint, and Ford Madox Hueffer (soon to be Ford). There was even a poem by James Joyce – 'I Hear an Army', published to little fanfare in *Chamber Music* (1907), was recommended to Pound by Yeats. The same year the first anthology appeared, Pound abandoned the movement to take up the cause of vorticism with Lewis. Lowell, working with H. D. and Aldington, brought out three annual anthologies between 1915 and 1917 under the title *Some Imagist Poets*. Pound considered this later phase of imagism, which also included D. H. Lawrence and John Gould Fletcher, to be watered down and hardly worth the name – he declined involvement and gave it the pejorative name of 'Amygisme'. A revival anthology edited by Aldington appeared in 1930 and featured virtually all the imagists from previous anthologies; the main exceptions were Lowell, who died in 1925, and Pound. Vorticism, which was led by Lewis, shared imagism's expressed desire for 'hardness' and clarity. In his autobiography, *Rude Assignment* (1950), however, Lewis mourned the fact that the contributions of Pound and others to *Blast* (1914–1915), the vorticist magazine, did not always live up to its fiery rhetoric. 'I wanted a battering ram that was all of one metal', he wrote. 'A good deal of what got in seemed to me soft and highly impure. Had it been France, there would have been plenty to choose from.'

Imagism's place in literary history is highly contested, and its shine has faded somewhat since the mid-twentieth century when it was viewed as one of the central achievements of modernism. Though its impact on especially American twentieth-century poetry is still widely acknowledged, vorticism has been a subject of greater interest in recent decades. As Patrick McGuinness has pointed out, it is an odd fact that, while imagism purported to value clarity and exactitude, 'its principles . . . were from the start unclear, disputed, and even conflicting'. It is also odd that T. E. Hulme, the movement's founding figure in Pound's account, was only briefly a poet and published only a handful of very short lyrics, none of which was included in the anthologies. Hulme's 'poetry year' of 1909 was just one of several distinct phases in a short but richly varied career. In November 1908, Hulme delivered his 'Lecture on Modern Poetry' to the Poets' Club. By March 1909, the restless Hulme had already set up what he called the 'Secession Club' with the poet and translator F. S. Flint. Ezra Pound joined this offshoot the following month. He first referred to 'Les Imagistes, descendents of the forgotten school of 1909', in a prefatory note to the ironically titled 'Complete Poetical Works of T. E. Hulme' – actually five short poems – which were included in Pound's *Ripostes* (1912). By 1910, Hulme had abandoned poetry for philosophy, leaving Pound to take control of the movement. Pound renamed it *imagisme* in keeping with the contemporary association of Paris with the avant-garde. (In 1909, for example, the first manifesto of Italian futurism was published not in Italian but in French, in the Paris daily newspaper *Le Figaro*.)

Imagism may be understood in part as a reaction to the impressionist movement that immediately preceded it. Imagist poetry demanded that readers be active rather than passive, their minds bridging the gap between juxtaposed images rather than simply receiving impressions. Pound, writing to *Poetry* editor Harriet Monroe in 1912 about the poetry of H. D., summed up the qualities of imagism: 'Objective – no slither; direct – no excessive use of adjectives; no metaphors that won't permit examination. It's straight talk, straight as the Greek' (Pound, 1971, p. 11). Both imagism and impressionism represented reactions against narrative, whether in poetry or painting, but their reactions were different in kind. Pound's anti-manifesto of imagism, 'A Few Don'ts by an Imagiste' (1912), established a list of commandments for the aspiring poet. (Pound, who would later write *The ABC of Reading* [1934], always took his role as teacher seriously.) 'Go in fear of abstractions' was one important rule. Craft, as opposed to romantic inspiration, was also emphasized. 'Don't imagine that the art of poetry is any simpler than the art of music', in other words it requires long practice. The musical analogy, common in aestheticism and particularly employed by the artist Whistler, whom Pound admired, was important in other ways. As in music, for example, narrative and 'views' were to be kept to a minimum. The poet should 'behave as a musician, a good musician', in matters such as cadence and rhythm. (Pound later cited Walter Pater's dictum that 'All art constantly aspires to the condition of music' as part of vorticism's 'ancestry'.) Science was another discipline worth imitating, for its innovation as well as its precision. In the same issue of *Poetry*, another description of imagism appeared – this time under the byline F. S. Flint, although it has since been attributed mainly to Pound. This companion piece described the movement from an outsider's perspective, as if members of the group had been interviewed. Interestingly, it attempted to set the group apart from other 'isms' like futurism and post-impressionism: they had no manifesto (despite evidence to the contrary), they were not revolutionary, and they did not abhor the past. Again the emphasis fell on free verse, precise images, the aspiration to music, and the use of 'no word that did not contribute to the presentation'.

Vorticism also defined itself in relation to futurism, the leading avant-garde movement of the time. However, the resemblance this time was much closer, and critics often described vorticism as the 'English futurism', or worse yet, a pale imitation. *Blast*'s striking visual style and numerous manifestos were obviously indebted to Marinetti. It was radical and provocative, rather than affecting calm disinterest like imagism. It sought to make an impact outside the domain of art: 'A VOR-TICIST KING! WHY NOT?' Moreover, like futurism (and later dada and surrealism), vorticism was a pan-artistic movement: *Blast* featured examples of poetry, drama, prose fiction, sculpture, and drawing. Its artists included Lewis, Edward Wadsworth, Jessica Dismorr, Helen Saunders, Frederick Etchells, William Roberts, and the sculptor Henri Gaudier-Brzeska. The first issue of *Blast* included writing by the ubiquitous Ford and Rebecca West, and the second included poems by T. S. Eliot, but the bulk of writing came from Lewis himself. One key difference with futurism was vorticism's relationship to modernity. As Peter Nicholls wrote in *Modernisms* (1995), vorticism tried 'to respond to the exciting challenge of modern dynamism and technology without capitulating to the sentimental lure of modernity's "eternal present"'. It would not worship the automobile as Marinetti did, in other words; harking back to Baudelaire, however, it would seek to reflect the new urban environment, especially through geometrical abstract art.

The vortex was, in Pound's words, something 'from which, and through which, and into which, ideas are constantly rushing'. In another sense, London itself was the titular 'vortex', the centre of energy. The attempt to establish a more specific definition runs into difficulty: Pound and Lewis gave contradictory explanations, and the movement itself thrived on contradiction. It was simultaneously dynamic and still, an extension of aestheticism and its refutation. In practical terms, scholarship has established that much of the first issue of *Blast* was put together before the name 'vorticism' and the accompanying manifestos came into being. But unlike futurism, the *Blast* manifestos only occasionally describe a serious platform. More often, they anticipate the nihilistic manifestos of Tristan Tzara's dada, preferring to attack sense rather than to make it. During the war, Lewis gained a commission as a war artist and was forced back to a more realist style of painting. Although he later returned to abstraction and even tried to revive vorticism in 1919, the English avant-garde had run its course and would be replaced by the high modernism of Woolf, Joyce, and Eliot. Imagism and vorticism both demonstrated how inhospitable Britain could be to such projects. After the war, the closest thing to a movement in literary modernism was the loose coterie of Bloomsbury, which never issued a manifesto or proclaimed a collective viewpoint. Pound, whom Lewis compared to Baden-Powell, the founder of the Scout movement, for his desire to organize, label, and invent doctrine for artistic movements, abandoned London for Paris shortly after the war.

See also: *Contexts*: Cities and urbanization, Culture, Fascism, War; *Texts*: Aestheticism and decadence, Avant-garde, Bloomsbury, Dada and surrealism, Futurism, Manifesto, Music, Violence.

Further Reading

Cork, Richard, *Vorticism and Abstract Art in the First Machine Age*, 2 vols (London: Gordon Fraser, 1976).

Dasenbrock, Reed Way, *The Literary Vorticism of Ezra Pound and Wyndham Lewis: Towards the Condition of Painting* (Baltimore: Johns Hopkins University Press, 1985).

Gage, John T., *In the Arresting Eye: The Rhetoric of Imagism* (Baton Rouge and London: Louisiana State University Press, 1981).

Hughes, Glen, *Imagism and the Imagists: A Study in Modern Poetry* (Stanford, CA: Stanford University Press, 1931).

Munich, Adrienne, and Melissa Bradshaw, eds, *Amy Lowell, American Modern* (New Brunswick, NJ: Rutgers University Press, 2004).

Wees, William C., *Vorticism and the English Avant-Garde* (Manchester: Manchester University Press, 1972).

Impersonality

T. S. Eliot introduced his 'Impersonal theory of poetry' in the landmark essay, 'Tradition and the Individual Talent' (1919). The theory is also reflected in his use of the 'objective correlative', the indirect expression of emotion in art: that concept was introduced in an essay on *Hamlet* published the same year. He begins 'Tradition and the Individual Talent' by making the seemingly paradoxical, or at least surprising, case for tradition in a modernist context. Indeed, Eliot recognizes how unfashionable tradition has become: 'Seldom, perhaps, does the word appear except in a phrase of censure.' Being 'traditional' is unpopular, while novelty is held in great esteem, even for its own sake. But Eliot argues compellingly that the 'historical sense' – feeling the 'simultaneous existence' of a Western tradition going back to Homer – gives the writer a sense 'of his own contemporaneity'. The 'individual talent' of the title must be seen and see himself, in this larger framework. 'You cannot value him alone', Eliot insists; 'you must set him…among the dead'. This view of the artist contrasts starkly with the pre-war iconoclasm of F. T. Marinetti, who called on people to 'set fire to the library shelves' in the first futurist manifesto of 1909. It was the futurists who declared: 'Time and Space died yesterday.' Other avant-garde movements, including dada, followed their example. Eliot's essay, in contrast, was part of a post-war 'call to order' seen across the arts, and it set the tone for 'high' modernism in Britain. It would be formally innovative, but, it claimed, politically neutral; it would appeal to a small, learned audience; and it would uphold the idea of a Western canon ('a living whole'), which Eliot and others, including contemporaries like F. R. Leavis, would articulate in their criticism.

Eliot calls for the artist's 'self-sacrifice' and 'continual surrender' to the larger culture. 'It is in this depersonalization', he states at the end of the first section, 'that art may be said to approach the condition of science'. Eliot proceeds to use the scientific analogy of the catalyst to argue that 'the more perfect the artist, the more completely separate in him will be the man who suffers and the mind which creates'. The 'passions', in other words, will be no more than 'material' for the artist. Eliot compares the artist's 'feelings' and 'emotions' to 'particles' that 'unite to form a new compound'. Art – the 'fusion of elements' – is superior to the raw emotions that may be involved in the artistic process. Eliot seeks to relegate personality and emotion, and with them the Romantic conception of art, to a lower tier of importance and to promote a classical model of stylistic restraint. Eliot refutes the Romantic poet William Wordsworth's famous definition of poetry as 'emotion recollected in tranquility'. He considered the emphasis on emotion and imagination put forth by Wordsworth and Coleridge to be a sign of artistic immaturity; a phase that younger poets might pass through on their way to a mature style. 'Poetry is not a turning loose of emotion, but an escape from emotion', he declares in the essay's famous closing lines; 'it is not the expression of personality, but an escape from personality'. All of this was anticipated in the previous century by Gustave Flaubert, who outlined in detail his view of the artist in a letter to a reader in 1857. He wrote:

Madame Bovary is based on no actual occurrence. It is a *totally fictitious* story; it contains none of my feelings and no details from my own life. The illusion of truth (if there is one) comes, on the contrary, from the book's impersonality. It is one of my principles that a writer should not be his own theme. An artist must be in his work like God in creation, invisible and all-powerful; he should be everywhere felt, but nowhere seen.

Furthermore, Art must rise above personal emotions and nervous susceptibilities. It is time to endow it with pitiless method, with the exactness of the physical sciences.

(Qtd in Ellmann and Feidelson, 1965, p. 132)

Other influences on Eliot's theory, aside from Flaubert, include older models like the metaphysical poets; Baudelaire's ironic spectator, the *flâneur*; and Wilde's idea of the mask, which was handed down to Yeats. As the dramatist in Wilde recognized, 'Man is least himself when he talks in his own person. Give him a mask, and he will tell you the truth.' Wilde made a virtue of artifice, claiming, in a quip that loosely anticipates Eliot: 'All bad poetry springs from genuine feeling.' Anti-Romantic theories like Eliot's were at work, explicitly or implicitly, in the modernism of Ezra Pound, T. E. Hulme, Wyndham Lewis, and James Joyce and form the basis of movements like imagism and vorticism. Pound, who worked closely with Yeats from 1913 to 1916, can be seen developing the doctrine of impersonality in his translation method. Rather than simply rendering foreign words into English, Pound's 'translations' of great writers of the past like Dante or the Confucian poet Li Po often resembled something closer to 'channelling', with Pound acting as a conduit or medium for the dead. (Critics have noted the strangely passive role this gives to the poet, which does not seem to agree with the 'hard' view of modernism expressed by Pound, Lewis, and others.) Pound's use of 'personae' is a central device in his work, and bears strong resemblance to Eliot's theory of impersonality. Pound the poet is an elusive figure, hiding in the background of his work, while various personae – writers and historical figures, 'elaborate masks' – speak in turns. The technique not only allowed Pound to escape from his own personality but also allowed him (as it did Eliot) to include voices from across the 'tradition', not merely the modern, and across history. In the poetry of Pound and Eliot, time is collapsed and a host of literary voices from diverse periods exist simultaneously. Eliot's successor, W. H. Auden, espoused a similar kind of poetic detachment, heard, for example, in the undramatic narrative voice of 'Musée des Beaux Arts' (1938), even while it speaks of the human response to suffering. Joyce, who was indebted to Flaubert in many ways, including his detached method of presentation, used Stephen Dedalus, in *A Portrait of the Artist as a Young Man* (1916), to voice his conception of the artist. 'The artist, like the God of creation', says Stephen, sounding very much like Flaubert, 'remains...invisible, refined out of existence, indifferent, paring his fingernails'.

See also: *Contexts*: Culture, Language, Science and technology; *Texts*: Aestheticism and decadence, Futurism, Imagism and vorticism.

Further Reading

Ellmann, Maud, *The Poetics of Impersonality: T. S. Eliot and Ezra Pound* (Cambridge, MA: Harvard University Press, 1987).

Ellmann, Richard, and Charles Feidelson, Jr., eds, *The Modern Tradition: Backgrounds of Modern Literature* (New York and Oxford: Oxford University Press, 1965).

Irish Literature

Irish writing accounts for a disproportionately large segment of the modernist canon, particularly as it was conceived for much of the twentieth century. The contribution of Wilde, Yeats, Joyce, and Beckett loomed large enough to prompt the critic Hugh Kenner, who contributed more than any other scholar to the Hibernicization of modernism, to declare that 'English' modernism was the work of Irish (and American) writers. Nor did Irish writers depend exclusively on English literary and philosophical traditions but instead looked to France, Russia, Italy, Germany, and the Far East for inspiration. This is not to suggest that Dublin was a thriving centre of literary production – far from it. Apart from Yeats's Irish Literary Theatre, founded in 1899, the Hibernian metropolis was even less hospitable to artistic innovation than London. Yeats was the only major Irish modernist to actually live and work in Ireland. (The novelist Flann O'Brien might also be counted here, but his writing is more often considered post-modernist.) Wilde lived in London, Beckett in Paris, and Joyce, as the closing signature of *Ulysses* tells us ('Trieste-Zürich-Paris'), moved around a lot. Yeats also had a strong foothold in London, but as he grew older he spent less and less time there. He was always deeply, if ambivalently, involved in Irish cultural and political life, even serving two terms in the Irish Senate where he spoke passionately against the prohibition of divorce and on other key issues. Although Yeats and Joyce can both be considered anti-colonial, nationalist writers, their two visions of Ireland differed significantly: for Yeats, Ireland was a Celtic nation, an island unto itself; for the cosmopolitan Joyce, Ireland was a European nation. Although some aspects of the Celtic Revival left him cold, the young Joyce was inevitably influenced by Yeats and the Irish Literary Theatre. In *A Portrait of the Artist as a Young Man* (1916), Stephen Dedalus refuses, as Joyce did, to sign a letter of protest against *The Countess Cathleen* (1899), choosing to support artistic freedom against a narrower nationalism.

It is Joyce, of course, whose name is most emblematic of Anglophone modernism, and perhaps of the modernist spirit in general. It was Ireland's great fortune that its most famous writer in exile chose to set all of his fiction in Dublin and that he attempted, as Stephen famously declares in *A Portrait*, 'to forge in the smithy of my soul the uncreated conscience of my race'. Much has also been written, however, about Yeats's transition to a modernist style, especially under the influence of the young poet Ezra Pound, and his contributions to modernist poetry. During the war, in the winters of 1914–1915, 1915–1916, and 1916–1917, Yeats worked closely with Pound at Stone Cottage in Sussex, and the two shared many ideas about art. This collaboration is often seen as a crucial event in the history of modernist poetry; this was where Pound began work on *The Cantos*. It should be noted, however, that the relationship contributed not only to the modernization of Yeats's poetic style under the influence of the younger generation but also worked in the other direction: the older poet transmitted to Pound his views on history and the occult, for example. In fact Yeats had already shown modernist tendencies by 1914–1915, having largely abandoned the old-fashioned diction of his early verse and embraced a plainer style in *The Green Helmet and Other Poems* (1910) and *Responsibilities* (1914). Pound's influence, fused with an apocalyptic view of events beginning with the Easter Rising of 1916, would result in some of Yeats's strongest and most influential work in the collections that followed: *The Wild Swans at Coole* (1919), *Michael Robartes and the Dancer* (1921), and *The Tower* (1928).

An intriguing and often overlooked figure of modern Irish literature is George Moore, who spent much of his career in London and Paris and was close to many of the French impressionists. Moore showed himself to be a modern, if not quite modernist, writer with novels like *A Drama in Muslin* (1886) and *Confessions of a Young Man* (1888), which influenced Joyce's *A Portrait*. Moore's novels – 15 in all – represent a broad mix that includes Zolaesque naturalism, symbolism, musical influences, a concern for style, and a slightly risqué, bohemian flavour. Some of the writers Moore became acquainted with in Paris in the 1870s included Zola, Turgenev, and Mallarmé. Moore occupies a pivotal place in Irish history, having acted as both absentee landlord and pro-Gaelic nationalist. Moore Hall, which he inherited in 1870, was built on an estate of over 12 thousand acres in County Mayo and was eventually torched in 1923, shortly before the end of the Irish Civil War. (Although Moore himself was recognized as a nationalist, his brother Maurice, the caretaker, expressed pro-treaty sympathies.) Moore was also an outspoken defender of women's rights and the poor, and with Yeats and Lady Gregory he helped to establish the Irish national theatre. Another friend of Yeats and a writer associated with the *fin de siècle* was the poet, critic, social reformer, and mystic AE (George Russell), who held well-attended literary evenings with Moore in Dublin during the first decade of the twentieth century. From 1905 to 1923, Russell edited the *Irish Homestead*, which had in the previous year published Joyce's short story, 'The Sisters', later to be revised and included in *Dubliners* (1914).

There were, of course, many other innovative Irish writers of the period. James Stephens, who wrote *A Story-Teller's Holiday* (1918), was the novelist Joyce suggested might finish *Finnegans Wake*, if he should die before it was completed. Then there was Austin Clarke, who had the unenviable job of writing poetry after Yeats, and whose collections, such as *The Vengeance of Fionn* (1921), bore the mark of the older poet. The Belfast-born poet Louis MacNeice, one of W. H. Auden's circle, is perhaps best known for *Autumn Journal* (1939). Eva Gore-Booth, a poet and suffragist and the sister of Constance Markievicz, the famed 'rebel countess' of the 1916 Easter Rising, was commemorated as the Utopian dreamer in Yeats's poem, 'In Memory of Eva Gore Booth and Constance Markievicz', written in 1927. Her dedicated activity as a suffragist in England included mentoring, for a time, the young militant Christabel Pankhurst. She published ten volumes of poetry, most of which dealt with themes of folklore and mysticism and was supported in her efforts by Yeats. The writer, surgeon, and senator Oliver St John Gogarty, author of *As I was Going Down Sackville Street* (1937), is familiar to readers of modernist literature primarily for his turn as the 'Stately, plump Buck Mulligan' who appears in the opening line of Joyce's *Ulysses*. Joyce and Gogarty were close friends for many years, and in 1904 Gogarty had occupied the Martello tower in Sandycove, Dublin, where Joyce, and later his character Stephen Dedalus, also lived for a time.

See also: *Contexts*: Cities and urbanization, Class, Empire, Fascism, Nationalism, Race; *Texts*: Aestheticism and decadence, Apocalypse, Drama, Epiphany, Music; *Criticism*: Postcolonialism.

Further Reading

Ellmann, Richard, *James Joyce*, rev. ed. (New York and Oxford: Oxford University Press, 1982).

Foster, John Wilson, ed., *The Cambridge Companion to the Irish Novel* (Cambridge and New York: Cambridge University Press, 2006).

Foster, R. F., *W. B. Yeats: A Life*, 2 vols (New York and Oxford: Oxford University Press, 1997–2003).

Kenner, Hugh, *A Colder Eye: The Modern Irish Writers* (London: Allen Lane, 1983).

Longenbach, James, *Stone Cottage: Pound, Yeats, and Modernism* (New York and Oxford: Oxford University Press, 1988).

Manifesto

In modernism, the manifesto may be defined as a declaration of artistic aims and principles loosely based on the revolutionary political form of the nineteenth century (for example *The Communist Manifesto*). It is usually a pamphlet-length, polemical, public declaration and may be issued by a group or an individual. The etymology is Latin, meaning 'struck by hand'. The word 'manifesto' entered into common English usage in the seventeenth century, with early examples being the rebellious tracts of the Diggers and Levellers. Samuel Johnson's *Dictionary* of 1755 defines 'manifesto' as 'a public protestation or declaration'. As a literary genre, the manifesto has failed to earn itself a place beside the novel and the short story, but the form did enjoy a brief spell of notoriety in the modernist period, especially in the wake of F. T. Marinetti's 'The Founding and Manifesto of Futurism' (1909). This incendiary manifesto conveys an enthusiasm for all things modern (airplanes, automobiles, factories), as the name of the movement suggests, and a strong rejection of anything considered *passé* or antithetical to progress. Controversially, this includes institutions dedicated to preserving cultural heritage ('We will destroy museums, libraries, academies of every kind'). Futurist manifestos are distinguished from earlier declarations of artistic intent by the close correspondence that exists between their shocking rhetorical style and the bold, aggressive art futurism produced. The line is blurred, in other words, between what is said in artistic manifestos and what is done in 'manifesto art'. One could even argue, as Martin Puchner has done, that the manifesto is 'the central genre of futurism', the fullest realization of the futurist aesthetic that futurism produced. The movement is closely linked to the birth of Italian Fascism, and this history has tainted the manifesto's reputation with associations of violence, misogyny, and jingoistic nationalism. More than this, however, futurism was about young artists escaping the weight of Italy's cultural history, and in this sense it is predominantly an artistic struggle, and a quintessentially modernist one, given expression in the language of politics.

The new form of manifesto that began with Marinetti quickly spread across Europe and the world, and for every 'ism' there was one or a dozen manifestos to defend it. Just as the many artistic movements formed in the early twentieth century carved out a niche with a particular name (imagism, vorticism, futurism, surrealism), so also the manifesto was a crucial form of advertisement: it was loud, bold, sensational, and succinct. Using the manifesto, a movement would make its bid for public attention: in the case of Wyndham Lewis's *Blast* (1914), which was composed almost entirely of manifestos, the puce wrappers and tabloid typography of the first issue gave an indication of the startling 'newness' to be found within. Little magazines were a common venue for manifestos, but they also appeared independently as posters, leaflets, or pamphlets, or even in mainstream newspapers (the first futurist manifesto appeared on the front page of *Le Figaro*). The most detailed 'guide' to manifesto writing is contained in Tristan Tzara's 'Dada Manifesto' of 1918. It begins: 'To proclaim a manifesto you have to want: A.B.C., thunder against 1,2,3, lose your patience and sharpen your wings to conquer.' Novelty, audacity, and fearlessness are all essential manifesto ingredients. 'Each page ought to explode, either from deep and weighty seriousness, a whirlwind, dizziness, the new, or the eternal, from its crushing humour, the enthusiasm of its principles or its typographical appearance.' Manifestos, like the 'isms' they promoted, were often used to mask shortcomings in terms of actual product. Futurism, imagism, and vorticism all issued manifestos using the collective 'we', when in fact they were written by an 'I' (Marinetti, Pound), and little, if any, art or literature had yet been produced.

As Puchner has stated, 'Futurism taught everyone how the manifesto worked.' Imagism and vorticism put the lesson to good use, although they disguised their imitation as reaction. Pound's 'A Few Don'ts by an Imagiste' (1913) and the explosive manifestos contained in *Blast* drew heavily upon the confident swagger of Marinetti, who paid several visits to London between 1910 and 1914. During the First World War, dada used the extravagant nihilism already associated with the genre to protest the inhumanity of the war and to reflect the perceived collapse of civilization. The 1920s were, according to Michael Levenson, 'a period when the urge to manifesto seemed as great as the urge to poetry'. Landmark essays such as Virginia Woolf's 'Modern Fiction' and T. S. Eliot's 'Tradition and the Individual Talent' (both 1919) might also be considered manifestos of modernism. The 1930s saw the manifesto increasingly used by writers and artists to speak out on political issues, including the Spanish Civil War. Examples from this decade include André Breton and Leon Trotsky's 'Manifesto: Towards a Free Revolutionary Art' (1938), Woolf's *Three Guineas* (1938), and William Butler Yeats's late polemic, *On the Boiler* (1939).

See also: *Contexts*: Culture, Fascism, Nationalism, Women and gender; *Texts*: Avant-garde, Dada and surrealism, Futurism, Imagism and vorticism, Violence; *Criticism*: Cultural materialism/New Historicism, Feminist and gender criticism, Marxist criticism.

Further Reading

Caws, Mary Ann, ed., *Manifesto: A Century of Isms* (Lincoln and London: University of Nebraska Press, 2001).

Lyon, Janet, *Manifestoes: Provocations of the Modern* (Ithaca, NY: Cornell University Press, 1999).

Puchner, Martin, *Poetry of the Revolution: Marx, Manifestos, and the Avant-Gardes* (Princeton and Oxford: Princeton University Press, 2006).

Somigli, Luca, *Legitimizing the Artist: Manifesto Writing and European Modernism, 1885–1915* (Toronto: University of Toronto Press, 2004).

Winkiel, Laura, *Modernism, Race and Manifestos* (Cambridge: Cambridge University Press, 2008).

Memory

In the opening scene of Virginia Woolf's *Mrs. Dalloway* (1925), Clarissa Dalloway steps over the threshold into the air of Westminster and is immediately 'plunged' into the first of a series of memories of her adolescence in the Cotswold village of Bourton:

> What a lark! What a plunge! For so it had always seemed to her, when, with a little squeak of the hinges, which she could hear now, she had burst open the French windows and plunged at Bourton into the open air.

The action of the novel, like Joyce's *Ulysses* (1922), takes place on a single day in June. Although events do occur – a suicide in the afternoon and a party in the evening – plot has for the most part been replaced by perception, conveyed in the stream-of-consciousness style, and reflection on the past. Bourton is in many ways remote from the bustle and noise of London in 1923: located in a rural setting, in the previous century, before the Great War, and before she became 'Mrs Richard Dalloway', it represents a crucial turning point not only in Clarissa's life (it was here she met and 'chose' Richard) but in the larger history of Europe. On the other hand, while in this sense it is distant, the past for Clarissa (and her 'double', Septimus Smith) is also always 'present' and still ongoing.

Characters in *Mrs. Dalloway* are defined not by their actions in the present but by events in the past. This is what Woolf called her 'tunnelling' technique: 'I dig out beautiful caves behind my characters', she wrote in her diary in 1923; 'I think that gives exactly what I want; humanity, humour, depth.' At the time she was in the process of drafting the novel she called 'The Hours', later to become *Mrs. Dalloway*. Reflection, often of a melancholy nature, largely replaces action and anticipation for Clarissa. As she recalls past relationships with Peter, Hugh, and Sally (all of whom attend her party), she wonders how her life might have been different: what if she had married Peter instead of Richard? Or chosen Sally over both men? Leopold and Molly Bloom are caught up with similar thoughts in Joyce's *Ulysses*. Both reflect on their life together and return in thought to Howth, north of Dublin, where they shared their first kiss. Bloom, sitting in Davy Byrne's pub, is also sitting in the gorse and rhododendrons on the Ben of Howth:

> She kissed me. I was kissed. All yielding she tossed my hair. Kissed, she kissed me.
>
> Me. And me now.

Bloom wanders the streets of Dublin as various stimuli in the present trigger memories of the past – of Rudy, the son who died an infant, of his marriage – while at home, in the closing chapter, Molly unleashes an unbroken torrent of memory starting from her adulterous affair with Blazes Boylan that afternoon and ending with Bloom's marriage proposal and her breathless answer: 'yes I said yes I will Yes'. Living half in the reality of the present and half in the promise of the past may be taken as a sign of middle age. But it also infects the young Stephen Dedalus, whose eyes were so firmly set on the future in *A Portrait of the Artist as a Young Man* (1916). Stephen now broods over the death of his mother, one cause of his return to Dublin from Paris. The two novels, *Mrs. Dalloway* and *Ulysses*, are shaped not by the forward progression of the main characters through space and time, in the chronological manner of the *bildungsroman*, for example, but more randomly through memories of the past – love, war, and other traumas – recollected in the static present. We perceive characters as the sum total of their memories, not of their actions. The model of the apparently stable public self, with a far deeper and more complex and changing true self (or assortment of selves) below the surface, and 'involuntary memory' as the conduit between them, comes from the French philosopher Henri Bergson. In *An Introduction to Metaphysics* (1903), translated into English by the critic and philosopher T. E. Hulme, Bergson contrasted the 'frozen surface' of the projected, external self with the 'continuous flux' of the multiple selves that lie beneath. In his influential early work, *Time and Free Will* (1889), Bergson argued that 'our past life' remains with us in the present, in its entirety, if we can only gain access to it. It is 'preserved even to the minutest details; nothing is forgotten; all we have perceived, thought, willed, from the first awakening of our consciousness, persists indefinitely'.

Beyond the tendency of their characters to live simultaneously in past and present, *Ulysses* and *Mrs. Dalloway* also depict a present dominated and haunted by larger historical events. Memories of the recent war haunt all the characters in Woolf's novel, in particular Septimus, who is plagued by survivor's guilt and the spectre of his dead commanding officer, Evans. *Ulysses*, set in 1904, is dominated not by the war but by Ireland's colonial history, including the narrower forms of Irish nationalism. Stephen tried to escape this history by fleeing to Paris at the end of *A Portrait*, but we find him back in Dublin at the start of *Ulysses*, still caught up in the 'nets' of 'language, nationality, [and] religion'. 'History', he famously tells Mr Deasy, the English headmaster of the school where he teaches, in response to Mr Deasy's anti-Semitic comments, 'is a nightmare from which I am trying to awake'. Bloom, of half-Jewish descent, is forced to confront the history of religious and ethnic persecution as he faces off against the Citizen, a bigoted Irish nationalist who is a stand-in for the Cyclops of Homer's *Odyssey*, with his monocular view of things. In Joyce's short story 'The Dead' (1914), the principal character Gabriel Conroy is haunted by the 'ghost' of Michael Furey, a boy his wife had once loved and who died seemingly out of his love for her. The boy represents a passion and authenticity of emotion that is inaccessible to Gabriel, the urbane, educated aesthete. The figure of Michael Furey stands between Gabriel and his wife and mocks him, not unlike the remark made earlier in the story by the nationalist Molly Ivors, who had whispered the unsettling name 'West Briton!' in Gabriel's ear.

See also: *Contexts*: Psychology; *Texts*: Consciousness, Stream of, Epiphany, Fragmentation; *Criticism*: Psychoanalytic criticism.

Further Reading

Kern, Stephen, *The Culture of Time and Space, 1880–1918* (Cambridge, MA: Harvard University Press, 1983).

McIntyre, Gabrielle, *Modernism, Memory, and Desire: T. S. Eliot and Virginia Woolf* (Cambridge and New York: Cambridge University Press, 2007).

Randall, Bryony, *Modernism, Daily Time and Everyday Life* (Cambridge: Cambridge University Press, 2007).

Music, Influence of

The 'Sirens' episode of James Joyce's *Ulysses* (1922) – one of the most musical passages in modern literature – begins, appropriately, with an overture. The chapter's main motifs are compressed into a few pages, starting with 'Bronze by gold heard the hoofirons, steelyringing', a shorthand reference to the barmaids Lydia Douce (bronze) and Mina Kennedy (gold) listening to the sound of horses from the viceregal cavalcade passing outside. The overture, like the episode it introduces, ends with the sound of Bloom farting over the famous last words of the Irish nationalist hero Robert Emmet, which he is reciting in his mind, while a convenient passing tram covers the noise: 'Then, not till then. My eppripfftaph. Be pfrwritt. / Done.' (Here Bloom, or Joyce, is also passing judgement on windy nationalist rhetoric.) Next follows the word 'Begin', and the episode proper starts. The eye takes a backseat to the ear in 'Sirens', which finds Bloom sitting in the bar of the Ormond Hotel thinking with melancholy resignation of his wife's affair with Blazes Boylan. ('As easy stop the sea. Yes: all is lost.') Their meeting, Bloom knows, is set to take place at that very hour: a refrain of 'jingle jingle' marks the progress of Boylan to Bloom's house and then describes the imagined noise of bedsprings. But Bloom is conducting an epistolary affair of his own, responding to a letter from Martha Clifford under the penname Henry Flower: 'P. P. S. La la la ree. I feel so sad today. La ree. So lonely. Dee.' The musical sound of these lines is characteristic of the chapter. Various styles are imitated: the staccato effect, for example, is rendered by short, choppy sentences, laden with punctuation, which also simulates Bloom's halting and scattered interior monologue. A fleeting comparison of himself with the energetic Boylan becomes: 'I. He. Old. Young.' The episode is replete with sounds and musical references, including lyrics, song titles, and puns ('tenors get women by the score'). The sound of Stephen Dedalus's father Simon singing with others in the next room reaches Bloom's ears, and the lyrics mingle with Bloom's thoughts.

Joyce used a musical title for his first published book, *Chamber Music*, in 1907. In 'Sirens' Bloom alludes to a possible pun in the title: 'Chamber music. Could make a kind of pun on that. It is a kind of music I often thought when she. Acoustics that is. Tinkling.' Punning aside, the musical analogy was a common feature of modernism, and it can be traced back to Walter Pater's famous declaration in *The Renaissance* (1873) that 'All art constantly aspires towards the condition of music'. Ezra Pound acknowledged Pater's influence on vorticism in the avant-garde magazine *Blast* (1914) because he championed form over content or narrative. Music's pure, non-linguistic expression made it a prime example for literary formalism. Pater argued that the 'mere matter' of a poem or painting was subordinate to the form in which it was expressed, and advocated that 'this form...should become an end in itself'. This paved the way for pure abstraction in the visual arts, but literature was more firmly tied to the outside world. It could only approximate the purer form of music by focusing attention on language itself and the repetition of motifs and reducing its dependence on the outside world by downplaying narrative and moral didacticism. Another of vorticism's influences, the American expatriate artist Whistler, called his works 'harmonies' and 'nocturnes' to discourage the viewer from looking 'through' the painting for the story or moral lesson rather than focusing on the arrangement of line and colour on the canvas. Joseph Conrad called music 'the art of arts' in his 'Preface' to *The Nigger of the Narcissus* (1897). Musical rhythm is central not only in Joyce's 'Sirens' episode but also in much of Woolf's writing. In *The Waves* (1931), for example, a character remarks that 'rhythm is the main thing in writing'. In Samuel Beckett's first published novel *Murphy* (1938), a failure of communication between Murphy and his lover Celia prompts her to think: 'It was like difficult music heard for the first time.' This sentence could also describe Beckett's style more generally. Music also becomes a euphemism for sex in *Murphy*, 'chosen with care' to evade, or simply mock, the censors.

   Modernism in music, as in literature, was marked by an initial period of shock and disruption followed by an increasingly cerebral sort of formalism. The pre-war period, coinciding with movements like cubism, futurism, and vorticism, was the revolutionary phase of Arnold Schoenberg's hauntingly atonal one-act opera *Expectation* (1909) and the Dionysian exuberance of Igor Stravinsky's *Rite of Spring* (1913). Along with Béla Bartók, these composers represent the turn towards dissonance and atonality. Their innovations built on previous departures from strict tonality in the work of Richard Wagner (whom Nietzsche championed in *The Birth of Tragedy*), Richard Strauss, and Gustav Mahler. Stravinsky and Bartók drew heavily on the folk music traditions of Russia and Hungary, respectively, in this pre-war period, in a way that matched the primitivist tendencies of painting and literature at this time. Also at this time, the futurist composer Luigi Russolo's manifesto, *The Art of Noises* (1913), translated the futurist adoration of the machine into the realm of music. Novelty was sought in 'the noises of trams, backfiring motors, carriages and bawling crowds', and futurist performances of music or poetry often involved the emulation of machine noise. Meanwhile, two of Schoenberg's pupils in Vienna, Anton Webern and Alban Berg, also took up the challenge of the new atonality, though in a rather more academic vein. 'Serialism', as Schoenberg's technique was called, used the 12 chromatic notes of an octave in a methodical, fixed system of composition. After the Second World War, serialism became the basis for the next generation of avant-garde composers, including Karlheinz Stockhausen and Oliver Messiaen. It was another of Schoenberg's students, John Cage, however, who eventually rejected the extreme rationality of this school and advocated a 'postmodern' indeterminacy. Cage was strongly influenced by Eastern philosophies and musical forms, seen for example in his use of the *I Ching* as a composition tool from the 1950s onwards.

   Popular music of the period was heard in the cabaret, music halls, and other venues. Increasingly, it was also mediated through phonograph recordings and radio broadcasts. (By the 1920s, most people in Britain either owned or had access to a wireless set.) Live music was also heard in the cinema, usually in the form of a pianist or a small string ensemble. Shortly before the First World War, American ragtime music 'invaded' Europe – France in particular, and to a lesser extent Britain. This was also preceded and accompanied by other forms of 'Negro music', as it was loosely known, such as the cakewalk. Ragtime, with its syncopated rhythms, influenced composers from Stravinsky to Claude Debussy, as well as modernist poets like the St. Louis-born T. S. Eliot. This was of course followed in the 1920s and 1930s by jazz: the 'Jazz Age' in American literature being roughly contemporaneous, even synonymous, with American modernism. Harlem Renaissance poets, including Langston Hughes, Claude McKay, and Jean Toomer, employed the rhythms of jazz and blues and vernacular speech as a means of representing and paying tribute to African-American culture and heritage. It was also a means of formal innovation, used alongside other modernist techniques like fragmentation and allusion.

See also: *Contexts*: Culture, Science and technology; *Texts*: Allusion, Consciousness, Stream of, Futurism, Harlem Renaissance, Irish literature, Primitivism.

Further Reading

Adorno, Theodor W., *Essays on Music*, trans. Susan H. Gillespie (Los Angeles: University of California Press, 2002).

Albright, Daniel, ed., *Modernism and Music: An Anthology of Sources* (Chicago: University of Chicago Press, 2004).

Bowen, Zack, *Musical Allusions in the Works of James Joyce: Early Poetry Through Ulysses* (Albany: SUNY Press, 1974).

Bucknell, Brad, *Literary Modernism and Musical Aesthetics: Pater, Pound, Joyce, and Stein* (Cambridge and New York: Cambridge University Press, 2001).

Primitivism

'From blackness, let us extract light. Simple, rich luminous naivety', declared the dadaist leader Tristan Tzara in his 'Note on Negro Art' (1917). 'Art, in the infancy of time', he continued, 'was prayer. Wood and stone were truth.' While we may read the 'naivety' in this passage as Tzara's own, his enthusiastic primitivism was characteristic of the time. For many modernist writers and artists, the 'naive' art of temporally and spatially distant cultures served to reinvigorate the dying culture of the West, which was seen as being too cerebral, bound by convention, and a slave to its own past achievements. Primitivism came in many forms, from the carelessly ignorant pillaging of museum artifacts for anything that would suggest novelty to a more careful anthropological interest in other cultures and religions. In most cases, however, it is fair to say that modernists used other cultures as raw material to feed their own artistic growth. What the modernists considered primitive was basically any culture other than their own, including European culture before the Renaissance (the Pre-Raphaelites were primitivist in this sense, for example). Although it was often uninformed and prone to romanticizing the 'other', the primitivist view nearly always regarded other societies as superior to the repressed, corrupted, mechanized West. Taking the opposite view, Adolf Hitler regarded primitivism itself, alongside cosmopolitanism and insanity, as one of the ills afflicting German culture. In his speech inaugurating the 1937 exhibition of 'Degenerate Art' in Munich, which included, in his own words, 'Cubism, Dadaism, Futurism, Impressionism, etc.', he railed against 'those prehistoric stone-age culture-vultures... [who] may just as well retreat to the caves of their ancestors to adorn them with their primitive international scribblings'.

Borrowing from the primitivist tendencies of European avant-garde movements like cubism and futurism, vorticism proudly proclaimed its 'savage' nature. 'The Art-instinct is permanently primitive', declared Wyndham Lewis in the first issue of *Blast* (1914). 'The artist of the modern movement is a savage.' One of the earliest examples of this kind of primitivism, Picasso's *Les Demoiselles d'Avignon* (1907; first exhibited publicly in 1916), depicted a brothel scene using African masks as the inspiration for three of his prostitutes' faces. Primitivism appealed to the desire of the avant-garde to shock with raw, visceral imagery and to radically alter the course of contemporary art. In a broader sense, primitivism had long existed in the arts: this is particularly true of the pastoralism and romantic idealization of 'simpler' and 'truer' ways of life, seen at times in the novels of D. H. Lawrence or the poems of W. B. Yeats. Primitivism in this sense is part of modernism's search for authenticity and value and an escape from 'civilized' culture. Lawrence wrote to Bertrand Russell in 1915, for example, describing the contrast he saw between 'mental consciousness' and 'blood consciousness', and the tyranny of the former over the latter in Western society. Indigenous peoples, Lawrence believed, had a closer connection to the 'blood consciousness', the instinctual life that he craved.

But for some at least, the interest in other cultures was more nuanced. The English philosopher and critic T. E. Hulme, for example, wrote several essays on Byzantine art and abstraction that suggest more than either romantic 'orientalism' or the desire for shock-value. Hulme first saw Byzantine mosaics in Ravenna, Italy, in 1911 and soon after had his ideas about Byzantine art confirmed by Wilhelm Worringer's influential book, *Abstraction and Empathy* (1908). 'I am moved by the Byzantine mosaic', he wrote, 'not because it is quaint or exotic, but because it expresses an attitude I agree with'. He maintained that this and other examples of early abstraction were 'abstract and stylized because these peoples wanted it to be so, not because they were incapable of anything more complex'. He saw an affinity between the worldview expressed in diverse examples of early abstract art, in which the outside world is seen as hostile and arbitrary, and the modern sense of alienation from one's surroundings. In both cases, the artist, rather than being in harmony with his or her subject matter, must attempt to impose order on an otherwise chaotic world. Rejecting the Renaissance humanist tradition, Hulme found his alternative in a mixture of neo-classicism, 'primitive' abstraction, and the modern abstract art of vorticism.

See also: *Contexts*: Anthropology, Cities and urbanization, Culture, Empire, Race, Sex and sexuality; *Texts*: Avant-garde, Dada and surrealism, Fragmentation, Futurism, Harlem Renaissance, Imagism and vorticism, Manifesto, Violence; *Criticism*: Postcolonialism, Psychoanalytic criticism.

Further Reading

Bell, Michael, *Primitivism* (London: Methuen, 1972).
Torgovnick, Marianna, *Gone Primitive: Savage Intellects, Modern Lives* (Chicago and London: Chicago University Press, 1990).

Realism and Naturalism

Although the terms 'realism' and 'naturalism' are often used interchangeably, there are important differences between them. Realism, as the name suggests, attempts to get closer to reality, closer to life as it is lived by the majority of people. Realist novels generally feature a reliable narrator, local colour and a contemporary setting, a straightforward plot, and ordinary speech. The movement owed much to journalistic style and scientific accuracy, as well as to the historical perspective. Where the French novels of Honoré de Balzac emphasized the careful recording of social life down to the smallest details of manners, clothing, furniture, food, and domestic space, English realist novels like George Eliot's *Middlemarch* (1872) added an important moral dimension. (French realist novels, moreover, were generally considered risqué in Britain.) Realism as a literary movement was closely connected to Victorian rationalism and empiricism. In their attempt to move away from Romantic escapism, realist novels tended to focus on the mundane facts of middle- or working-class life. Both tendencies are most often associated with the novel, because it is generally considered the most 'realistic' genre for its ability to present detailed characters and their progressive movement through time and space. In fact, as practitioners of the 'anti-novel' (like B. S. Johnson) later found, the difficult task is *not* to produce a novel that is in some sense realistic. No matter how often a modernist or postmodernist novel signals to readers its own fictionality, we as readers quickly slip back into our old habits of imagining living, breathing characters in actual situations.

The realist novel dominated the second half of the nineteenth century, and in the simplest terms modernism can be seen as a reaction against this legacy. In English literature, realism is associated with authors such as Elizabeth Gaskell, Charles Dickens, and George Gissing. It also has strong associations with French painting, beginning with Gustave Courbet's *Realist Manifesto* (1855), which should remind us that realism at one time represented a radical new direction in art and literature. Just as surrealism evolved from dada, naturalism as a movement developed out of realism. With naturalism, the desire to present a faithful and minutely detailed description of observable phenomena – the novel as a social document – was carried out with even greater diligence and scientific exactitude. Moreover, its 'scientific' outlook became more prominent with the added dimension, post-Darwin, of a deterministic perspective on human behaviour. Just as a distinction must be made between 'modernism' and 'modernity', so 'realism' should not be confused with 'reality'. The term 'realism' denotes an artistic style that places primary emphasis on a close and faithful representation of reality. But what is reality? And how is it represented most faithfully?

Near the end of the nineteenth century, some realist authors tested the limits of the form in ways that anticipated modernism. Gissing's late-realist fiction, for example, acquired a self-reflexivity that made it almost modernist. In his most famous book, *New Grub Street* (1891), Gissing took as his subject matter the writing 'industry' in London. One of his struggling author-characters, Harold Biffen, writes an ultra-realist novel called *Mr Bailey, Grocer*, which he describes as 'the true story of Mr Bailey's marriage and of his progress as a grocer' (Mr Bailey is Biffen's actual grocer). It is a simple yet noble tale of unadorned reality, probably unsellable and possibly unreadable; Biffen manages to get the book published shortly before he commits suicide. The grim determinism of Gissing's novels brings them close to the naturalism of Emile Zola, although in late-Victorian English literature the distinction between realism and naturalism is often very slight. Thomas Hardy was another novelist of the 1880s and 1890s who pushed the boundaries of realism. With his last published novel, *Jude the Obscure* (1895), Hardy's frank depictions of sexuality also succeeded in pushing the public's patience. D. H. Lawrence would extend Hardy's earthy investigations into English village life in *Sons and Lovers* (1913), before moving more decisively into modernist territory with *The Rainbow* (1915) and *Women in Love* (1920). He always emphasized a primitivist vitality, however, and sided with a certain type of realism in his essay 'Surgery for the Novel – Or a Bomb' (1923). Here Lawrence criticized the self-conscious experiments of 'serious' novelists like James Joyce, Marcel Proust, and Dorothy Richardson for being overly cerebral, self-conscious to the point of obsession, and divorced from 'true feeling'.

The transition to modernism is marked by a number of widely divergent trends, including the extremes of naturalism and aestheticism. Depending on your view, these styles may herald the beginning of modernism or, on the other hand, may represent the decadent close of the Victorian era. The more moderate view would see both styles as transitional. Gustave Flaubert's emphasis on artistic autonomy and 'writerly' precision, for example, distinguished *Madame Bovary* (1857) from the 'readerly' and rather baggy three-decker novels of the period. His preoccupation with language was passed on to Henry James and then to 'high' modernists like Joyce. Joseph Conrad, Polish-born but raised with an awareness of contemporary French art and literature, expanded the vocabulary of conventional realism with a new emphasis on impressionism. Apart from the French influence, Russian novelists like Fyodor Dostoevsky and Ivan Turgenev were pushing a new psychologism that contributed to the development of the modernist novel in English.

Although in the mid-nineteenth century it represented a radical departure from Romanticism, the realist approach had gone stale and was ripe for overthrow in the early twentieth century. Virginia Woolf saw the Edwardian novels of 'materialists' like Arnold Bennett, John Galsworthy, and H. G. Wells as upholding tired literary conventions that were ill suited to represent changing ideas of consciousness and the dynamism of modern life. She also questioned the reality they claimed to represent with such objectivity and accuracy – was this real life? Eschewing the careful cataloguing of external facts, Woolf, along with other stream-of-consciousness writers like Proust and Dorothy Richardson, pursued in an impressionist manner the reality of perception. It is important to understand that these modernists were, at least up to a certain point in their careers, trying to get *closer* to reality through newer means, rather than abandoning reality for fantasy or pure formalism. The first half of Joyce's *Ulysses* (1922), for example, is often read as an example of late naturalism for its extreme fidelity to the mundane observations of daily life. Joyce's naturalism can also be seen in the way his characters are formed largely by their history and environment – a determinism that Stephen Dedalus, who left Dublin at the end of *A Portrait of the Artist as a Young Man* (1916) only to reappear, against his will, at the beginning of *Ulysses*, clearly demonstrates.

See also: *Contexts*: Censorship, Cities and urbanization, Class, Market, Psychology; *Texts*: Aestheticism and decadence, Consciousness, Stream of, Irish literature, Primitivism; *Criticism*: Cultural materialism/New Historicism, Marxist criticism.

Further Reading

Morris, Pam, *Realism* (London: Routledge, 2003).

Violence

Violence in Anglo-American modernism is most often associated with the aggressive rhetoric of Wyndham Lewis, Ezra Pound, and T. E. Hulme. Other modernists like Yeats and D. H. Lawrence are also included in this category, chiefly for their vitriolic hatred of the 'mob'. A statement by Pound in a letter to James Joyce in December 1913 is characteristic: 'From what [Yeats] says I imagine we have a hate or two in common.' To some extent violence is present in all works of modernism and may be explained as a necessary component of modernism's artistic rebellion: its words and images were meant to shock readers and gallery goers out of their complacency. This much is to be expected. But even its adherents will admit that modernism's reputation has been tarnished by the prevalence of certain types of violence. Misogynistic, anti-Semitic, homophobic, elitist, and fascistic violence mars the work of some of the most prominent modernists. As early as 1917, in 'The Death of Futurism' (published in the *Egoist*), the novelist and critic John Cournos attacked 'Vorticism and all those "brother" arts, whose masculomaniac spokesmen spoke glibly...of "the glory of war" and "contempt for women"'. Hulme, who was by most accounts an intimidating figure, was a primary source of this violent, reactionary strain of modernism. Hulme was emblematic of early modernism's violent tendencies: he carried a brass knuckleduster, custom made for him by the sculptor Henri Gaudier-Brzeska (both men were killed in the war). He once famously responded to the critic Anthony Ludovici's negative judgement of avant-garde sculpture by suggesting that 'the most appropriate means of dealing with him would be a little personal violence'. Hulme also translated Georges Sorel's influential book on French syndicalism, *Reflections on Violence* (1908, translated 1914), which defended as 'heroic' the use of violence by syndicalist workers in a general strike. Sorel, a morally conservative critic of bourgeois democracy, later influenced the totalitarianism of Mussolini and Stalin, especially through his emphasis on the importance of myth in social and political movements. Sorel believed that violent events, such as the martyrdom of a revolutionary leader, served as useful symbols that reinforced the mythical quality of the larger movement. In *The Art of Being Ruled* (1926), Wyndham Lewis described Sorel as the 'key to all contemporary political thought'.

Violent action by anarchists, trade unionists, and Suffragettes was part of the political climate of the pre-war period. At the height of anarchist activity, dynamite attacks became common and several heads of state were assassinated, among them President Carnot of France (1894), Prime Minister del Castillo of Spain (1897), King Umberto of Italy (1900), and the American President McKinley (1901). Joseph Conrad's *The Secret Agent* (1907) was based on the death of French anarchist Martial Bourdin in Greenwich, London in 1894, when the bomb he was carrying exploded. The climactic event in D. H. Lawrence's novel *Aaron's Rod* (1922), often described as one of his 'leadership' novels (with *Kangaroo* and *The Plumed Serpent*), occurs when an anarchist or fascist in post-war Florence throws a bomb into the café where Aaron is sitting, destroying Aaron's flute (his 'rod') and killing a man at the next table.

Rhetorical violence was another defining characteristic of early modernism. It was most prominent in avant-garde manifestos and polemical writings before the war, especially those of the Italian futurists, which were replete with the violent imagery and jingoistic slogans that Cournos found so repellent. Aggression was a central point of the futurist platform. 'Except in struggle, there is no more beauty', the first manifesto of 1909 declared. 'No work without an aggressive character can be a masterpiece.' In her striking 'Manifesto of Futurist Woman' (1912), Valentine de Saint-Point's refutation of Italian futurism's violent misogyny, de Saint-Point overturns expectations by asserting the equally violent force of women, declaring: *Let woman find once more her cruelty and her violence*. The manifestos included in the vorticist magazine *Blast* (1914), published on the eve of the First World War, followed the example of futurism by using militaristic language. It described the vorticist movement as 'primitive mercenaries' whose aim was to 'stir up Civil War among peaceful apes'. (Much later, Lewis explained his tactics: 'It was essential that people should believe that there was a kind of army beneath the banner of the Vortex.') Within weeks of the first issue of *Blast*, and still closer to the outbreak of war, Lewis published 'Kill John Bull with Art'. In the essay, he described the 'racial attraction' of the Italian futurist Marinetti, which he argued was Marinetti's native 'violence and vitality'. He recommended that the English – and English artists – should learn from this example and shed their respectable Victorian image: 'What English people have not got is fury...I hold the opinion that the more fury they can develop the better.'

When the 'War Number' of *Blast* came out a year later, much had changed. The bright puce wrapper of the first issue was replaced by a sombre khaki. Lewis admitted: 'The War has exhausted interest for the moment in booming and banging.' Violent rhetoric was now considered distasteful. It gave way to the subtler language, less focused on shocking the public, which defined the high modernism of the 1920s. But the violence associated with the war, on the battlefield or at home, did receive treatment by modernist writers. Lawrence's short story 'Tickets, Please' (1919), published in the popular magazine the *Strand*, is an interesting example that plays on public anxiety surrounding women in the workplace and other changes that were forced in part by the war. The battle of the sexes takes place in 'the darkness and lawlessness of war-time', when most able-bodied men were at the Front and 'ladies and cripples' (like Lawrence himself, who was judged unfit for service) were running the show. In the story, the caddish John Thomas is attacked *en masse* by the very women, now 'filled with supernatural strength', that he had victimized in the past. 'You ought to be *killed*', one woman tells him, with 'a terrifying lust in her voice'. John Thomas, in his fear, 'started to struggle as an animal might', but his attackers also resemble animals, acting as if by instinct and spurred on by the taste of blood; when they cease their attack they stand 'with mute, stupefied faces'.

More common than this revolt against male tyranny, however, was the depiction of violence against women. The violent rape scene in Lewis's novel *Tarr* (1918), for example, is depicted through the cold, geometrical lens of vorticism. Yeats's poem 'Leda and the Swan' (1924) similarly recasts its ancient subject, the rape of Leda by Zeus in the guise of a swan, in the stark and dissonant language of modernism (Leda is 'mastered by the brute blood of the air'). In the pre-war avant-garde (or 'rear guard') of Pound, Lewis, and Hulme, misogynistic language was used to depict the decadence from which they sought to depart. In Pound's *Hugh Selwyn Mauberley* (1920), for example, Europe is derided as 'an old bitch gone in the teeth'. This of course was in line with futurism's 'scorn for women', which Marinetti explained as contempt for soft sentimentality and old-fashioned romantic ideals. In 'The Work of Art in the Age of Mechanical Reproduction' (1936), the Marxist critic Walter Benjamin wrote about futurism's glorification of violence in the form of technological warfare and its alliance with fascism. In the famous concluding passage, he mourned the fact that: '[Mankind's] self-alienation has reached such a degree that it can experience its own destruction as an aesthetic pleasure of the first order. This is the situation of politics which Fascism is rendering aesthetic. Communism responds by politicizing art.' Benjamin saw the futuro-fascist aestheticization of violence as 'the consummation of *"l'art pour l'art"* ' rather than its rejection. Possibly thinking of Brecht, he presented the use of art by the Left as the dialectical antidote to this kind of inhumanity.

See also: *Contexts*: Fascism, War, Women and gender; *Texts*: Anti-Semitism, Apocalypse, Avant-garde, Futurism, Imagism and Vorticism, Manifesto, Primitivism; *Criticism*: Feminist and gender criticism, Marxist criticism.

Further Reading

Houen, Alex, *Terrorism and Modern Literature* (Oxford and New York: Oxford University Press, 2002).

Johnsen, William A., *Violence and Modernism: Ibsen, Joyce, and Woolf* (Gainesville: Florida University Press, 2003).

3 Criticism: Approaches, Theory, Practice

Introduction

The entries in this section fall into two broad categories: critical trends of the modernist period and criticism since the poststructuralist 'turn' of the late 1960s. The former category includes figures such as F. R. Leavis and the American New Critics. In *New Bearings in English Poetry* (1932), Leavis sided strongly with the modernist innovations and critical interventions of T. S. Eliot and Ezra Pound. He was fiercely critical of late Victorian and Edwardian poetry, promoting instead the poetry of John Donne, Alexander Pope, and Samuel Johnson. Advocates of the American New Criticism sought, like Leavis, but without any particular moral emphasis, to develop a critical practice that would adequately address the rigorous demands modernist poetry placed on the reader. Eliot, Leavis, and the New Critics all agreed that criticism deserved serious recognition as a discipline and that it must earn this recognition by conducting its analysis in a careful, systematic, and professional manner.

Modernist-era Marxism also comes under this first category. Important figures here include the Hungarian critic Georg Lukács, the Italian Antonio Gramsci, and the Frankfurt School critics Walter Benjamin, Theodor Adorno, Max Horkheimer, and Herbert Marcuse. All these critics were strongly influenced by Hegel's dialectical method, and of course by the social theory of Marx, though all reformulated and reinterpreted Marxism in different ways. Lukács is perhaps atypical of this group in his criticism of 'decadent' modernist literature (in *Theory of the Novel*, 1920) and his advocacy of 'socialist realism'. Most of the other critics share modernism's desire to move beyond traditional modes of representation and its concerns about the effects of mass culture. Horkheimer and Marcuse favoured a sociological approach to culture, although Marcuse was also interested in psychoanalytic theory. Benjamin and Adorno, meanwhile, wrote directly and extensively on literature, music, film, and other cultural productions of the modernist period. Unlike Lukács, they viewed modernism in a positive light for its ability to maintain critical distance from the ideology of the State, a revolutionary potential they found lacking in the mass culture of which Adorno was particularly dismissive.

The psychoanalysis of Freud and Jung, the first-wave feminism of Virginia Woolf, and the structuralism of Saussure also belong to the modernist phase. The great leaps in the understanding of human consciousness made by the relatively new field of psychology in the early twentieth century had a profound impact on literature. The links to modernist writers, including Joyce, Lawrence, and Woolf, were particularly close. Woolf's essays 'A Room of One's Own' (1929) and *Three Guineas* (1938), meanwhile, became foundation texts for the second-wave feminist criticism that began in the 1960s. Saussure, who is also discussed at length in the 'Contexts' section, is linked to modernism especially through his influence on Russian formalists like Roman Jakobson and Viktor Shklovsky, who were among the first to apply Saussure's theories to literature. In *Art as Technique* (1917), a key statement of formalism, Shklovsky introduced the concept of *ostrenenie*, or 'defamiliarization', the ability of art to renew language and to save us from our habit of falling into unconscious routines, not least in our use of language. The ability of poetry to revitalize language became a central tenet of many avant-garde movements in Europe, particularly Russian and Italian futurism but also imagism and vorticism.

Theory since the 1960s, the second major category, is dominated by the anti-foundationist streams that originated with Jacques Derrida, Michel Foucault, Julia Kristeva, and others. By the 1980s, poststructuralism had itself achieved institutional status in the academy. The earlier point of origin for these theories is Saussure, who is largely responsible for the linguistic turn in twentieth-century theory. The current tendency in literary criticism is to combine various approaches: for example, a post-structuralist reading of Joyce's *Ulysses* (1922) that analyses postcolonial themes, issues of gender, psychoanalytic perspectives, and other aspects of the text by drawing on scholars as diverse as Homi K. Bhabha, Hélène Cixous, and Jacques Lacan. Another side of this eclecticism is the rise of interdiscipinarity that has gone hand in hand with the rise of theory since the 1960s. Theory in its contemporary form is broadly interdisciplinary in nature, as the categories in this section demonstrate (psychoanalysis, feminism, New Historicism, and so forth). So the rise of theory has meant not only studying literary texts using extra-literary methods but also in some cases moving away from strictly literary texts to other cultural forms like television, film, and music. This has caused some anxiety in English departments over boundary lines, but it has also brought fresh insights to the field, and it shows an understanding that literary texts are part of a larger world.

Of course, literary criticism goes back much further than the twentieth century. And the description of theory since the 1960s as a largely poststructuralist endeavour perhaps does not do justice to the return of historicist approaches in the past two decades, which have borrowed from thinkers like Foucault but which can also be seen as a reaction against the ahistorical close readings performed by Derrida. The present list does, however, include the most widely used, or in some cases the most historically relevant, critical approaches to modernism. The descriptions offered here do not pretend to be exhaustive – how can one describe, for example, Freud's importance to literature and literary criticism in a few paragraphs? Instead, they introduce essential figures and concepts, outline the historical development of the approach, and provide suggestions for the application of these reading practices to specific modernist texts. Readers should take away a working knowledge of these key theoretical positions, while keeping in mind the complexities and contradictions that such a brief overview will necessarily conceal. The suggestions for further reading that follow each entry are intended to help readers build on the foundations provided here, and wherever possible I have suggested texts that serve as relatively accessible entry points to a given body of criticism.

Further Reading

Castle, Gregory, *The Blackwell Guide to Literary Theory* (Oxford and Malden, MA: Blackwell, 2007).

Klages, Mary, *Literary Theory: A Guide for the Perplexed* (London and New York: Continuum, 2006).

Whitworth, Michael, ed., *Modernism: A Guide to Criticism* (Cambridge and Malden, MA: Blackwell, 2006).

Cultural Materialism/New Historicism

These two approaches are often, and justifiably, seen as related critical traditions that grew up on different sides of the Atlantic. Both are part of the larger category of cultural studies, and both are informed by recent developments in Marxist, feminist, and postcolonial theory. Both represent, in literary studies, a return to historical and cultural contexts after the long reign of formalism under New Criticism and similar approaches. Moreover, both may be seen as reactions against traditional historicist approaches but also against the extreme textuality of structuralist and deconstructionist trends. Cultural materialism, the older of the two movements, evolved out of the work of Marxist critic Raymond Williams, author of *Culture and Society: 1780–1950* (1958) and *The Long Revolution*

(1961). In *Culture and Society*, Williams calls for an expansion of literary analysis to include a range of disciplines and cultural sources such as 'institutions, manners, customs, [and] family memories'. A similar approach was being developed elsewhere at the time in E. P. Thompson's *The Making of the English Working Class* (1963). Meanwhile, the field of cultural studies found institutional acceptance in 1964 with the opening of the Centre for Contemporary Cultural Studies at the University of Birmingham. Its first director was Richard Hoggart, author of *The Uses of Literacy: Changing Patterns in English Mass Culture* (1957), followed by Stuart Hall in 1968. Williams defined the term 'cultural materialism' in *Marxism and Literature* (1977), and it was given a significant boost by Jonathan Dollimore and Alan Sinfield's *Political Shakespeare: New Essays in Cultural Materialism* (1985). Since the 1980s, Dollimore, Sinfield, Catherine Belsey, and others have contributed to the development of the approach. Williams identified minority (including 'emergent' and 'oppositional') cultures as a focus of cultural studies. Sinfield and Dollimore's recent co-founding of the interdisciplinary Centre for the Study of Sexual Dissidence and Cultural Change at the University of Sussex highlights this focus, specifically in relation to queer theory.

New Historicism also seeks to examine literature in its historical and cultural contexts. It is more sceptical, however, of the Marxist view and less interested in the stance of political engagement which cultural studies shares with feminism and other approaches. Initiated by Stephen Greenblatt in the 1980s, the New Historicist project took its inspiration from the American cultural anthropologist Clifford Geertz and his idea of 'thick description', defined in the first essay of his groundbreaking work, *The Interpretation of Cultures* (1973). In literary studies, this provided the impetus for New Historicism's reading of literature within a broader cultural context, alongside other forms of cultural discourse or 'texts'. New Historicism also followed closely the example of French philosopher and pioneer of poststructuralism Michel Foucault. Foucault, whose works include *The Birth of the Clinic* (1963), *The Archeology of Knowledge* (1969), *Discipline and Punish: The Birth of the Prison* (1975), and *The History of Sexuality* (1976), read historical subjects in radically unconventional, 'anti-historical' ways. Using 'archeological' and 'genealogical' approaches, the latter being derived from the philosopher Friedrich Nietzsche, Foucault drew attention to power structures in society without resorting to chronological historical narratives; one of his main discoveries was the way in which social power is rooted in 'discursive formations', ideological structures embedded in and authorized by language. The ideas of authority and dissidence or subversion are central to both cultural materialism and New Historicism, but in different ways. New Historicists, for example, have generally been less optimistic than cultural materialists about the power of literary texts to subvert cultural norms, arguing that subversive texts are easily co-opted and 'contained' within the larger cultural discourse by adjustments to the literary canon and other accommodations.

Both views adhere to the principle that there is no single, authoritative, chronological narrative of history but many alternate and subjective histories or genealogies. Modernism, for example, would not be viewed as a single, unified movement but as 'modernisms': a diverse and often contradictory field of movements and figures, united only by similar claims to literary and artistic innovation. Both theoretical trends have found subjects in the Renaissance particularly productive; however, modernism has also benefited from New Historicist and cultural materialist approaches. As Cheryl Herr's groundbreaking study, *Joyce's Anatomy of Culture* (1986), demonstrates, social and historical contexts are of fundamental importance to understanding Joyce. *Ulysses*, for example, is a compendium and critique of the myriad cultural discourses of daily Dublin life: the language of the Catholic Church and British colonial rule, and the vernacular of the music hall and tabloid journalism. In the 'Nausicaa' episode, Gerty McDowell's view of Leopold Bloom sitting on the beach is represented in the idiom of the romance novel, while Bloom sees her through the image of the lingerie advertisement, the pornographic snapshot, and the popular song ('Those girls, those girls, those lovely seaside girls / All dimples smiles and curls, your head it simply whirls'). A tension that sometimes arises in cultural-historical approaches to literature, especially from a Marxist perspective, is the conflicting desire to celebrate and elevate popular culture – marginalized for so long in literary criticism – and to recognize and critique the manipulative role the mass media often plays in shoring up the dominant ideology of a culture. Modernists like Joyce and Eliot had the same problem: intrigued by the possibilities and novelty of popular culture in songs, films, print journalism, and advertising, they were also horrified at the power the new media, especially in its baser forms, apparently held over its consumers.

Further Reading

Brannigan, John, *New Historicism and Cultural Materialism* (Basingstoke and New York: Palgrave Macmillan, 1998).

Gallagher, Catherine, and Greenblatt, Stephen, *Practicing New Historicism* (Chicago and London: University of Chicago Press, 2000).

Sinfield, Alan, *Faultlines: Cultural Materialism and the Politics of Dissident Reading* (Oxford: Clarendon Press, 1992).

Deconstruction

The theoretical approach more or less synonymous with linguistic philosopher Jacques Derrida is in a sense the original 'post-structuralism'. Born in the atmosphere of social upheaval in 1960s France, deconstruction (which can be traced back to philosophical terms used by Martin Heidegger and Edmund Husserl) represented both a radical overhaul of structuralism and, in the larger sense, a critique of the very structures of Western thought. Derrida trained as a philosopher at the *Ecole normale supérieure* in the 1950s, where his mentors included Louis Althusser and Michel Foucault. His dissertation and early scholarship centred on the German phenomenologist Edmund Husserl, but his major breakthrough came with a paper on structuralism presented in 1966 at a conference hosted by Johns Hopkins University in Baltimore. The paper, 'Structure, Sign, and Play in the Discourse of the Human Sciences' (published the following year in Writing and Difference), effectively deconstructed structuralism just as it was making inroads to American academia, and this provocative gesture brought him international recognition. His writings paved the way for some of the most important 'anti-foundationist' streams of contemporary theory, including feminist, postcolonial, and New Historicist approaches. Exploding onto the American academic scene in the mid-1970s, particularly at Yale University where Derrida taught for a time, alongside leading advocates such as Paul De Man, J. Hillis Miller, and Geoffrey Hartman, deconstruction remained a dominant force in American English departments for the next two decades. In contrast to other areas of poststructuralism, deconstruction is firmly and meticulously focused on the text, rather than contexts. Derrida declared in his most famous work, *Of Grammatology* (1967): 'there is nothing outside the text'; 'nothing outside', that is, because meaning within a system is always relative, defined by difference. This close-reading approach, which aligns deconstruction with various formalisms, including the 'practical criticism' of I. A. Richards in Britain and the American New Criticism, has been viewed as a weakness of deconstruction: it ignores the social, political, and historical contexts out of which texts arise.

However, although it relies predominantly on textual analysis, the implications of deconstructive practice are nothing, if not political. (This is evident in deconstruction's influence on later theoretical trends, such as postcolonial studies or queer theory.) Derrida's critique of the 'logocentrism' ('word-centredness') of Western philosophy, for example, can be extended to a broader critique of Western ethnocentrism. Logocentrism basically refers to the assumption of a stable, closed system, based in language, which originates (in the Judeo-Christian tradition) with God: 'In the beginning was the Word...and the Word was God.' For Derrida, logocentrism is also related to 'phonocentrism', the privileging of speech over the written word. These concepts are bound up with another privileged term: 'presence'. Speaking implies presence, whereas writing is associated with absence; the spoken word is considered to be the primary, 'natural' source of meaning, while writing is secondary and derivative. In Derrida's view, language is not simply the expression of pre-existing, 'natural' ideas about the world: thought actually happens *through* language. Our worldview is embedded in our language system, which itself is entirely arbitrary (following Saussure) rather than 'natural'.

There is no natural connection, either, between words or signs and the objects or ideas they have come to represent. Working from anthropologist Claude Levi-Strauss's identification of binary opposites ('speech/writing', 'presence/absence') as the basic units or building blocks of culture, Derrida focused on the idea that in each of these pairs, one term (the first) is always dominant. By challenging the hierarchies of the binary oppositions structuring Western thought – white/black, men/women, inside/outside, and so on – deconstruction reveals the processes by which power is defended and reinforced, and abuses of power are justified or 'naturalized'. Furthermore, and again following Saussure, the terms of the binary opposition have 'value' only in relation to each other and are thus defined by what Derrida calls '*différance*', a pun on 'difference' and 'deferral'. This too has political implications, as one term depends upon and defines its meaning only in relation to the other. Hence, in the pair 'reason/madness', 'madness' can only be defined in opposition to, and from the perspective of, 'reason', based on the assumption of 'reason' as the privileged term. The hierarchy, as Derrida showed, is inherently unstable because it can always be inverted. Deconstruction considers categories like history, philosophy, and literature – indeed all systems of categorization – as rhetorical constructs, products of language. The Western perception of self and other, subject and object, inside and outside, and so on is no longer seen as the 'natural' or 'true' one, but as one 'narrative' among many others – no longer stable or absolute but unstable, contingent, and relative.

The relationship between deconstruction and modernism is longstanding and can be traced in part to Derrida's interest in James Joyce. 'Theoretical Joyce', now a mainstay of Joyce criticism (the so-called Joyce industry), really began in the 1970s and 1980s with essays on Joyce by Derrida, Roland Barthes, and other poststructuralist critics who were particularly interested in the possibilities opened up by *Ulysses* and *Finnegans Wake*. In 1984, at the height of deconstruction's influence, Derrida was invited to give the keynote lecture, titled 'Ulysses

Gramophone: Hear Say Yes in Joyce', at the Ninth Annual International James Joyce Symposium in Frankfurt. Derrida's analysis, like the text on which it was based, is replete with 'play': fluid and circuitous, unfixed and unstable, shifting and multivocal (Derrida even employed a cassette recorder in his delivery), it frequently lapses into wordplay, etymology, and digression. There is also a personal narrative running through the essay in the form of an autobiographical travelogue (Ithaca, New York; Oxford, Ohio; Tokyo, Japan). Like *Finnegans Wake*, it worries aloud over its own signification to the reader, auditor, or translator ('how will the sentences that I have just thrown out at you be translated?'), who will bring his or her own highly personal associations to the text.

So what, finally, does a deconstructionist reading look like? In the view of deconstruction, it is impossible to speak 'outside' of a system. It is impossible to critique a particular system of thought, for example, without employing the terms and 'logic' of that same system. The best we can do, therefore, is to constantly draw attention, as Derrida does (and as much postmodern literature does), to the system as a construct and to highlight the fact that meaning in the system (and the interpretation) is unstable and provisional, though it may appear otherwise. Joyce's *Ulysses*, of course, is hardly a random example: with techniques like parody and pastiche, and a good dose of Derridean 'play', Joyce deconstructs the novel using its own vocabulary; from the inside, as it were. Rather than 'solving' the text by discerning a single, stable meaning, a deconstructionist reading will end in the endless – endless pluralities, irreducible oppositions, and unresolved tensions. The frequently (mis)punctuated title of *Finnegans Wake* is a good example of this plurality, suggesting not simply the name of a popular Irish ballad, but infinite (and indeterminate) Finnegans infinitely waking. It is little wonder that Derrida and other poststructuralists found so much value in Joyce's later writings. Like the 'bricoleur'-figure of Lévi-Strauss and Derrida, who makes use of a system while acknowledging that it is unstable, a construct, Joyce demonstrated with *Ulysses* that the old 'truths' no longer held, the mirror was cracked but that a new novel could still be cobbled together from the old discourses.

Further Reading

Culler, Jonathan, *On Deconstruction: Theory and Criticism After Structuralism* (Ithaca, NY: Cornell University Press, 1982).

Derrida, Jacques, *Acts of Literature*, ed. Derek Attridge (London: Routledge, 1992).

Norris, Christopher, *Deconstruction: Theory and Practice*, 3rd rev. ed. (London: Routledge, 2002).

Feminist and Gender Criticism

Contemporary feminist theory grew out of the 'second-wave' feminism of the 1960s and 1970s and came to prominence as an institution in the early 1980s. There were, and in some respects still are, divergent strands of feminist criticism, in particular the French poststructuralist school of Hélène Cixous, Luce Irigaray, and Julia Kristeva, and the humanist-based Anglo-American school exemplified by Sandra Gilbert and Susan Gubar's *The Madwoman in the Attic* (1979), or Elaine Showalter's 'gynocriticism' (the study of the unique history of women's writing). American feminists in particular, including Bonnie Kime Scott, have emphasized canon revision as a central project of feminist criticism. Gender criticism, which is not confined to women alone, also found widespread recognition in the 1980s. Two pioneers of gender theory are Eve Kosofsky Sedgwick, author of *Epistemology of the Closet* (1990), and Judith Butler, author of *Gender Trouble: Feminism and the Subversion of Identity* (1990). Gender criticism raises questions about the construction of gender and sexuality that had been articulated earlier in Simone de Beauvoir's *The Second Sex* (1949), where the author famously stated: 'One is not born, but rather becomes, a woman.'

The issue of being and becoming, of 'nature' and 'nurture', has been a key subject of debate between certain strands of feminist and gender criticism. The 'essentialist' point of view, followed by some feminists and queer theorists on both sides of the Atlantic, argues basically that there are inherent, 'natural' differences between women and men, or between homosexuals and heterosexuals. Cixous, Kristeva, and Irigaray, drawing on Lacanian theory, have all posited a link between female bodies – as maternal, for example, or as experiencing sexual pleasure differently than men (expressed in the concept of *jouissance*) – and female writing, or *l'écriture féminine*. The 'constructionist' or 'performative' view, on the other hand, challenges the category of 'sex' and even the notion of a stable subject, arguing instead that gender and sexuality, and other forms of identity, are always socially constructed.

The feminist and gender criticisms that rose to prominence in the 1980s have deep roots in the modernist era. The first-wave feminism of the late nineteenth and early twentieth century brought forward a wealth of new ideas about sex, gender, and desire. This period saw the advent of the New Woman, high-profile campaigns by suffragists and suffragettes, and finally the gaining of the vote for women in most Western countries. Modernist writers including Virginia Woolf and James Joyce raised important questions about gender and literature, in terms of style, point of view, characterization, and other aspects. In Joyce's *Ulysses* (1922), for example, Leopold Bloom bears little resemblance to the hero of Homer's *Odyssey* or to the Western image of the hero in general. Nor does Molly Bloom resemble the conventional heroine. As Vicki Mahaffey argues in her essay '*Ulysses* and the End of Gender' (1998), Joyce challenges the reader's expectations by upsetting such stereotypical images, making Bloom 'neither brave nor vengeful' and Molly neither passive nor naively innocent. 'The only men in the novel who pride themselves on their physical prowess', Mahaffey points out, 'are an adulterer and a bigot: the exaggeratedly hot Blazes Boylan and the hypocritical Citizen'. Gerty McDowell, the woman Bloom encounters on the beach in the 'Nausicaa' episode, tries to adhere to the image of perfect femininity that she has learned from popular romance; her view of Bloom, too, is conditioned by her reading habits. Joyce highlights the destructive effect this has on Gerty as a woman: as Mahaffey explains, 'Gerty relentlessly censors her thoughts and perceptions, vigilantly replacing them with sentimental pictures'.

Woolf stands in relation to later feminist theory much as T. S. Eliot does to New Criticism, as an influential and pioneering figure. Her essay 'A Room of One's Own' (1929), based on lectures given at Girton College, Cambridge, in 1928, is seen by many critics as a key point of origin for feminist literary theory. In the essay, Woolf confronts injustices like the exclusion of women from formal education (something from which she herself suffered), the lack of a female literary tradition, and the barriers to becoming a woman writer. She also invents a sister ('Judith') for William Shakespeare to illustrate the dearth of opportunities afforded to women:

> Meanwhile his extraordinarily gifted sister, let us suppose, remained at home. She was as adventurous, as imaginative, as agog to see the world as he was. But she was not sent to school. She had no chance of learning grammar and logic, let alone of reading Horace and Virgil. She picked up a book now and then, one of her brother's perhaps, and read a few pages. But then her parents came in and told her to mend the stockings or mind the stew and not moon about with books and papers.

> (pp. 60–61)

More controversial, but equally important, is Woolf's exploration of the relationship between writing and gender, where she raises the possibility of a 'feminine' subjectivity and prose style. This was later developed by Cixous as the concept of *l'écriture féminine*, in her landmark essay-manifesto 'The Laugh of the Medusa' (1975).

Cixous performs her argument by shunning the conventions of scholarly rhetoric, which she sees as a 'masculine' style. She writes instead in a fluid, 'feminine' style, using wordplay and metaphor, like the central metaphor of the medusa, to convey her meaning. Following Derrida, her essay critiques Western logocentrism and phallocentrism (or 'phallogocentrism'). Interestingly, however, the theory of feminine writing pursued by Cixous and other French feminist critics is not necessarily limited to female authors. Just as Woolf found Marcel Proust to be a highly androgynous writer, even tending to a 'feminine' style, Cixous considered the writing of Joyce to be 'feminine' in some respects. (Cixous chose Joyce as the focus of her dissertation, published in 1972 as *The Exile of James Joyce*.) Woolf does not argue decisively for a feminine style in 'A Room of One's Own', but instead, in Showalter's influential phrase, she takes 'flight into androgyny'. Drawing on Samuel Taylor Coleridge's theory of androgynous writing, Woolf states near the conclusion of her essay: 'It is fatal to be a man or woman pure and simple; one must be woman-manly or man-womanly.... Some collaboration has to take place in the mind between the woman and the man before the art of creation can be accomplished.' Showalter viewed this as a retreat from the feminist position articulated earlier in the essay, but other (especially gender) critics have found Woolf's exploration of androgyny to be equally groundbreaking.

Further Reading

Butler, Judith, *Gender Trouble: Feminism and the Subversion of Identity* (London and New York: Routledge, 1990).

Cixous, Hélène, *The Hélène Cixous Reader*, ed. Susan Sellers (London and New York: Routledge, 1994).

———, 'The Laugh of the Medusa', *Signs* 1.4 (Summer 1976): 875–93.

Goldman, Jane, *The Feminist Aesthetics of Virginia Woolf* (Cambridge and New York: Cambridge University Press, 1998).

Moi, Toril, *Sexual/Textual Politics: Feminist Literary Theory*, 2nd rev. ed. (London and New York: Routledge, 2002).

Scott, Bonnie Kime, *Refiguring Modernism, Vol. 2: Postmodern Feminist Readings of Woolf, West, and Barnes* (Bloomington and Indianapolis: Indiana University Press, 1996).

Showalter, Elaine, *A Literature of Their Own: British Women Novelists from Brontë to Lessing* (Princeton, NJ: Princeton University Press, 1977).

Woolf, Virginia, *A Room of One's Own and Three Guineas* (Oxford and New York: Oxford University Press, 1992).

Leavisite Criticism

One of the great figures of English literary criticism, and very much of the modernist period, Cambridge English professor F. R. Leavis is remembered in different ways. For some poststructuralist critics, Leavis was an unrepentant humanist and moralist in the Arnoldian tradition, a supporter of elitist literature, and a defender of the establishment. Others recognize that, in making the 'tradition of the modern', Leavis did some radical things: he taught twentieth-century literature at Cambridge beginning (as a 'freelance' lecturer) in the 1920s, when such a thing was unspeakably modern; he read Eliot's *The Waste Land* (1922) to his students through a megaphone; he got in trouble with the authorities for trying to have the banned *Ulysses* (1922) accepted as a course text. Leavis also worked to increase the circulation of literature among all classes in society through the education system, even while upholding the value of 'difficult' literature. In addition, he held a lifelong interest in the widely misunderstood D. H. Lawrence, beginning with a pamphlet in 1930, shortly after Lawrence's death, and later extended with a full-length study, *D. H. Lawrence: Novelist* (1955).

Leavis, like William Empson and I. A. Richards, is sometimes thought of as an English 'New Critic', but in his case the label is misleading. Although he did seek to raise the calibre and the profile of literary criticism as a distinct profession through his influential journal, *Scrutiny* (1932–1953), Leavis refused to isolate literature from social and historical concerns. The study of literature, for Leavis, was ultimately the study of human nature, and as such it could not be confined to a merely aesthetic realm. Rather, it would be a sort of index or measure of national achievement and therefore a matter of concern to everyone. Articles in *Scrutiny*, many of which were also written by his wife, Q. D. Leavis, advocated the fostering of an educated elite who would protect English literature and culture in an age of mass media and falling standards. But Leavis also campaigned for the dissemination of literature into the state school system, ostensibly to ensure a 'moral' education but also to provide wider access to 'great' literature for all classes in society. It has been argued that Leavis and *Scrutiny* contributed to the rise of cultural studies in Britain, by bringing notice to and encouraging analysis of popular culture, albeit to underline the superiority of 'serious' literature. Raymond Williams, the Marxist critic and pioneer of cultural materialism, took Leavis's landmark study, *The Great Tradition* (1948), as both an inspiration and a departure point for his work beginning in the 1950s, and was also inspired by Leavis's dual role as critic and educator. In this respect, Leavis must be acknowledged as an early influence on cultural criticism in Britain.

Leavis made a significant impact with two early forays into criticism, *Mass Civilization and Minority Culture* (pamphlet, 1930) and *New Bearings in English Poetry* (1932). Both works aligned Leavis with the concerns of high modernism: the former reflected Ezra Pound and T. S. Eliot's extreme selectivity in judging a few works 'worthy' of inclusion in a narrow literary canon, while the latter presented a robust argument for new additions to this canon, including Eliot, Pound, Yeats, and the proto-modernist Gerard Manley Hopkins. In this sense, Leavisite criticism is arguably closest to the view of the 'major' modernists themselves, Eliot in particular, although he may have differed with Pound and Eliot over his concern for the interests of the 'common reader'. The judgements made in *New Bearings* and subsequent works had a pervasive influence on the shape of twentieth-century poetry in English, as they helped to establish the validity of the high modernist position, and to gain acceptance not only for the modernist poets themselves but also for the revamped literary tradition that Leavis shared in many respects with the modernists. Central aspects of his critical style, including the focus on individual authors and the privileging of a narrow canon, fell out of fashion with the rise of literary theory from the 1970s onwards. There are still, however, humanist critics in the Leavisite line, including public intellectuals like John Carey, author of *The Intellectuals and the Masses* (1992).

Further Reading

Bell, Michael, *F. R. Leavis* (London and New York: Routledge, 1988).

Leavis, F. R., *D. H. Lawrence: Novelist* (London: Chatto and Windus, 1955).

———, *The Great Tradition: George Eliot, Henry James, Joseph Conrad* (London: Chatto and Windus, 1948).

———, *New Bearings in English Poetry: A Study of the Contemporary Situation* (London: Chatto and Windus, 1932).

———, ed., *A Selection from Scrutiny*, 2 vols (Cambridge: Cambridge University Press, 1968).

Marxist Criticism

Rather than acting as interpreter for the text, Marxist criticism, in Terry Eagleton's words (in *Criticism and Ideology*, 1978), 'show[s] the text as it cannot know itself'. The Marxist critic analyses literature not by uncovering the hidden meaning contained within a text, but by situating the text in history, placing it beside other, non-literary forms, and seeing it as both a product of labour and an expression of ideology. Literary texts can also be said to do certain types of work themselves, either by promoting and reinforcing hegemonic power structures, or by challenging and subverting the dominant powers, or sometimes both. Marxism employs a dialectical approach borrowed from the German philosopher Hegel, in which a 'thesis' and an 'antithesis' produce a new 'synthesis'. Dialectical materialism grounds the dialectic in 'material' elements like social, political, and economic effects. In his essay, 'The Author as Producer' (1934), Walter Benjamin wrote: 'The dialectical approach...has absolutely no use for such rigid, isolated things as work, novel, book. It has to insert them into the living social context.' (Cultural materialism also employs this form of analysis.) The central example for Marxism of this type of materialist dialectic is the struggle between two classes, the bourgeoisie and the proletariat, which will (in theory) yield a classless society.

A Marxist analysis pieces together the social and economic conditions surrounding the production of a text. This might include, for example, its relationships with class, race, and gender. Marx and Engels distinguished society's economic 'base', the mode of production, from its 'superstructure', principally law and politics, but also (for most Marxists) social and cultural institutions, which develop out of this material foundation. The mode of production in a capitalist society normally involves a ruling bourgeoisie, a proletariat class of wage labourers, a factory system, a bureaucracy, and so on. Work is considered an essential part of life in the Marxist view, but under capitalism workers are 'alienated' from the products of their labour, and the workers themselves are reified as 'products' to be bought and sold by the ruling class. Philosophy and religion fall into the category of 'consciousness', which also arises from material conditions, and which relates to the dominant 'ideology' – the set of beliefs, laws, principles, and traditions used by the ruling class to keep the other classes in place. As Marx himself states in *The German Ideology* (1846): 'Life is not determined by consciousness, but consciousness by life.' In its original form, the base/superstructure model is very simple: economic reality determines ideology. However, later Marxists, and even Marx and Engels in their later careers, have reworked central concepts of Marxist theory like ideology and the relationship between base and superstructure in various ways, and as a result widely divergent schools of Marxism have developed. Marx and Engels both wrote about literature, providing examples of what a Marxist literary analysis might look like. It was far from their main concern, however, and a Marxist theory of literature was not articulated as such. That job has been left to their disciples, including (to name a few): Georg Lukács, Antonio Gramsci, Walter Benjamin, Theodor Adorno, Max Horkheimer, Jürgen Habermas, Herbert Marcuse, Louis Althusser, Fredric Jameson, and Terry Eagleton.

Of the many varieties of Marxist criticism, the so-called critical theory of Benjamin, Adorno, and others is particularly relevant to modernist literature. A critique of modernity that is firmly rooted in the modernist period, critical theory drew on contemporary examples of literature, film, music, and art. Horkheimer, Adorno, Marcuse, and Erich Fromm were all associated with the Institute for Social Research at Frankfurt University, but more particularly with the Frankfurt School, a group of dissident or neo-Marxist social critics that formed under Horkheimer's directorship of the Institute beginning in 1930. Benjamin was an 'unofficial' member of the group, and his Marxism was of a particularly eclectic kind, blending in equal parts of German Romanticism and Jewish mysticism (both of which went against the materialist view). Despite his unorthodox and often difficult approach, however, he is seen as a central figure of Western Marxism and a key critic of modernity. Benjamin wrote extensively on a number of modernist authors, many of whom he knew personally, including Charles Baudelaire and Marcel Proust (both of whose works he also translated), Franz Kafka, and Bertold Brecht, as well as the surrealists, whom he admired, and the Italian futurists, whom he did not. He theorized the figure of the *flâneur* and his milieu, the crowd, as well as the notions of spectacle and commodity. Benjamin's prose portraits of cities like Moscow, Berlin, Paris, Marseille, and Naples are themselves a fascinating part of the European modernist canon. The Institute for Social Research, which published Benjamin's most famous essay, 'The Work of Art in the Age of Mechanical Reproduction' (1936), moved to Columbia University in New York, in 1934, following Hitler's rise to power. (Benjamin's own apparent suicide occurred at the Spanish border in 1940, as he fled Nazi-occupied France en route to America.) The School returned to Frankfurt in the 1950s under the directorship of Horkheimer and then, in the 1960s, under Adorno. Also associated with the school was Jürgen Habermas, whose rise to prominence at the Institute in the 1960s inaugurated the next phase of critical theory.

As a 'structuralist Marxist' who also wrote on the importance of Freud and Lacan, the French philosopher Louis Althusser has been a pivotal figure in the development of Marxist criticism in recent decades. This is particularly true for Britain, where Althusser served as a conduit between the poststructuralist theories of Lacan and Foucault (a former student) and the British Left. In *For Marx* (1965) and *Lenin and Philosophy* (1971), Althusser mounted a rigorous critique of twentieth-century Western Marxism and advocated a return to the 'true' Marx of his writings. Althusserian Marxism sought to uncover the scientific Marx, de-emphasizing (as a structuralist would) the humanist and historicist

Marx that was chiefly the legacy of Hegel. Since the 1980s, the literary critic Terry Eagleton has been the public face of Marxism in Britain, and he has done much to clarify the application of Marxist theory to literary analysis, both for experts and for general readers. Utilizing Marxist theory, including Gramsci's concept of cultural hegemony, he has read Ireland's colonial history through Irish literature from Swift to Joyce in *Heathcliff and the Great Hunger: Studies in Irish Culture* (1995). Above all, his insistence has been on the fundamental importance of material production to social and cultural forms – this, ultimately, is what separates Marxism from other forms of literary criticism.

Further Reading

Arato, Andrew, and Gebhardt, Eike, eds, *The Essential Frankfurt School Reader* (New York: Continuum, 1997).

Benjamin, Walter, *Illuminations*, ed. Hannah Arendt, trans. Harry Zohn (New York: Harcourt, Brace and World, 1968).

Eagleton, Terry, *Marxism and Literary Criticism* (London and New York: Routledge, 2002).

Eagleton, Terry, and Milne, Drew, eds, *Marxist Literary Theory: A Reader* (Oxford and Malden, MA: Blackwell, 1996).

Jameson, Fredric, *The Political Unconscious* (London: Methuen, 1981).

Lukács, Georg, *The Theory of the Novel* (Cambridge, MA: MIT Press, 1971).

Marx, Karl, and Engels, Friedrich, *The Marx-Engels Reader*, ed. Robert C. Tucker (New York: Norton, 1972).

Trotsky, Leon, *Literature and Revolution*, trans. Rose Strunsky (London: RedWords, 1991).

Williams, Raymond, *Marxism and Literature* (Oxford: Oxford University Press, 1977).

New Criticism

The New Criticism of the American South in the 1930s and 1940s was roughly contemporaneous to and shared many of the concerns of modernist literature. The close attention to language and the emphasis on textual autonomy, on the one hand, and the disregard for biographical, social, or political contexts on the other made New Criticism a natural ally of modernism. Furthermore, the New Criticism was a response to the increasing difficulty and sophisticated irony of modernist writing, and particularly modernist poetry as practised by T. S. Eliot, William Butler Yeats, Ezra Pound, and Archibald MacLeish, whose 'Ars Poetica' (1925) concludes with a classic statement of formalist modernism: 'A poem should not mean/But be.' In other words, poetic language is different from ordinary language, which we expect to convey a message: a poem, on the contrary, expresses nothing but itself. Cleanth Brooks conveyed a similar view when he coined 'the heresy of paraphrase' to suggest that the meaning of a poem was inextricably bound up with its form and could not be summarized or extracted in simpler terms. Building on this idea of a poem not as something that 'does', but as something that 'is', William K. Wimsatt and Monroe C. Beardsley coined the terms 'affective fallacy' and 'intentional fallacy' in the 1940s in two essays bearing these respective titles. The 'affective fallacy' tried to get at a poem's meaning through its psychological effects on the reader, something the New Critics found far too vague and 'impressionistic' (although reader-response criticism has focused on precisely this element). The 'intentional fallacy' warned against using diaries, letters, interviews, and other biographical sources to ascertain an author's intention, conscious or unconscious, in producing a work. Wimsatt and Beardsley considered this approach to be mere guesswork, hopelessly imprecise, and wholly irrelevant and preferred to focus only on the end result, that is, the text itself. Instead, the New Critics focused their talents on discovering wit, irony, paradox, ambiguity, and imagery and described how these poetic elements contributed to the unified structure that was the hallmark of any good poem.

The American poet and critic John Crowe Ransom's volume of essays, *The New Criticism* (1941), gave the tendency a name, but it is better thought of as a broad-based critical approach than as an organized theoretical school or movement. Ransom, along with some of his students at Vanderbilt University in Nashville, Tennessee, notably Allen Tate and Robert Penn Warren, had originally formed a circle called the Fugitives and published a literary magazine, *The Fugitive* (1922–1925). It was here that some of the main tenets of New Criticism first took shape. The work of the English critics I. A. Richards (*Practical Criticism*, 1929) and William Empson (*Seven Types of Ambiguity*, 1930) later became an important contributing influence and were given a chapter in Ransom's titular book. These critics emphasized the 'close reading' favoured by New Criticism and the 'objective' analysis that led to the acceptance of literary criticism as a serious academic discipline. (Empson differed from Brooks, however, on the issue of the acceptable use of paraphrase.) The ideas of the New Critics also bore the mark of modernists like Eliot and Pound, especially in their close attention to poetic form, their classical values, and their interest in the English metaphysical poets. With the modernists, the New Critics sought to protect 'high' culture from the perceived threat of 'mass' culture. As Southern intellectuals, however, they also argued that the separation of culture from society was a product of modern capitalism and that a return to the pre-industrial integration of culture and, say, livelihood was desirable. Their critique of modern industrial America (traditionally associated with the North but also with the New

South) led Tate, Ransom, Warren, and other members of the Fugitives to form a movement called the Agrarians in the late 1920s. They published a manifesto in the form of a book of essays, *I'll Take My Stand* (1930), demonstrating an activist side that has often been omitted from accounts of the New Criticism.

Like F. R. Leavis, the New Critics had a profound impact on literary criticism as a serious profession. Their highly selective tastes helped to shape the twentieth-century American literary canon and the criteria by which great works of literature would be judged. Educational curricula were also significantly affected, particularly at the university level: textbooks like *Understanding Poetry* (1939) and *Understanding Fiction* (1943) by Brooks and Warren guided the way literature was read in American universities for decades to come. Their influence was also felt in the Creative Writing departments that were beginning to appear in the mid-twentieth century and in college-based literary journals like the *Kenyon Review* (where Ransom was founding editor) and the *Sewanee Review*. With the rise of literary theory at the expense of evaluative criticism, however, the New Criticism lost its dominant position in the 1970s, giving way to linguistically based approaches like deconstruction. From the 1980s onwards, New Criticism also came under fire from a range of approaches (Marxist, feminist, psychoanalytic, New Historicist, and cultural materialist) that argued for the importance of extra-literary contexts in literary analysis. Where the New Critic once searched for a poem's unifying metaphor, the idea of unity now seemed hopelessly naïve. A poem like *The Waste Land* would now be studied in its social context or read for its displays of adjection and desire, rather than as a perfectly self-contained unit; and rather than finding ambiguities resolved in an organic whole, the contemporary critic might find only local coherence and unresolved (yet 'productive') tensions. Nevertheless, the methods developed by the New Critics were useful, if limited (they never worked particularly well with longer texts or non-literary ones): particularly in reading modernist poetry, for which their tools were purpose-built.

Further Reading

Brooks, Cleanth, *The Well Wrought Urn: Studies in the Structure of Poetry* (New York: Harcourt, Brace, 1947).

Jancovich, Mark, *The Cultural Politics of the New Criticism* (Cambridge and New York: Cambridge University Press, 1993).

Ransom, John Crowe, *The New Criticism* (Norfolk, CT: New Directions, 1941).

Wimsatt, William K., *The Verbal Icon: Studies in the Meaning of Poetry* (Lexington: University of Kentucky Press, 1954).

Postcolonialism

As a theoretical position concerned with the history of imperialism and the impact of colonial rule, postcolonialism has developed alongside other areas of cultural studies since the 1970s. Like feminism, postcolonial criticism has led to a diversified literary canon and raised questions about canon formation and the 'classics' of Western literature. One of the most significant controversies of the emergent postcolonial criticism was the debate over Joseph Conrad's *Heart of Darkness* (1902) that began in the 1970s and remains contentious to this day. In 1975, the Nigerian writer Chinua Achebe gave a lecture, entitled, 'An Image of Africa: Racism in Conrad's *Heart of Darkness*', charging that 'Conrad was a bloody racist' and declaring that the 'offensive and totally deplorable book' should not be categorized as a great work of literature. A few years later, a former Conrad scholar, Edward Said, published one of the founding texts of postcolonial theory, *Orientalism* (1978). Drawing, as many postcolonialist critics have since, on Jacques Derrida's deconstructionist critique of Western logocentrism and binary oppositions like 'west/east', *Orientalism* lays bare the Western view of the Orient and Islam as it has been constructed in literary and other texts, and as this image has changed in the past two centuries. Central to Said's thesis, which also draws on Michel Foucault, is the idea that the 'Orient' is a construct of Western discourse that has served to authorize the imperial domination of the oriental 'other' by Europe and America. Contributing to this image of the 'other', according to Said, are stereotypes of, for example, the Orient as static and incapable of progress, the oriental woman as sexually exotic, and so on. Said attempts to deconstruct this image and unsettle the binaries of 'self/other', 'presence/absence', and 'light/dark' and to challenge received notions of Western liberalism and progress.

Another pioneer of postcolonial theory is the Bengali critic Gayatri Spivak, who draws on a range of Marxist, feminist, and other approaches in her writings and interviews. A student of the Yale deconstructionist Paul de Man, Spivak translated and wrote a preface to Derrida's *Of Grammatology* in 1977 and helped to import the terms of deconstructionist critique into a postcolonial framework. The 'subaltern' identified in her most famous essay, 'Can the Subaltern Speak?' (1985), is a term borrowed from the Italian Marxist critic Antonio Gramsci. Gramsci appropriated it from military terminology, where it refers to a person of inferior rank, and applied it to the underclass in society. In postcolonial criticism, and particularly 'subaltern studies' (also the name of a series of essays edited by Ranajit Guha), it refers to people on the margins of society, specifically South Asian society, who are 'subordinate' in some way, whether in terms of class, caste, or gender. Homi K.

Bhabha, another Indian-born critic, is known for his writings on nation-hood, colonial discourse and the 'other', and 'mimicry'. This last concept, outlined in 'Of Mimicry and Man: The Ambivalence of Colonial Dis-course' (1984), describes the behaviour of colonial subjects who are forced to abandon their native culture and learn instead to 'mimic' the culture of the colonizer. Another possible step in this process, according to Bhabha, is 'hybridity', in which colonization and migration unsettle the apparently stable boundaries of language and cultural and racial identity, opening up a 'Third Space' and causing new 'hybrid' identities to form.

The historical connection between modernism and imperialism is a complex and important one. The second major phase of colonial expan-sion began in the Victorian period and ended with the start of the First World War; in terms of sheer size, the British Empire reached its peak in 1920, at the height of modernism. However, the end of the First World War also marked the beginning of the end of European imperialism: at the Treaty of Versailles in 1919, the United States introduced self-determination as a major concern. Following World War II, the event traditionally seen as marking the end of modernism, a wave of decolo-nization quickly spread through Africa, Asia, and Latin America, resulting in the independence of most former colonies of Britain, France, Belgium, and other European countries. Coinciding with these events, the decades that followed also saw publication of many key texts of postcolonial liter-ature and theory, including Achebe's *Things Fall Apart* (1958), with its title drawn from a line in Yeats's 'The Second Coming' (1920); Franz Fanon's *Black Skin, White Masks* (1950) and *The Wretched of the Earth* (1961); and Ngũgĩ wa Thiong'o's *A Grain of Wheat* (1967), set during the struggle for independence in Kenya. Earlier, in the 1930s, students and writers from francophone colonies in Africa and the West Indies like Léopold Senghor (Senegal) and Aimé Césaire (Martinique) started the *négritude* movement in Paris, co-opting and embracing negative stereotypes of the bodily and the sensual and promoting a sense of solidarity and pride in African her-itage and culture. The movement drew inspiration from the writers and activists of the Harlem Renaissance in New York, and in the postwar period Fanon and others gave the theory of *négritude* relevance for a new generation.

Further Reading

Ashcroft, Bill, Griffiths, Gareth, and Tiffin, Helen, *The Empire Writes Back: Theory and Practice in Postcolonial Literatures* (London and New York: Routledge, 1989).
Attridge, Derek, and Howes, Marjorie, eds, *Semicolonial Joyce* (Cambridge and New York: Cambridge University Press, 2000).

Bhabha, Homi K., *The Location of Culture* (London and New York: Routledge, 1994).

Booth, Howard J., and Rigby, Nigel, eds, *Modernism and Empire* (Manchester and New York: Manchester University Press, 2000).

Cheng, Vincent, *Joyce, Race, and Empire* (Cambridge and New York: Cambridge University Press, 1995).

Said, Edward, *Culture and Imperialism* (London: Chatto and Windus, 1993).

————, *Orientalism* (London and New York: Routledge, 1978).

Spivak, Gayatri Chakravorty, *A Critique of Postcolonial Reason* (London and Cambridge, MA: Harvard University Press, 1999).

Postmodernism

In 1986, when postmodernism was still regarded as a fairly radical concept, Andreas Huyssen described the shift from modernism to post-modernism in his book *After the Great Divide*, which remains one of the clearest summaries of the postmodernist position. According to Huyssen, modernism's 'adversary culture' had fossilized over time, and 'the high modernist dogma ha[d] become sterile'. Just as modernism sought to supplant outdated Victorian modes with new forms of expression in the early twentieth century, postmodernism – a term that gained currency in literary discussions in the 1960s – found the modernist outlook unsuited to 'current cultural phenomena'. In particular, Anglo-American modernism's rigid dichotomy of 'high' and 'low' culture was regarded as obsolete and was being challenged by critical trends from deconstruction to cultural materialism and New Historicism. Charges of racism, sexism, and elitism began to plague the modernist legacy, but more generally it was their seriousness, their Romantic belief in the importance of the artist ('the antennae of the race', in Pound's words), that appeared rather old fashioned in the era of postmodern playfulness. As culture moves forward, Huyssen argued, modernism 'is being replaced by a new paradigm ... which is itself as diverse and multifaceted as modernism had once been'. Futurism had predicted in 1909 that before long 'younger and stronger men will probably throw us in the wastebasket like useless manuscripts – we want it to happen!' Postmodernism effectively consigned modernism to history, but whether it is a distinct movement or simply a late phase is still open to debate.

Theories of postmodernism often depict the new postmodern aesthetic in stark contrast to the old modernism. Characteristics of modernism are commonly said to include an emphasis on inward consciousness and perception, rather than external 'reality'; departures from stable and unified forms in the use of fragmented narrative and collage; a high degree of self-consciousness about the status of the work of art, in particular how it is constructed and consumed; and an interest, often laced with scepticism, in technology and time. As a departure from modernism, postmodernism is said to emphasize space over time, and copies (or 'simulacra') over valuable originals. (For example, the luxury-signed first edition of Joyce's *Ulysses* attempts to retain the 'aura' of authenticity in a way that the assembly line silk-screens and Brillo boxes of Andy Warhol do not.) Postmodernism also privileges play, parody, and pastiche over serious purpose and blurs or erases genre distinctions and high/low boundaries. Even where there is crossover between the two categories, the crucial difference is said to be attitude: modernism mourns the loss of unity and meaning even while it chronicles their collapse, while postmodernism celebrates the new anti-humanist vision of a de-centred, destabilized, and disorderly universe, made up of small stories and local meaning rather than master narratives and universal truths.

This binary opposition between modernism and postmodernism is itself a construct, however, and one that can be challenged on many levels. Increasingly, as postmodernism too becomes a chapter of history, it is viewed not as modernism's opposite but as an extension or development of modernism that builds on advances that took place in the first half of the twentieth century. If some texts seem to adhere particularly well to the 'modernist' side of the binary – T. S. Eliot's *The Waste Land* (1922), for example, read as mourning the loss of cultural meaning and coherence ('These fragments I have shored against my ruins') – others do not. Where does the latter half of *Ulysses* (1922) fit in, with its catalogue of styles (journalistic, epic, legal, scientific), not to mention the extremely slippery *Finnegans Wake* (1939), both texts that inspired Jacques Derrida and other poststructuralists? What about Marcel Duchamp's 'readymades', like the urinal-turned-sculpture, *Fountain* (1917)? Why should the provocations of dada or the play-filled language experiments of Gertrude Stein be read as modernist rather than postmodernist? At the same time, modernism itself is increasingly viewed by scholars as a range of innovations influenced by and responding to the changes wrought by modernity, rather than as a coherent movement – the modernism of Eliot, Pound, Yeats, Woolf, and Joyce – that could be superseded by an equally monolithic postmodernism.

What we have been discussing so far are modernism and postmodernism as aesthetic categories. But there is another very different distinction to be made: the distinction between the social conditions of modernity and postmodernity. Modernity is defined at the beginning of this book as being older, broader in scope, and quite different from, or even opposed to, the values and tendencies of modernism. It corresponds in many ways to a humanistic or Enlightenment view of the world: the facts of the world are knowable and can be apprehended through objective, rational science; the self is a knowable, stable, and coherent entity, and so on. Modernism witnessed the decline of this worldview in the first half of the twentieth century. Postmodernity, by contrast, replaces universal truths and grand narratives with meaning that is partial, contingent, temporary, and relative: 'this is my truth, tell me yours'. Moreover, it represents a critique of the universalizing tendency, the desire to impose a grand narrative or 'metanarrative' (to use a term favoured by the postmodernist philosopher Jean-François Lyotard), bringing artificial order where there is diversity, contradiction, and instability. Examples of grand narratives include the concepts of universal freedom or historical progress, or the belief that science has the power to explain everything. Metafiction, the style favoured by postmodernism, constantly reminds us that what we are reading is fiction, dispelling the illusory effect of traditional storytelling. The opposition between modernity and postmodernity seems to hold up better than any clear aesthetic distinction between modernism and postmodernism. Evidence for this can be found in the work of Lyotard himself. He draws mainly on examples from the modernist period – *Ulysses* in particular, as a wildly playful and (inter)textual departure from the Victorian realist novel – to illustrate his theories. Metafiction was, of course, also a feature of modernist art and literature. The key distinction made by postmodernist theorists, however, is that postmodernism neither laments the loss of coherence and meaning nor does it put its faith in art as a 'new religion'.

Further Reading

Foster, Hal, ed., *The Anti-Aesthetic: Essays on Postmodern Culture* (New York: The New Press, 2002).

Jameson, Fredric, *Postmodernism, or The Cultural Logic of Late Capitalism* (London: Verso, 1991).

Lyotard, Jean-François, *The Postmodern Condition: A Report on Knowledge*, trans. Geoff Bennington and Brian Massumi (Manchester: Manchester University Press, 1979).

Poststructuralism

Considering how often the term 'poststructuralism' is heard in English departments these days, it may be surprising to learn just how loose and ambiguous this term actually is. Then again, since challenging apparently stable and commonsense meanings is the *raison d'être* of poststructuralist critical practice, one can hardly expect a straightforward definition. Bearing in mind this caveat, it is possible to identify some of the main concepts and practices referred to by the term. First and foremost, poststructuralism represents a critique of structuralism that is performed using the vocabulary developed by structuralists like Ferdinand de Saussure and Claude Lévi-Strauss. Jacques Derrida argued in his landmark essay 'Structure, Sign and Play in the Discourse of the Human Sciences' (1966) that structures always posit a 'centre'. 'The function of this centre', Derrida wrote (or spoke, since it was first delivered as a lecture), was to 'limit what we might call the *play* of the structure. By orienting and organizing the coherence of the system, the centre of a structure permits the play of its elements inside the total form' (Derrida, 1978, pp. 278–79). As attractive as this model might be, Derrida argued that it is also invalid; its coherence, its permanence, and truth, are illusory, being based on an appeal to an authority that being godlike (or indeed, God) is unverifiable. The authority that validates the system or structure is also external and not central at all. 'The center is not the center', as Derrida famously stated. Poststructuralists working after Derrida have continued to question the structuralist model, seeking not to 'discover' universal structures in the world but instead to 'deconstruct' systems of meaning of all kinds by demonstrating their instability, artificiality, and contradictory nature. Furthermore, building not only on Derrida but on the writings of another pioneering figure, Michel Foucault, poststructuralism presents a challenge to the seemingly unquestionable 'natural' or absolute authority of systems. This challenge, moreover, forms a central part of the Marxist and feminist varieties of poststructuralism.

Related to the anti-foundationist, anti-universalizing tendency is another important aspect of poststructuralism – the emphasis on language. Like structuralism, poststructuralism views consciousness more as the product than the origin of language. Language, a repository of meaning, teaches us how to view the world; we then reinforce and reproduce meanings through our use of language. The word 'wife', for example, suggests more than the simplest meaning of a 'married woman'; it also carries connotations of dependence, domesticity, and so on. But poststructuralists also believe in the possibility, to some degree, of actively changing meaning through language so that if we use the term 'partner' rather than 'wife', we might alter, however slightly, the perception of the role that person plays. 'Politically correct' language has come in for a lot of criticism over the past few decades, but many would agree that by consciously replacing (or, in some cases, rehabilitating) previously commonplace yet discriminatory words like 'queer' we move some way towards actually changing norms in our society: raising standards of equality, for example. If language is constantly evolving, not least through the coining of neologisms in literature, then why not take an active part in its development, especially if we believe (as post-structuralists do) that language directly influences our relationships with other people and the world?

Another key tenet of poststructuralist theory, borrowed directly from Saussure, is that, in Catherine Belsey's words, 'meaning is differential, not referential' (Belsey, 2002, p. 10). Belsey uses the example of 'modern' as a term denoting a particular timespan: there is no one meaning of 'modern', only many instances of its use in different contexts – modern architecture, modern languages, modern civilization. Each usage suggests a different timespan and timeframe, and in each case the meaning is not positive but negative, defined by difference – 'not medieval', for example. Difference in poststructuralism, however, is taken from its original linguistic context and applied to non-linguistic phenomena. For example, an investigation of power is at the heart of all of Foucault's works, whether they treat power relations in sexuality, discipline, medicine, or madness. Power, however, only has meaning through difference, and in this case resistance is the corollary that gives power meaning.

Roland Barthes, another key figure of poststructuralism, made his reputation with a collection of short essays on culture titled *Mythologies* (1957). These essays, originally published as journalistic pieces, put into practice Saussure's idea for a 'science of semiology', described in his *Course in General Linguistics* (1913). Semiology or 'semiotics' (the two are more or less interchangeable) is the study of signs; in *Mythologies*, Barthes draws examples of signifying practices from a wide range of cultural activities, from advertising to professional wrestling. In other words, linguistic theory is used to analyse sign systems apart from language. *Mythologies* laid the groundwork for the discipline of Media Studies and represented an important step forward in the application of theory to the analysis of popular culture. This was still, arguably, within the realm of structuralism; or, if it was less intent on finding universal truths, it was at least still heavily dependent upon the structuralist methods of Saussure and Claude Lévi-Strauss. More than a decade later, however, with the extremely close reading of Honoré de Balzac's short story 'Sarrasine' in *S/Z* (1970), Barthes truly moved beyond the universal claims of structuralism to an acceptance that meaning was more likely to be transitory, arbitrary, and local. It was also in this book that Barthes introduced his influential distinction between two types of texts – 'readerly' (*lisible*) and 'writerly' (*scriptible*, a neologism coined by Barthes). A 'readerly' text is the traditional sort of storytelling: it obscures its own machinery and limits the possibilities of meaning to the narrowly conventional. It is essentially a product to be consumed by the reader, without prompting undue thought on the reader's part. A 'writerly' text, in contrast, is full of subversive possibilities, an open site for the production of meaning by the reader. Modernist texts are virtually by definition the 'writerly' kind – they are highly indeterminate and consciously difficult, challenging conventions of plot and characterization and inviting multiple, even contradictory readings. (Think of Joyce's *Finnegans Wake*.)

Two years earlier, Barthes had published another famous essay on literature, 'The Death of the Author' (1968). Barthes saw writing not as a manifestation of authorial intent, but as precisely the opposite: 'writing is the destruction of every voice, of every point of origin ... [the] space where our subject slips away'. The modernist doctrine of impersonality, articulated most clearly by T. S. Eliot, but also by Joyce and Pound, anticipates Barthes's theory. For Barthes, the author does not control meaning; meaning, through language, controls the author. 'The text is a tissue of quotations drawn from the innumerable centres of culture ... the book itself is only a tissue of signs.' Rather than seeing the author as the beginning and the end of meaning, Barthes transfers the origin of meaning to the reader: 'a text's unity lies not in its origin but in its destination'. But the reader is an ideal reader, 'without history, biography, psychology'. That this essay was published in the revolutionary year 1968 is not a coincidence: Barthes gives his theory a social and political dimension, even closing the essay with a call to arms: 'To give writing its future, it is necessary to overthrow the myth: the birth of the reader must be at the cost of the death of the Author.'

Further Reading

Attridge, Derek and Ferrer, Daniel, eds, *Post-Structuralist Joyce: Essays from the French* (Cambridge and New York: Cambridge University Press, 1984).

Barthes, Roland, *Image-Music-Text*, trans. Stephen Heath (New York: Hill and Wang, 1978).

Belsey, Catherine, *Poststructuralism: A Very Short Introduction* (Oxford and New York: Oxford University Press, 2002).

Foucault, Michel, *The Foucault Reader*, ed. Paul Rabinow (London and New York: Penguin, 1991).

Psychoanalytic Criticism

To start at the beginning, in the psychoanalytic fashion, is to start with Sigmund Freud. Freud is the point of origin for all psychoanalytic theory, a body of theory that can scarcely be summarized in a few paragraphs, even in its immediate relation to literature. Nevertheless, some key points of orientation will be helpful. The first point to keep in mind is that psychoanalysis involves a kind of close reading – though not the kind practised by the New Critics. Freudian analysis places great emphasis on language – slips of the tongue, for example. One route to the unconscious, that vast treasure trove of repressed desires that is inaccessible to the conscious mind, is through verbal slips ('parapraxes'). Another is through jokes, as Freud explained in *Jokes and Their Relation to the Unconscious* (1905), including one of James Joyce's favourite varieties, the pun. Parapraxes and puns act as outlets for our repressed wishes, which usually relate to sex. Another route to the unconscious is through dreams. These are 'read' as texts by the analyst, again for what they say about our repressed wishes and fantasies. (The purpose of psychoanalysis, in one sense, is to cure the patient's neurotic disorders by discovering where their intellectual development from childhood to adulthood has gone wrong. This has a lot to do with the desires we force into our unconscious.) To read dreams, one must be familiar with their two most common guises, as outlined in *The Interpretation of Dreams* (1900): 'condensation' and 'displacement'. Like metaphor, condensation uses a single image to express a complex idea or set of ideas or to act as the meeting point for various associations. Displacement works by a kind of substitution or metonymy (usually, naming the part for the whole) to use the linguistic equivalent (as Jacques Lacan does). If an image is too painful, for example, it will appear instead as an associated image, which then displaces the original. Condensation and displacement also figure in other manifestations of the unconscious, such as jokes.

Lacan, a French psychiatrist who merged Freudian psychoanalysis with the structuralism of Saussure and Lévi-Strauss, is the other major figure for psychoanalytic criticism. He departed from Freud in his insistence, which was important for later poststructuralist theories, that the self – Freud's 'ego' – is entirely illusory, a construct of the unconscious. Freud's theories had started to undermine the stability of the self, but Lacan travelled much further along this path, questioning the reality of the 'I'. Under Saussure's influence, Lacan also came to see the unconscious as being structured like a language, with its signifiers in a constant state of what Derrida would call 'play'. To become an adult with a sense of self is to limit the amount of play and to impose a kind of stability – albeit an artificial one – on meaning. Like Freud, Lacan places great emphasis on the first years of life: he calls the initial stage of the inseparable infant and mother the state of 'nature' or the Real. Next is the 'mirror stage' or the Imaginary, where the child sees itself in a mirror and develops a sense of self as 'other', as something whole and external – an error, argues Lacan, that remains with us into adulthood. Our idea of ourselves is really the image of the other, the image in the mirror; self *is* other, through mistaken identification. The next stage, where true separation occurs and language intrudes, is the entrance into the realm of the Symbolic. When we begin to use language, and to call ourselves 'I', we enter into the Symbolic – which is, in essence, the structure of language. Lacan, like Freud, views this order as a patriarchal one, and calls it the Law of the Father. The centre of this system is the Other, also called the Phallus (after Freud's Oedipal theory). We want to be the centre, to merge with it, but our existence in language, in the Symbolic, is built on our desire, or Lack, and the centre is thus unattainable.

It will be useful at this point, given the difficulty of these concepts, to provide a sense of what psychological criticism in general looks like. One approach, for example, might borrow from 'reader-response' theory to focus on the psychological effects a text has on the reader. Or the critic might treat the characters in a novel as real people and analyze their underlying motivations and hidden desires, as manifested through their behaviour. Or the text itself could be said to have an unconscious, and the condensations and displacements of a text could be read much as a therapist reads the symbolism of dreams. In his essay 'Creative Writers and Daydreaming' (1908), Freud views fiction as a kind of dreaming. This opens up the possibility of analyzing the author through his or her work, as if the whole text was a manifestation of the author's unconscious. Joyce might be read in terms of the preoccupation with bodily processes in *Ulysses* (1922), or the endless punning and evasive, constantly shifting wordplay in *Finnegans Wake* (1939). Joyce would have been interested, at least, in such approaches: as rough contemporaries of Freud and Carl Jung, many of the modernists followed the development of psychoanalysis closely. The imagist poet H. D., for example, was in therapy with Freud himself and later wrote about her experiences in a memoir and diary, published together as *Tribute to Freud* (1956). Freud's links with Bloomsbury and the Hogarth Press, and D. H. Lawrence's two books on psychoanalysis are discussed elsewhere in this book, as is Jung's treatment of Joyce's daughter, Lucia. Lacan was deeply interested in Joyce's later works; the explorations of the unconscious in the 'Circe' and 'Penelope' episodes of *Ulysses* in particular have attracted much interest from psychoanalytic criticism. In recent decades, Lacanian psychoanalysis has been extended by poststructuralist feminist critics like Julia Kristeva, and in the writings of the Slovenian philosopher (and former presidential candidate) Slavoj Žižek, who has read a wide array of cultural phenomena, from Hitchcock to the American-led occupation of Iraq (in *Welcome to the Desert of the Real!*, 2002), through Lacanian theory.

Further Reading

Brivic, Sheldon, *Joyce Through Lacan and Žižek* (Basingstoke and New York: Palgrave Macmillan, 2008).

Freud, Sigmund, *The Freud Reader*, ed. Peter Gay (New York: W. W. Norton, 1995).

Lacan, Jacques, *Écrits: A Selection*, trans. Alan Sheridan (London: Tavistock, 1977).

Žižek, Slavoj, *The Žižek Reader*, eds Elizabeth Wright and Edmond Wright (Oxford and Malden, MA: Blackwell, 1999).

Structuralism

Saussure's contribution to twentieth-century structuralist and poststructuralist theory (which covers much of what goes on in English departments today) has been immense. His *Course in General Linguistics* (1913), a posthumous record of his lectures at the University of Geneva between 1906 and 1911, as reconstructed by his students, is the central text of structuralist linguistics. Saussure's idea of 'sign' and 'signified', his theory about the 'arbitrary nature of the sign', and his claim that language is a closed system in which terms gain their value by their difference from other words, have all been of crucial importance to later theorists like Jacques Derrida and Jacques Lacan. It was Derrida's groundbreaking work *Of Grammatology* (1967), in fact, that deconstructed Saussurean linguistics and delivered a fatal blow to structuralism – but even in their departure from Saussure, Derrida and others use his terms as their frame of reference, much as cultural materialists might use Marxist terms while breaking away from orthodox Marxist theory. One example is the system of binary opposites described by the structuralist anthropologist Claude Lévi-Strauss (for example in *The Raw and the Cooked*, 1969) as underlying the way all human cultures perceive the world. While Derrida drew attention to the potential instability of such binary systems (they could be inverted, for example), the very idea of the existence of such systems was crucial to his arguments: as Derrida himself would admit, it is impossible to speak outside the system.

The structuralist approach is all about breaking things down into their basic elements. Just as a scientist might study the molecules and atoms that make up matter, so the structuralist linguist will try to find the building blocks of a language. The structuralist anthropologist will seek to discover the primary elements of a culture, and the structuralist literary critic will look for the basic units of a text. In fact, the literary critic working within a structuralist framework will inevitably begin with the structure of a language – phonemes, words, grammar, and so on. Or he or she might look more generally at narrative structures – how, for example, they are similar in folktales from different parts of the world. It should already be apparent that structuralism is to a great extent about finding universal patterns, things in common – between cultures or literary texts. This aspect of structuralism is at odds with later poststructuralist theories that question the universality and stability of systems. But this objective, 'scientific' approach represented an important departure from the wholly subjective criticism that preceded it. Saussurean linguistics is based on a key distinction of two terms – *langue* and *parole*. *Langue* is the overall system of a language, while *parole* is the 'actual' spoken and written language – the 'rules', on the one hand, and the 'behaviour' on the other. Structuralism, as might be guessed, is more interested in the *langue*, the system.

Saussure viewed language as a system of signs, and called the study of this system 'semiology' ('semiotics' is another term denoting the general science of signs). A sign, according to Saussure, comprises two parts – 'signifier' and 'signified'. The first is the 'form' a sign takes, and the second is the 'concept' or 'meaning' it is meant to suggest. For example, there is the English sound-image 'bicycle', and then there is the concept 'bicycle' that this signifier should evoke. The relationship between signifier and signified, according to Saussure, is arbitrary, and it works by a negative rather than a positive connection. A word signifies something not because of an inherent or 'natural' link but because of a negative one: it does *not* mean something else. The system works by contrast or difference. Jonathan Culler provides the following explanation by example: 'the letter *b* may be written in any number of different ways (think of different people's handwriting), so long as it is not confused with other letters, such as *l*, *k*, and *d*. What is crucial is not any particular form or content, but differences, which enable it to signify.' The arbitrary nature of language is demonstrated by the range of words in different languages for a given concept. Even onomatopoeic words, which might seem closer to the thing they describe, vary between languages and cultures: an American rooster says 'cock-a-doodle-do', for example, while a Spanish rooster says *quiquiriquí*. Importantly, for Saussure and much theory since, language does not refer to an inherent, ideal, pre-existing, or external reality but actually shapes or structures our view of reality. In this sense, literature that reinvents language or pushes the meaning of words – as modernist literature so often does – can also challenge our ways of seeing the world.

Further Reading

Barthes, Roland, *Mythologies*, trans. Annette Lavers (New York: Hill and Wang, 1973).

Culler, Jonathan, *Structuralist Poetics: Structuralism, Linguistics and the Study of Literature* (Ithaca, NY: Cornell University Press, 1976).

Saussure, Ferdinand de, *Course in General Linguistics*, trans. Wade Baskin (New York and London: McGraw-Hill, 1966).

Chronology

1890   The Rhymers' Club founded
The Kelmscott Press founded by William Morris
James McNeill Whistler, *The Gentle Art of Making Enemies*
James George Frazer, first two volumes of *The Golden Bough*
(1890–1915)
William James, *Principles of Psychology*
Henrik Ibsen, *Hedda Gabler*
Knut Hamsun, *Hunger*

1891   Paul Gauguin visits Tahiti
George Gissing, *New Grub Street*
Oscar Wilde, *The Picture of Dorian Gray* and *Intentions*
Thomas Hardy, *Tess of the D'Urbervilles*

1892   Walt Whitman dies
Max Nordau, *Degeneration*
Rudyard Kipling, *Barrack Room Ballads*
George Bernard Shaw, *Mrs Warren's Profession*

1893   William Butler Yeats, *The Celtic Twilight*
George Egerton, *Keynotes*

1894   Alfred Dreyfus arrested for treason in France
Demise of the 'three-decker' novel
Yellow Book launched
Walter Pater dies
Sarah Grand, *The Heavenly Twins* and 'The New Aspect of the
Woman Question'
Kipling, *The Jungle Book*

1895   Wilhelm Roentgen discovers X-rays
Guglielmo Marconi invents telegraphy
Trials of Oscar Wilde
Wilde, *The Importance of Being Earnest*
Hardy, *Jude the Obscure*

1896   *Daily Mail* begins circulation in London
Savoy magazine founded by Arthur Symons and others
William Morris dies
A. E. Housman, *A Shropshire Lad*
Alfred Jarry, *Ubu Roi*

1897   Queen Victoria's Diamond Jubilee
Giacomo Puccini, *La Bohème* (opera)
Anton Chekhov, *Uncle Vanya*

H. G. Wells, *The Invisible Man*
Joseph Conrad, *The Nigger of the Narcissus*
Stéphane Mallarmé, *Un coup de dés*

1898   The Curies discover radium
Mallarmé dies
Hardy, *Wessex Poems*
Wells, *War of the Worlds*
Wilde, *Ballad of Reading Gaol*

1899   Boer War begins (1899–1902)
Henry James, *The Awkward Age*
Symons, *The Symbolist Movement in Literature*
Yeats, *The Wind Among the Reeds*

1900   British Labour Party founded
Wilde dies
Friedrich Nietzsche dies
Henri Bergson, *Laughter*
Sigmund Freud, *The Interpretation of Dreams*
Conrad, *Lord Jim*

1901   Queen Victoria dies, Edward VII accedes
US President McKinley assassinated, Theodor Roosevelt
takes over
First Nobel Prize for Literature awarded to Sully Prudhomme
Thomas Mann, *Buddenbrooks*
August Strindberg, *Dance of Death*

1902   Émile Zola dies
Vladimir Lenin, *What is to Be Done?*
Conrad, *Heart of Darkness*
André Gide, *The Immoralist*
Henry James, *The Wings of the Dove*
William James, *Varieties of Religious Experience*
Yeats, *Cathleen Ni Houlihan*

1903   Women's Social and Political Union founded by
Emmeline Pankhurst
First successful flight by the Wright brothers
Daily Mirror launched
Whistler dies
W. E. B. DuBois, *The Souls of Black Folk*
Henry James, *The Ambassadors*
G. E. Moore, *Principia Ethica*
Shaw, *Man and Superman*

1904   Entente cordiale between Britain and France
Abbey Theatre opens in Dublin
Conrad, *Nostromo*
James, *The Golden Bowl*
John Millington Synge, *Riders to the Sea*

1905   Albert Einstein announces special theory of relativity
Sinn Fein founded by Arthur Griffith

Shaw, *Major Barbara*
Wilde, *De Profundis*
Edith Wharton, *The House of Mirth*

1906   Dreyfus exonerated in France
Paul Cézanne dies
Ibsen dies
Upton Sinclair, *The Jungle*

1907   Kipling wins Nobel Prize
Pablo Picasso, *Les Demoiselles d'Avignon* (painting)
Conrad, *The Secret Agent*
James Joyce, *Chamber Music*
Shaw, *John Bull's Other Island*
Synge, *The Playboy of the Western World*
Bergson, *Creative Evolution*
Henry Adams, *The Education of Henry Adams*

1908   Herbert Asquith becomes Prime Minister
Pablo Picasso and Georges Braque begin cubism in painting
English Review founded by Ford Madox Hueffer
Gertrude Stein, *Three Lives*
Georges Sorel, *Reflections on Violence*
E. M. Forster, *A Room with a View*
Wilhelm Worringer, *Abstraction and Empathy*

1909   Freud lectures on psychoanalysis in America
National Association for the Advancement of Colored
People (NAACP) founded
Algernon Swinburne dies
Henri Matisse, *The Dance* (painting)
Gustav Mahler, *Symphony No. 9*
Filippo Tommaso Marinetti, 'The Founding and
Manifesto of Futurism'
Ezra Pound, *Personae*

1910   Edward VII dies, George V accedes
Mark Twain dies
First post-impressionist exhibition, London
Marinetti delivers his 'Futurist Speech to the English',
London
Igor Stravinsky, *The Firebird* (ballet)
Forster, *Howards End*
Pound, *The Spirit of Romance*
Yeats, *The Green Helmet*

1911   Der Blaue Reiter group formed in Munich
Rhythm magazine founded by J. M. Murry and others
D. H. Lawrence, *The White Peacock*
T. E. Hulme, 'Romanticism and Classicism'
Conrad, *Under Western Eyes*
Pound, *Canzoni*
Gertrude Colmore, *Suffragette Sally*

1912   Sinking of the *Titanic*
Second Post-Impressionist exhibition, London
Futurist exhibition, Paris
Poetry magazine founded, Chicago
Max Stirner, *The Ego and His Own* (1844), published in English
Marcel Duchamp, *Nude Descending a Staircase* (painting)
Pound, *Ripostes*
Carl Jung, *Psychology of the Unconscious*

1913   Woodrow Wilson becomes US President
The Armory Show, New York
Roger Fry founds Omega Workshops, London
Rabindranath Tagore awarded Nobel Prize for Literature
Igor Stravinsky, *The Rite of Spring* (ballet)
Ferdinand de Saussure, *Course in General Linguistics*
Edmund Husserl, *Phenomenology*
Freud, *Totem and Taboo*
Marcel Proust, *Swann's Way* (first volume of *In Search of Lost Time*, 1913–1927)
Lawrence, *Sons and Lovers*
Mann, *Death in Venice*

1914   Archduke Franz Ferdinand assassinated in Sarajevo
First World War begins
Wilson pledges US neutrality
Egoist (formerly the *New Freewoman*), *Blast*, and *Little Review* founded
Clive Bell, *Art*
Joyce, *Dubliners*
Lawrence, *The Prussian Officer and Other Stories*
Pound (ed.), *Des Imagistes*
Stein, *Tender Buttons*
Yeats, *Responsibilities*

1915   First transcontinental telephone call, New York to San Francisco
Sinking of the *Lusitania*
Henri Gaudier-Brzeska dies
Rupert Brooke dies
D. W. Griffith, *Birth of a Nation* (film)
Lawrence, *The Rainbow*
Ford Madox Ford, *The Good Soldier*
Dorothy Richardson, *Pointed Roofs* (first volume of *Pilgrimage*, 1915–1967)
Virginia Woolf, *The Voyage Out*

1916   Easter Rising in Dublin
Asquith resigns, Lloyd George becomes Prime Minister
First Dada performances at the Cabaret Voltaire, Zurich
Henry James dies
Joyce, *A Portrait of the Artist as a Young Man*

Pound, *Lustra* and *Gaudier-Brzeska: A Memoir*
Apollinaire, *Le Poète Assassiné*
Henri Barbusse, *Le Feu*
Georg Lukács, *Theory of the Novel*

1917   Bolshevik Revolution in Russia
T. E. Hulme dies
US enters the war
Marcel Duchamp, *Fountain*
T. S. Eliot, *Prufrock and Other Observations*
Yeats, *The Wild Swans at Coole*

1918   First World War ends
Franchise Act grants vote to women over 30
Apollinaire dies
Tristan Tzara, *Dada Manifesto 1918*
Gerard Manley Hopkins, *Poems* (posthumous)
Joyce, *Exiles*; *Ulysses* begins serialization
Lawrence, *New Poems*
Wyndham Lewis, *Tarr*
Lytton Strachey, *Eminent Victorians*
Oswald Spengler, *The Decline of the West* (1918–1922)
Willa Cather, *My Ántonia*

1919   Treaty of Versailles
Weimar Republic established
Bauhaus founded in Weimar
John Maynard Keynes, *The Economic Consequences
of the Peace*
Eliot, 'Tradition and the Individual Talent'
Claude McKay, 'If We Must Die'
Sherwood Anderson, *Winesburg, Ohio*
Woolf, *Night and Day*
Yeats, *Two Plays for Dancers*

1920   Prohibition in America
Women granted right to vote in US
First meeting of the League of Nations
Dial magazine founded
Roger Fry, *Vision and Design*
Freud, *Beyond the Pleasure Principle*
Eliot, *Poems* and *The Sacred Wood*
Katherine Mansfield, *Bliss and Other Stories*
Pound, *Hugh Selwyn Mauberley*
William Carlos Williams, *Kora in Hell*
Jessie Weston, *From Ritual to Romance*

1921   First trial of Joyce's *Ulysses* (based on serialization)
Shuffle Along jazz revue comes to Broadway
Irish Independence
Aldous Huxley, *Crome Yellow*
Lawrence, *Women in Love* and *Sea and Sardinia*
H. L. Mencken, *Prejudices*

André Breton, *The Magnetic Fields*
Luigi Pirandello, *Six Characters in Search of an Author*
Yeats, *Michael Robartes and the Dancer*

1922   Benito Mussolini's march on Rome
Irish Free State established, civil war breaks out (1922–1923)
British Broadcasting Corporation founded
Criterion magazine founded
Proust dies
Eliot, *The Waste Land*
Joyce, *Ulysses*
Woolf, *Jacob's Room*
McKay, *Harlem Shadows*
Lawrence, *Aaron's Rod* and *England, My England* (US)
Edith Sitwell, *Façade*
E. E. Cummings, *The Enormous Room*
F. Scott Fitzgerald, *Tales of the Jazz Age*
Bronislaw Malinowski, *Argonauts of the Western Pacific*
Ludwig Wittgenstein, *Tractatus Logico-Philosophicus*

1923   USSR founded
Stanley Baldwin elected British Prime Minister
Yeats wins Nobel Prize
Katherine Mansfield dies
Mary Butts, *Speed the Plough*
Jean Toomer, *Cane*
D. H. Lawrence, *Kangaroo*
Mina Loy, *Lunar Baedeker*
Wallace Stevens, *Harmonium*
Leon Trotsky, *Literature and Revolution*
William Carlos Williams, *Spring and All*
Italo Svevo, *The Confessions of Zeno*

1924   Ramsay MacDonald leads first Labour government in Britain
Italian Fascist State inaugurated
Lenin dies
Kafka dies
Joyce's 'Work in Progress' begins serialization in *transition*
Transatlantic Review founded in Paris by Ford Madox Ford
Forster, *A Passage to India*
Ernest Hemingway, *In Our Time*
Breton, *Manifesto of Surrealism*
Marianne Moore, *Observations*
T. E. Hulme, *Speculations*

1925   Shaw wins Nobel Prize
Sergei Eisenstein, *Battleship Potemkin* (film)
Adolf Hitler, *Mein Kampf*
John Dos Passos, *Manhattan Transfer*
Eliot, *Poems 1905–1925*
F. Scott Fitzgerald, *The Great Gatsby*
Kafka, *The Trial*

Alain Locke (ed.), *The New Negro*
Stein, *The Making of Americans*
Woolf, *Mrs. Dalloway* and *The Common Reader*
Yeats, *A Vision*

1926   General Strike in Britain
Fritz Lang, *Metropolis* (film)
Fire!! magazine founded in Harlem, NY
H.D., *Palimpsest*
William Faulkner, *Soldiers' Pay*
Hemingway, *The Sun Also Rises*
Langston Hughes, *The Weary Blues*
Lawrence, *The Plumed Serpent*
MacDiarmid, *A Drunk Man Looks at the Thistle*
Sean O'Casey, *The Plough and the Stars*
Wyndham Lewis, *The Art of Being Ruled*

1927   Charles Lindbergh's solo flight across the Atlantic
Henri Bergson wins Nobel Prize for Literature
Isadora Duncan dies
transition magazine founded by Eugene Jolas
Laura Riding and Robert Graves, *A Survey of
Modernist Poetry*
Wyndham Lewis, *Time and Western Man*
Joyce, *Pomes Penyeach*
Hemingway, *Men Without Women*
Woolf, *To the Lighthouse*
Kafka, *Amerika*
Jean Rhys, *The Left Bank and Other Stories*

1928   Vote extended to women over 21 in Britain
National Party of Scotland formed
Hardy dies
Djuna Barnes, *Ryder*
McKay, *Home to Harlem*
Pound, *Selected Poetry* (ed. T. S. Eliot)
Eliot, *For Lancelot Andrewes*
Joyce, *Anna Livia Plurabelle*
Lawrence, *Lady Chatterley's Lover*
Woolf, *Orlando*
Yeats, *The Tower*

1929   Wall Street stock market crash
MacDonald leads second Labour government
Thomas Mann wins Nobel Prize
John Grierson, *Drifters* (film)
Faulkner, *The Sound and the Fury*
Robert Graves, *Goodbye to All That*
Wyndham Lewis, *Paleface: The Philosophy of the Melting Pot*
Alfred Döblin, *Berlin Alexanderplatz*
Lawrence, *Pansies*
Woolf, *A Room of One's Own*
Nella Larsen, *Passing*

1930   D. H. Lawrence dies
Freud, *Civilization and Its Discontents*
William Empson, *Seven Types of Ambiguity*
F. R. Leavis, *Mass Civilization and Minority Culture*
W. H. Auden, *Poems*
Eliot, *Ash Wednesday*
Pound, *A Draft of XXX Cantos*
Faulkner, *As I Lay Dying*
Wyndham Lewis, *The Apes of God*
Robert Musil, *The Man Without Qualities* (first two parts)

1931   Financial crisis, Britain temporarily abandons gold standard
Woolf, *The Waves*
Samuel Beckett, *Proust*
Eugene O'Neill, *Mourning Becomes Electra*

1932   Lytton Strachey dies
Scrutiny magazine founded
Auden, *The Orators*
Aldous Huxley, *Brave New World*
Nathanael West, *Miss Lonelyhearts*
F. R. Leavis, *New Bearings in English Poetry*
Q. D. Leavis, *Fiction and the Reading Public*

1933   Hitler becomes Chancellor of Germany
F. D. Roosevelt elected US president, ushers in New Deal
Prohibition ends
American ban on *Ulysses* lifted
Yeats, *The Winding Stair and Other Poems*
Stein, *The Autobiography of Alice B. Toklas*
Eliot, *The Use of Poetry and the Use of Criticism*

1934   Beckett, *More Pricks Than Kicks*
Eliot, *After Strange Gods*
George Orwell, *Down and Out in Paris and London*
Pound, *The ABC of Reading*
Nancy Cunard (ed.), *Negro: An Anthology*
Wyndham Lewis, *Men Without Art*
Fitzgerald, *Tender is the Night*
Rhys, *Voyage in the Dark*

1935   Italy invades Abyssinia
Moore, *Selected Poems*
Eliot, *Murder in the Cathedral*
Pound, *Jefferson and/or Mussolini*
George Dangerfield, *The Strange Death of Liberal England*

1936   Spanish Civil War
Beginning of Stalin's 'Great Purge' (1936–1938)
BBC television begins broadcasting
Charles Chaplin, *Modern Times* (film)
Faulkner, *Absalom! Absalom!*
Barnes, *Nightwood*

Dylan Thomas, *Twenty-five Poems*
Yeats (ed.), *The Oxford Book of Modern Verse 1892–1935*
Michael Roberts (ed.), *The Faber Book of Modern Verse*
Walter Benjamin, 'The Work of Art in the Age of Mechanical Reproduction'

1937   'Degenerate Art' exhibition held in Munich
Neville Chamberlain pursues policy of appeasement (1937–1940)
Mass Observation movement launched in Britain
Picasso, *Guernica* (painting)
Wyndham Lewis, *The Revenge for Love* and *Blasting and Bombardiering*
Zora Neale Hurston, *Their Eyes Were Watching God*
Orwell, *The Road to Wigan Pier*
Woolf, *The Years*

1938   *Krystallnacht* ('Crystal Night') across Germany, November 9–10
Breton, Trotsky, and Diego Rivera, *Manifesto: Towards a Free Revolutionary Art*
International Surrealist Exhibition, Paris
Elizabeth Bowen, *The Death of the Heart*
Pound, *Guide to Kulchur*
Beckett, *Murphy*
Orwell, *Homage to Catalonia*
Woolf, *Three Guineas*

1939   Second World War begins
Yeats dies
Freud dies
Joyce, *Finnegans Wake*
Yeats, *Last Poems and Two Plays*
John Steinbeck, *The Grapes of Wrath*
Louis MacNeice, *Autumn Journal*
Flann O'Brien, *At Swim-Two-Birds*
Nathanael West, *The Day of the Locust*

1940   Winston Churchill forms coalition government
The London Blitz begins
Fall of France
Walter Benjamin dies
F. Scott Fitzgerald dies
Charles Chaplin, *The Great Dictator* (film)
Hemingway, *For Whom the Bell Tolls*
Richard Wright, *Native Son*
Stein, *Paris France*

1941   Japanese attack on Pearl Harbor
Joyce dies
Woolf dies
Trotsky assassinated in Mexico
Pearl Harbour bombed, US enters war

John Crowe Ransom, *The New Criticism*
James Agee, *Let Us Now Praise Famous Men*
Fitzgerald, *The Last Tycoon*
Woolf, *Between the Acts*

1942   Allied bombing raids begin on German cities
Wallace Stevens, *Notes Toward a Supreme Fiction*
Albert Camus, *The Outsider*

1943   Warsaw Ghetto Uprising in Poland
MacDiarmid, *Lucky Poet*

1944   D-Day landings, liberation of Paris
Wassily Kandinsky dies
Eliot, *Four Quartets*
Tennessee Williams, *The Glass Menagerie*
William Carlos Williams, *The Wedge*

1945   Atom bombs dropped on Hiroshima and Nagasaki
Allies liberate Auschwitz
Second World War ends
United Nations founded
Ezra Pound imprisoned in Italy, writes *The Pisan Cantos* (1948)
Evelyn Waugh, *Brideshead Revisited*
Orwell, *Animal Farm*

References

Armstrong, Tim, *Modernism: A Cultural History* (Cambridge and Malden, MA: Polity, 2005).

Bradbury, Malcolm and James McFarlane, eds, *Modernism: 1890-1930* (Harmondsworth: Penguin, 1976).

Butts, Mary, 'Bloomsbury', *Modernism/Modernity* 5.2 (1998): 32-45.

Carpenter, Humphrey, *A Serious Character: The Life of Ezra Pound* (Boston: Houghton Mifflin, 1988).

Derrida, Jacques, *Writing and Difference*, trans. Alan Bass (Chicago: University of Chicago Press, 1978).

Eliot, T. S., *The Letters of T. S. Eliot, Volume I, 1988-1922*, ed. Valerie Eliot (London: Faber, 1988).

Ellmann, Richard and Charles Feidelson, Jr, eds, *The Modern Tradition: Backgrounds of Modern Literature* (Oxford and New York: Oxford University Press, 1965).

Ford, Ford Madox, *Mightier Than the Sword: Memories and Criticisms* (London: George Allen and Unwin, 1938).

Forster, E. M., *Commonplace Book*, ed. Philip Gardner (Stanford: Stanford University Press, 1985).

Lawrence, D. H., *The Collected Letters of D. H. Lawrence, Volume I*, ed. Harry T. Moore (London: Heinemann, 1962).

Levenson, Michael, *A Genealogy of Modernism: A Study of English Literary Doctrine 1908-1922* (Cambridge and New York: Cambridge University Press, 1984).

Lukács, Georg, *Realism in Our Time*, trans. John and Necke Mander (New York: Harper and Row, 1964).

Marinetti, F. T., *Critical Writings*, ed. Günter Berghaus, trans. Doug Thompson (New York: Farrar, Straus and Giroux, 2006).

Nordau, Max, *Degeneration* (London: Heinemann, 1895).

Orwell, George, *Critical Essays* (London: Secker and Warburg, 1946).

Perloff, Marjorie, 'Epilogue: Modernism Now', in David Bradshaw and Kevin J. H. Dettmar, eds, *A Companion to Modernist Literature and Culture* (Oxford and Malden, MA: Blackwell, 2006), pp. 571-78.

Pound, Ezra, *Selected Letters of Ezra Pound*, ed. D. D. Paige (New York: New Directions, 1971).

Rainey, Lawrence, ed., *Modernism: An Anthology* (Oxford and Malden, MA: Blackwell, 2005).

Schuchard, Ronald, 'Burbank with a Baedeker, Eliot with a Cigar: American Intellectuals, Anti-Semitism, and the Idea of Culture', *Modernism/Modernity* 10.1 (2003): 1-26.

Stein, Gertrude, *Paris France* (New York: Scribners, 1940).

Surette, Leon, *The Birth of Modernism* (Montreal and Kingston: McGill-Queen's University Press, 1993).

Trilling, Lionel, *Beyond Culture: Essays on Literature and Learning* (New York: Viking, 1965).

Yeats, William Butler, *The Letters of W. B. Yeats*, ed. Allan Wade (London: Hart-Davis, 1954).

General Index

Postcolonialism, 20, 123, 124, 127, 140–2
Postmodernism, x, 17, 91, 103, 112, 116, 129, 142–4
Poststructuralism, 122, 123, 124, 125, 127–9, 130, 133, 136, 143, 144–7, 148, 150, 151
Pound, Ezra, x, xii, xiii, 2, 6, 13, 14, 18, 21, 23, 25, 28, 29, 34, 39, 48, 50–1, 52, 53, 54, 57, 60, 64–5, 67, 70, 74, 83, 90, 91, 93, 95, 96–9, 102, 103–5, 107, 111, 118, 120, 122, 134, 137–8, 142, 143, 147
Primitivism, 2, 7, 35, 37, 82, 112, 113–15, 117, 119
Proust, Marcel, 45, 55, 65, 77, 79, 88–9, 117, 132, 136
Psychoanalysis, 6, 32–4, 44–5, 79, 122, 123, 139, 148–50
Psychology, 4, 11, 13, 32–4, 35, 37, 44, 71, 77, 79, 82, 89, 117, 123, 138, 147, 148–50
Publishing, 26–9, 45, 72

Queer theory, 125, 127, 130

Race, 5, 7, 20, 30, 34–7, 54, 62–6, 68, 77, 95, 103, 119, 135, 140–2
Radcliffe-Brown, A. R., 5
Radio, 16, 21, 27, 43, 64, 112
Rainey, Lawrence, 28–9, 58, 61, 91, 94
Ransom, John Crowe, 138–9
Ray, Man, 65, 75, 81
Realism, xii, 58, 99, 115–18, 122, 144
Religion, xi, 3, 5–6, 30, 38–40, 41, 63, 67, 84, 87–8, 91, 109–10, 113, 135, 144
Rhys, Jean, 50, 54
Richardson, Dorothy, 29, 34, 50, 54, 55, 76, 77, 117
Romanticism, 2, 14, 15, 34, 39, 40, 51, 59, 60, 68, 82, 101–2, 115, 117, 136, 142
Rosenburg, Harold, x
Ruskin, John, 24, 59
Russell, Bertrand, 35, 48, 72–3, 114
Russell, George (AE), 104
Russolo, Luigi, 92, 112

Said, Edward, 21, 38, 140
Saint-Point, Valentine de, 119
Saussure, Ferdinand de, 24, 26, 123, 128, 145, 146, 148, 150–2
Schoenberg, Arnold, 112
Science and technology, 5–6, 12, 23, 35, 37, 40–4, 98–9, 101, 143–4
Scott, Bonnie Kime, xii, 50–1, 130, 132
Secularism, 38–9, 63, 90
Sex and sexuality, xii, 3, 8–10, 29, 32, 34, 44–6, 51, 56, 57, 73, 74, 77, 112, 116, 120, 125, 130, 140, 146, 148
Shakespeare, William, 25, 31, 63–4, 79, 86, 125, 131
Shaw, George Bernard, 35, 48, 49, 84, 85
Shklovsky, Viktor, 25, 92, 123
Short story, the, 55–6, 89
Showalter, Elaine, 10, 130, 132
Simmel, Georg, 11
Sinclair, May, 29, 34, 46, 48, 50, 77
Sinfield, Alan, 125–6
Sociology, 3, 11, 32, 37, 83, 122
Sorel, Georges, 2, 21, 118–19
Spengler, Oswald, 68
Spivak, Gayatri, 140, 142
Stalin, Joseph, 17, 22, 65, 82, 118
Stein, Gertrude, 35, 37, 48, 50, 54, 65, 71, 74, 75, 77, 83, 94, 143
Stephens, James, 104
Stopes, Marie, 35
Strachey, Lytton, 31, 48, 72–4
Stravinsky, Igor, 112–13
Stream of consciousness, 33, 75, 77–80, 108, 111
Strindberg, August, 71, 85
Structuralism, 24, 92, 123, 127, 144–7, 148, 150–2
Suffrage, 1, 13, 49–51, 119, 130
Surette, Leon, 18, 22, 40, 66
Surrealism, 7, 12, 68, 70, 71, 75, 81–3, 86, 93, 99, 106, 116, 136
Svevo, Italo, 65, 72
Symbolism, 34, 57, 58, 71, 87, 88, 104
Synge, J. M., 18, 83

Theatre, 18, 28, 30, 69, 71, 83–6, 92, 103–4
Thomas, Dylan, 68, 83
Toklas, Alice B., 48, 65

Index of Works Cited